The Inner Journey
Views from the Jewish Tradition

Series Editor: Ravi Ravindra
Associate Series Editor: Priscilla Murray

The Inner Journey
Views from the Jewish Tradition

Edited by Rabbi Jack Bemporad

PARABOLA Anthology Series

MORNING LIGHT
P R E S S

MORNING
◯ LIGHT
P R E S S

Published by Morning Light Press 2007.

Editor: Rabbi Jack Bemporad
Series Editor: Ravi Ravindra
Associate Series Editor: Priscilla Murray
Copyright © 2007 Morning Light Press

Morning Light Press
323 North First, Suite 203
Sandpoint, ID 83864
morninglightpress.com
info@mlpress.com

Printed on acid-free paper in Canada.

Philosophy
SAN: 255-3252

Library of Congress Cataloging-in-Publication Data

The inner journey : views from the Jewish tradition / editor, Jack Bemporad.
    p. cm. -- (Parabola anthology series)
  "Material published in Parabola during its first thirty years"--General series introduction.
  Includes bibliographical references and index.
  ISBN-10: 1-59675-015-4 (alk. paper)
  ISBN-13: 978-1-59675-015-9 (alk. paper)
  1. Spiritual life--Judaism. I. Bemporad, Jack. II. Parabola (Mt. Kisco, N.Y.)
BM723.I56 2007
296.7--dc22
                    2007010952

To the path makers
and the pilgrims on the path

General Introduction to
The Inner Journey: A Parabola Anthology Series

When *Parabola: Myth, Tradition, and the Search for Meaning* was launched in 1976, the founder, D. M. Dooling, wrote in her first editorial:

> *Parabola* has a conviction: that human existence is significant, that life essentially makes sense in spite of our confusions, that man is not here on earth by accident but for a purpose, and that whatever that purpose may be it demands from him the discovery of his own meaning, his own totality and identity. A human being is born to set out on this quest. ... Every true teaching, every genuine tradition has sought to train its disciples to act this part, to become in fact followers of the great quest for one's self.

For over thirty years, *Parabola* has honored the great wisdom traditions of every culture, turning to their past and present masters and practitioners for guidance in this quest. Recognizing that the aim of each tradition is the transformation of human life through practice supported by knowledge and understanding, *Parabola* on behalf of its readers has turned again and again to Buddhist and Christian monks, Sufi and Jewish teachers, Hindu scholars, and Native American and other indigenous peoples, evoking from each of them illumination and insight.

Over the years *Parabola*, in each of its issues, devoted to a central theme of the human condition as it is and as it might be, has gathered remarkable material. "The Call," "Awakening," "Food," "Initiation," "Dreams and Seeing," "Liberation," "The Mask," "Attention": in these and in scores of other issues, a facet of the essential search is explored, always with the aim of casting light on the way.

The purpose of the *Parabola Anthology Series* is to gather the material published in *Parabola* during its first thirty years in order to focus this light and to reflect the inner dimensions of each of these traditions. While every religious tradition has both external and inner aspects, the aim of each is the transformation of the whole being. The insights and understandings that ring true and carry the vibration of an inner meaning can provide guidance and support for our quest, but a mere mechanical repetition of forms which were once charged with great energy can take us away from the heart of the teaching. Every tradition must change and evolve; it has to be reinterpreted and reunderstood by successive generations in order to maintain its relevance and application.

Search carries a connotation of journey; we set out with the hope for new insight and experience. The aim of the spiritual or inner journey is transformation, to become more responsible and more compassionate as understanding and being grow. This demands an active undertaking, and insights from those who have traveled the path can provide a call, bring inspiration, and serve as a reminder of the need to search.

For this series, selections have been made from the material published in *Parabola* relating to each of the major traditions and teachings. Subtle truths are expressed in myths, poetry, stories, parables, and above all in the lives, actions, and expressions of those people who have been immersed in the teaching, have wrestled with it and have been informed and transformed by it. Some of these insights have been elicited through interviews with current practitioners of various teachings. Each of the great traditions is very large, and within each tradition there are distinct schools of thought, as well as many practices, rituals, and ceremonies. None of the volumes in the present series claims to be exhaustive of the whole tradition or to give a complete account of it.

In addition to the material that has been selected from the library of *Parabola* issues, the editor of each volume in the series provides an introduction to the teaching, a reminder of the heart of the tradition in the section, "The Call of the Tradition," as well as a list of books suggested for further study and reflection. It is the hope of the publishers and editors that this new series will surprise, challenge, and support those new to *Parabola* as well as its many readers.

—*Ravi Ravindra*

CONTENTS

The Call of the Tradition

"With what shall I come before the Lord, and bow myself
before God on high? Shall I come before Him with
burnt offerings, with calves a year old?
Will the Lord be pleased with thousands of rams, with ten thousands of
rivers of oil? Shall I give my first-born for my transgression, the fruit of my
body for the sin of my soul?"
He has showed you, O man, what is good;
and what does the Lord require of you but to do justice,
and to love kindness, and to walk humbly with your God?[1]

—Micah 6:6-9

Thus says the Lord: "Let not the wise man glory in his wisdom,
let not the mighty man glory in his might, let not the rich man
glory in riches; but let him who glories glory in this,
that he understands and knows Me, that I am the Lord
who practices steadfast love, justice, and righteousness in the earth;
for in these things I delight, says the Lord."[2]

—Jeremiah 9:23-24

"Seek the Lord while He may be found, call upon Him
while He is near; Let the wicked forsake his way,
and the unrighteous man his thoughts;
let him return to the Lord, that He may have mercy on him,
and to our God, for He will abundantly pardon.
For My thoughts are not your thoughts,
neither are your ways My ways, says the Lord.
For as the heavens are higher than the earth,
so are My ways higher than your ways and My thoughts
than your thoughts. For as the rain and the snow
come down from heaven, and return not thither
but water the earth, making it bring forth and sprout,

giving seed to the sower and bread to the eater,
So shall My word be that goes forth from My mouth;
it shall not return to Me empty,
but it shall accomplish that which I purpose,
and prosper in the thing for which I sent it.[3]

—Isaiah 55:6-11

"Is such the fast that I choose: to loose the bonds of wickedness,
to undo the thongs of the yoke, to let the oppressed go free,
and to break every yoke? Is it not to share your bread with
the hungry, and bring the homeless poor into your house;
when you see the naked to cover him, and not to hide yourself
from your own flesh? Then shall your light break forth like the dawn,
and your healing shall spring up speedily;
your righteousness shall go before you,
the glory of the Lord shall be your rear guard.

Then you shall call, and the Lord will answer; you shall cry,
and He will say, Here I am.[4]

— Isaiah 58:6-9

Ben Bag Bag said: Turn it, and turn it again, for everything is in it.
Pour over it, grow old and gray over it.
Do not budge from it. You can have no better guide for living than it.[5]

—Avot 5:22

R. Meir used to say: Where do we find the proof
that even a Gentile who pursues the study of Torah
is like a high priest? From the assertion about Torah's ordinances
that "by pursuing their study man shall live:

Lev. 18:5, where Scripture speaks not of priest, Levite,
Israelite, but of man." So you learn that even a Gentile who pursues the
study of Torah is like a high priest.[6]

—B. Sanh. 59a

Torah demands forty-eight attributes (from its students):
study (aloud); attentive listening, distinct pronunciation;
alertness of mind; intuitive insight; awe (of one's master),
reverence (for God); humility; cheerfulness; cleanliness;
attendance on sages; intense examination of a matter
in the company of colleagues; subtle discussion
with disciples; unhurried reflection; persistence
in study of Scripture and Mishnah; strict moderation in
business, in sleep, in chitchat, in pleasure,
in hilarity, and in worldly interests; patience;
a good heart; faith in the sages; resignation to
afflictions; knowing one's place; contentment with one's lot;
restraint in one's words; refraining from claiming merit
for oneself; being loved; loving Him who is present everywhere;
loving fellow creatures; loving re-proof and rectitude;
shunning honor and avoiding pride in one's learning;
taking no delight in laying down the law; bearing
the yoke with one's fellow; judging him charitably;
guiding him to the true path (Halakhah);
urging him to reconciliation (in a dispute);
being systematic in study; asking and answering;
listening and being ready to answer (when asked);
learning in order to teach; studying in order to practice
(precepts); making his teacher wiser (by pointed questions);
noting with precision what he is hearing;
and giving credit for a comment to the one who made it."[7]

—Avot 6:6

Abraham's Prayer and Sodom's Sins
"Abraham drew near and said:
"Shall not the Judge of all the earth exercise justice?" (Gen.18:23 and 18:25).
According to R. Levi, the verse means that Abraham said:
If You seek to have a world, strict justice cannot be exercised;
and if You seek strict justice, there will be no world.
Do You expect to take hold of the well's rope at both ends? You desire a world
and You also desire justice? You can only have one of the two.
If You do not relent a little, the world will not endure.[8]

—Bereshit Rabba 39.6, 4.9

R. Joshua Ben Levi taught: When Moses went up on high,
the ministering angels dare say to the Holy One:
Master of the Universe, what business does one born of woman
have in our midst? God replied: He came to receive the Torah.
They argued: This precious thing, which has been stored with
You for nine hundred and seventy four generations
before the world was created, You are about to give
it to mere flesh and blood? "Oh Lord, our Lord,
how glorious is Thy Name in all the earth!
Let Thy majesty continue to be celebrated above the heavens…
What is man that Thou shouldst be mindful of him,
and the son of man that Thou shouldst think of him?"
(Ps. 8:2 and 8:5). Then the Holy One said to Moses:
Let you be the one to reply to the ministering angels.
Moses spoke right up: Master of the universe,
I fear that they will consume me with the fiery breath of their mouths.
God said: Take hold of the throne of My glory and reply to them.
Moses spoke up again: The Torah You are about to give me–
what is written in it? "I am the Lord thy God,
that brought thee out of the land of Egypt" (Exod.20:2).
Then, turning to the angels, he asked: Did you go down to Egypt?
Were you enslaved to Pharoah? What need have you for the Torah?

What else is written in it? "Ye shall have no gods that others worship"
(Exod.20:3)—do you live among nations who worship idols?
What else is written in it? "Thou shalt not take the
Name of the Lord thy God in vain" (Exod. 20:7)
are there business dealings among you
(that might lead to swearing a false oath)?
What else is written in it? "Remember the Sabbath Day,
to keep it holy" (Exod. 20:8)—do you do the kind of work
that requires you to rest? What else is written in it?
"Honor thy father and thy mother" (Exod.20:12)
—do you have a father or mother? What else is written in it?"
Thou shalt not murder, thou shalt not commit adultery,
thou shalt not steal" (Exod. 20:13)
—is there rivalry among you, is the impulse to evil within you?
At that, the angels conceded to the Holy One, for at the psalm's end,
they said once more, "O Lord our God, how glorious is
Thy Name in all the earth," although they did not add (as before),
"Let Thy majesty continue to be celebrated above the heavens."[9]

—B. Shabbat 88b-89a

"Go, get thee down" (Exod. 32:7). The Holy One said to Moses: Go,
Moses, get you down from your greatness. It was only
because of Israel that I bestowed such greatness upon you.
But now that Israel have sinned, what need I have of you?
At that Moses' strength was so depleted that he
did not have the strength to utter even a single word.
But when God said to him, "Let Me be, that I may destroy them"
(Deut. 9:14), Moses reasoned: So the outcome depends on me!
At once he rose up and prayed vigorously as he pleaded for mercy.
A parable: A king of flesh and blood became angry at his son
and beat him severely. Now, the king's friend, seated in the king's presence,
was afraid to utter even one word (in demurral). But when the king said
(to his son), "Were it not for my friend who is seated in my presence,

I would slay you," the friend said: "So the outcome depends on me!"
At once he rose up and rescued the son.
"And now let Me be" (Exod.32:10). R. Abbahu said:
Were Scripture not explicit, it would have been impossible to say such a thing.
For the verse implies that, like a man who grabs hold
of his fellow by his garment, Moses, if one dare say it, grabbed hold of the
Holy One and brazenly said to Him: Master of the universe,
I will not let You be until you pardon and forgive Israel.[10]

—B. Ber. 32a

And let not thy nature promise thee that the grave will be
thy refuge; for against your will thou wast framed
(Jer. 18:6), and against your will thou wast born, and against
your will thou livest, and against your will thou diest, and against
thy will shalt thou hereafter give account and reckoning before
the King of the kings of kings, the Holy One, blessed is He.[11]

—Avot 4:22

Moses had come and said: the Great God, Almighty and Awful.
Then came Jeremiah and said: "Aliens are destroying His Temple!
Where then are His awful deeds?"
Hence he omitted from his prayer the attribute awful.
Daniel came and said: "Aliens are enslaving His sons,
where are His mighty deeds?"
Hence he omitted from his prayer the attribute of "might."
How could these prophets dare abolish something established by Moses?
Rabbi Eleazar answered: "Since they knew that the Holy One insists on
truth, they will not ascribe false things to Him."[12]

—B. Yoma, 69b

The Inner Journey: Introduction

Judaism affirms that human beings are by nature religious. They require that certain basic psychological and spiritual needs be fulfilled, and it is religion that, for better or for worse, attempts to fulfill them. For in all of us there is a constant quest for some explanation of how things ultimately hang together, a sense of the whole of things. We need an explanation of the world, but more importantly, we strive to understand our place in it, our role in this vast cosmos of which we are a part.

Science tries to explain parts, sections, certain domains in our universe. But there is a need to put these domains together, and this needs a perspective that can connect facts and values; the true, the good, the beautiful, and the holy. This is beyond the work of science. A religious perspective is needed that tries to incorporate all these values into some overall framework to give us a sense of the world and our place in it.

Everyone has a profound need for reassurance; that things are going to be all right, that our lives are and will continue to be secure.

We also need recognition. We need to feel that on some level we are special and worthy of love and respect, that we are important and that our lives have meaning and significance; that we are valuable human beings; that in some sphere we can and will make a difference, and we spend our lives trying to find ways that will enable us to gain a sense of self that defines our humanity.

Finally we need a feeling of connectedness. Not just to our fellow human beings and the world but to a transcendent reality that connects us to something higher than ourselves, more noble, richer, more inclusive and valuable.

There are authentic and inauthentic ways of providing answers to these questions, and one of the major teachings of Judaism is the delineation of how these ways differ.

One can act so as to ascend to a higher level, which is the path toward a fuller sense of self, toward a dimension that links us to the true, the good, the beautiful and the holy; toward the divine. Or we can descend, giving up the higher for the lower so as to become less than that which we potentially can become.

The prophets Jeremiah and Hosea said we take on the character of what we pursue. Jeremiah says if we go after things of naught, then we become naught. Hosea says if we go after detestable things we become detestable. The prophets defined evil as the perversion, frustration and degradation of all that is the Divine in us. Its opposite, the good, is the development of the image of God within us, giving us the strength to turn away from vanity and to aspire to a higher ethical and spiritual life. But spiritual growth, the spirituality we are concerned with, is not and cannot be reduced to a growth in knowledge. It has to do with a growth in being, a transformation of self.

Personally and socially, Judaism makes the ethical the central focus of life and gives us a blueprint for living a meaningful life. It rejects intermediaries and hero worship of any single individual. In practicing Judaism, it is never an individual, be he Moses, Buddha, Jesus or Mohammed, who determines and defines our lives or acts as an intermediary or savior. Instead, there are many individuals—prophets, sages, ordinary people, including non-Jews, from whom we can learn how to live. As Ben Zoma says, the wise person is the one who can learn from everyone and everything.

Spirituality

The ancient rabbinic text, the Mishnah, in Sanhedrin 4:5, states: "A single man was created in the world, to teach that if any man has caused a single soul to perish, scripture imputes it to him as if he had caused a whole world to perish, and if any man saves alive a single soul, scripture imputes it to him as if he had saved alive a whole world. ... Therefore everyone must say, for my sake the world was created."[1]

Another Mishna in Eduyoth recounts a significant debate between the schools of Hillel and Shammai about whether or not it was better for man to have been created. After considerable discussion, a vote was taken and the school of Shammai, that claimed it was better for man not to have been created, got the most votes. Thereupon the Hillellites taught that since man was already created, people should examine their past deeds and future deeds, so that one's past would not necessarily become one's future. However, since everyone does not know whether in his/her particular case it would have been better or not if s/he were created, everyone should live one's life as if s/he were worthy of having been created.

Judaism teaches that if you want to raise yourself up to a Godly spiritual plane, to find the Divine spark in yourself and in others, you must honestly ask yourself: "Am I living my life in such a way that indeed I have the right to say for my sake the world was created?" and say that I am worthy of having been created.

What Judaism teaches is that if we genuinely and authentically and radically ask this question, we will find that we cannot help but be transformed spiritually.

Spirituality is inner growth nurtured by ethical behavior, which in turn nurtures the Divine spark within us. It deals with those potentialities in our natures that elevate us in moral worth and dignity and link us to God. The blossoming of that is what makes us uniquely human, the taking upon ourselves the tasks of character development, the paths of righteousness, the acceptance of responsibility to live an ethical life. It is the striving to realize and embody in ourselves and in others a higher, broader, enhanced way of life; for there is no spirituality without responsibility and without facing the burden of ascent. Through this work we can be transformed and transform others and the world. It is in this sense that spirituality gives us the possibility of growth in being.

The mark of the truly religious person is that he is willing to take on more than his share in the process of value enrichment, of the production and conservation of personal and group values. The prophets teach us that there is something at stake in every historical situation, and we can, by acting or failing to act, make a decisive difference in our lives, in the lives of those we connect to and in the world. This is what holiness and spirituality are all about.

The spiritual path or task begins with our awareness of those things in us that are conducive to our basest desires and motivations, and those things that are conducive to our highest aspirations of the good and Divine. It begins when we learn how to understand and manage both the "good" and "evil" we confront in ourselves. The connectedness between the spiritual, holy, sacred in oneself to that which transcends us, reinforces, feeds, nourishes, transforms us and lifts us to that higher spiritual plane.

If this is the true meaning of spirituality, then God's being must be a continuing process of the Creation, conservation and enhancement of value and personality; of the true and the good, the beautiful and the holy. God must be the ground for the creation of the world and life and mind and personality and spirit; the ever-continuing creation of all that is of worth in existence. Such creation of values requires not just an orderly and intelligible universe but also a universe that, especially in life and personal life, manifests values that qualify and integrate and realize this universe.

The question now emerges. How are we to accomplish this task? We need a guide, a direction, something to stabilize and integrate, in the proper manner, the all-too inchoate and scattered elements that constitute our ordinary selves.

The Significance of Torah

The Jewish people have a love affair with the Torah. The Torah is not simply the Five Books of Moses, or even the entire Bible. More correctly, it is the whole gamut of Jewish teaching and wisdom contained in the written law (*Torah sheh B'chtav*) and oral law (*Torah sheh Ba'al Peh*). While Torah has all too often been translated by the word "law," its literal and etymological meaning is more appropriately translated as direction, instruction and teaching.

The Torah is the prism through which one strives to understand the significance of one's self, the Jewish people, the world and the Divine. It is that body of teaching that transforms Jews into seekers of the truth that permits them to connect as a self to their people, to the cosmos and to the Divine. It embodies an ethic that directs behavior toward all human beings, other creatures and the environment.

One sage goes so far as to say that for the sake of the study of Torah, human beings were created. But what is of interest here is that Torah must be received and understood in our own unique way. Rabbi Jose says in *Pirke Avot* 2:17 "…What knowledge of Torah a man acquires is personal to himself. It cannot be inherited or bequeathed."

Herford explains that Torah is in essence a revelation of Divine Truth through the medium of the written and oral word. You may learn from your teacher how to interpret the word of Torah and may be instructed that such and such Truths are contained in it; you may be helped in your search for these Truths; you, in turn, may help others and teach what has been taught to you, but what you cannot receive of the Divine Truths revealed in the Torah is your own inward vision of "the deep things of God."[2]

Leo Baeck, in commenting on this same verse, says, "The Torah is far more than a book, far more than anything that has ever been written. Therefore, it was not merely to be read and known; it was to be rediscovered anew in every word, ever and continuously to be made our own."[3]

Learning Torah is a difficult task, and one that is not without pain. The process of appropriation, of making Torah one's own, of learning it with effort and struggle, is seen in Ben He He's statement *Pirke Avot* 5:26, "according to the *tza'arah* (the suffering) is the reward." One is reminded of Cushman's statement in reference to Plato "where things ultimate are at issue, Plato has no faith in borrowed findings, no faith in so-called truths which a man does not achieve for himself as a personal possession."[4]

The opening words in *Pirke Avot* 1:1 tell us, "The Torah was received by Moses on Sinai, transmitted to Joshua, from Joshua to the elders, from the elders to the prophets and the prophets handed it to the men of the Great Assembly."

This means that each of us must receive the Torah, and it is incumbent upon us to then transmit it. What does it mean to receive the teaching as the Rabbis taught it? *Tanchuma Yisro* 40a states: "Rabbi Jose ben Haninah said 'the word of God spoke to each man in his own power. Nor need you marvel at this. For the manna tasted differently to each; to the children, to the young; and to the old according to their power. If the manna tasted differently according to men's power, how much more the word?"

A similar passage is even more revealing: "God's voice went forth to each one in Israel according to his power and obedience. The elders heard the voice according to their capacity, the adolescents, the youths, the boys, the women, the sucklings each according to their capacity, and also Moses according to his capacity for it says that Moses kept speaking and God, himself, would answer him with the voice; that voice which Moses was able to hear." (*Tanchuma, Shemot* 5:25 90b).

One must prepare to receive the Torah; purification, struggle and transformation are demanded from us for it to be properly understood. We must also understand the full dimensionality of the Torah and all its vastness, and what is involved in receiving it and transmitting it.

As Slonimsky put it, "... The Torah, identified with the primeval Wisdom, is the blueprint, the objectified mind of God, but also the instrumental power, i.e., both the plan and the architect, which God employs in the creation of the world and of man."[5]

Just as God envisioned the Torah as His creative blueprint, and the world is constantly and creatively renewed, the Torah received by man is also continually and creatively renewed. The Torah exposes us to the depth of life. But it is the job of the individual to come to understand him/herself through it and creatively struggle to live and incorporate that wisdom into his being, into his essence, into his/her life. It is the Torah that orients us in our sense of self and motivates us to act, for Torah implies doing as well as receiving. For what good is knowledge if it is not applied?

When one applies Torah to life, it becomes part of the chain of transmittal, of the tradition that entails further receptivity and creativity. Thus the Psalmist's insight: "In thy Light we see the Light." In this way, new dimensions of truth are perceived, shared and carried forward. You become open to something higher, and receptivity moves you to decision and action. You stand before God and the other in the light of the Torah and its wisdom, whose significance is expressed in the blessing that is made after one reads from the scroll in the synagogue, "Blessed are you, God, Creator of the Universe, who has given us the Torah of truth."

Throughout Jewish history, the Torah was viewed as a sacred text. It was read, reread and meditated on because our forefathers believed that God revealed the truth about ultimate questions therein. *Pirke Avot*, the Ethics of the Fathers (5:22) expresses it clearly: Ben Bag Bag said, "Turn it and turn it for all is in it. Contemplate and contemplate it and grow gray and old in it and turn not from it; for there is no better measure [*middah*] for thee than it."

The Torah is not simply a history or story. It has cosmological significance and teaches wisdom that enables us to live and understand the ultimate truths of both human and cosmological creation. The cosmological significance is seen in such statements as, "… Therefore, our Sages said, all who involve themselves in Torah for its own sake are called *Rei'a*—'friend', it is as if he becomes a partner with the Creator, since it is he who is now maintaining the worlds with his Torah study, without which the world would revert to *tohu va vohu* [chaos] (*Nefesh HaChaim* 4:11-12).

The Torah contains many layers, including the "*Ma'aseh Bereishit*," the teaching as to Creation as well as the "*Ma'aseh Merkavah*" (lit. chariot), the truth about God. But one must be able to receive it. One must be prepared to accept it—and its obligations. Moses, Joshua, the Elders, the Prophets and the men of the Great Assembly were qualified to do so. But what qualified them to receive it? They were prepared to accept grace of the Torah while at the same time struggling mightily and painfully to be purified (remembering the *tza'aroh*, the suffering) and found worthy to receive it. (The Sabbath morning Amidah prayer says: "*Vetaher Leibeynu Le Avdecha b'Emet*" ("Purify our hearts that we may serve you in Truth."). This is part of what accepting the Torah means in all its forms.

And what is the Torah? The narrative of the Torah is just the beginning. There are layers upon layers beneath it that we study and learn to apply in order to become God's partners in Creation.

Baeck correctly points out that "Every story in the Bible not only told something, but also meant something. It did not describe what once was; what came to be or ceased to be, it revealed something permanent or absolute; something that once was; was still, and that despite the change of scene and time remained the same."[6]

There is the Chassidic tale of Reb Moshe of Uhely, who had a dream of heaven where the great sages were studying the Talmud for eternity. What did he see? A simple *beit medrash*, a house of study, and the sages sitting around long tables engrossed in study. He was disappointed and asked, "Is that all there is to heaven?" And a Voice responded, "You are mistaken. The sages are not in Heaven, Heaven is in the sages."

As a result, the learning is something that transforms us. There is a sense that the Torah is a manifestation of God's grace, and here Max Brod's definition of "grace" is strikingly appropriate. "Grace exists as to the divine power that makes possible within life what life itself can never admit by virtue of its own laws."[7]

Torah learning can only be done by examining the texts from every possible perspective. This leads us to the four basic levels of rabbinic exegesis, for the rabbis understood these matters often better than we do. They believed that the Bible and whoever wrote it—be it Moses, the Prophets, Ezra, etc.—knew what they were teaching about; that they said what they meant and knew how to use the Hebrew language.

This did not limit interpretation of their words to surface text, and, in fact, the rabbis saw a four-fold level of interpretation of the Torah as expressed in the acronym *Pardes*—*peh, resh, daled, samech*—the Hebrew word for orchard or citrus grove, a place that bears fruit. *Peh* stands for *Pshat*—the plain sense or literal interpretation of the text. *Resh* stands for *remez*—which means "hint"—for sometimes the Bible only offers hints to those who know how to appreciate a hint. *Daled* stands for *drash*—exegesis on a multiplicity of levels: parables, allegories, homilies and explanations of meaning and sense of context—of form and substance and even philosophy. Finally, the letter *samech* stands for *sod*—literally "secret"—which involves the mysticism of the Bible. And "In the Beginning," the mysterious and secret were alluded to as a process of the Creation. What was a person allowed to know? How much is revealed?

Mishnah Hagigah 2:1 states: "Do not comment [*darash*] on sexual matters with three (present), nor on the Work of Creation [*Maaseh Bereshit* = Gen 1] with two, nor on the Chariot [*Merkavah* = Ezek 1] with one, unless he is a sage [*hakham*] and contemplates what he knows ..."

In his introduction to *The Guide to the Perplexed*, Maimonides writes: "Our Sages laid down the rule. The *Ma'aseh Bereishit* must not be expounded in the presence of two. If an author were to explain these principles in writing, it would be equal to expounding them unto thousands of men. For this reason, the prophets treat these subjects in figures and our sages, imitating the method of scripture, speak of them in metaphors and allegories because there is a close affinity between these subjects and metaphysics—and indeed they form part of its mysteries. Do not imagine that these most difficult problems can be thoroughly understood by any one of us. This is not the case."

Thus, the attempt to read the Torah one-dimensionally on any level without awareness of the other levels would be tantamount to truncating its meaning.

Two points perhaps should be discussed here: the difference between much of modern exegesis and rabbinic exegesis. Modern study of the Bible treats it like any other historical text—which may or may not contain great insight but which is a product of historical factors, all of them explainable from within the confines of historical explanation and historical process. Anything that does not fit into this structure is viewed as purely subjective in the sense that the individuals reporting the events may have believed them to have taken place. But what is definitive is the critical conceptual imagination of the historian.

So, for example, the Pentateuch describes how Baalam's donkey speaks. The question as to whether the author actually believed the donkey spoke is apt only if one accepts the literal interpretation.

In this story, here is a famous seer who, with a curse, can destroy a whole people, but unlike his donkey, he cannot see an angel in front of him. Even more significantly, the great seer who had come to curse and destroy an entire people would need a sword to kill a lowly donkey. Today, it is the general opinion of scholars that even the Bible itself wrote this story as "ironical."

But to limit this to a one-dimensional, even non-literal interpretation is to miss what is basic to rabbinic exegesis. *Pirke Avot* mentions Balaam's donkey as an example. It was one of the last creations brought to life at twilight on the sixth day of Creation since it does not fit the order of things. More specifically, it is not enough for rabbinic interpretation to read the story as if it were solely about Balaam who was blind to the Angel of God. We are required to read the story in such a fashion so as to awaken in ourselves the sense of our own blindness. For the story is not simply about Balaam, his blindness and his pretentiousness, it is about our own blindness and our own pretentiousness to be seers (who in effect cannot see or accomplish great things through speech). Indeed, we cannot speak as truly as a dumb animal does.

Finally, it is important to note that it was easier for God to make an animal speak than to have a man change. And this is one of the most important elements in Jewish thinking which has to do with genuine repentance. While lip service is given to the Bible as the Book of Wisdom of the Western World, nevertheless, modern exegesis adapts a judgmental attitude towards it in the sense that the Bible must fit into the categories of historical investigation. There is nothing intrinsically wrong with this, and it serves a useful, even necessary purpose. The problem arises when the historical perspective is seen as the only one and all other interpretations are seen as superfluous.

The rabbis understood Torah differently. Life had to be seen and understood within the categories, concepts, teachings and truths of the Torah. It was viewed as the norm and touchstone of reality, and thus all was seen both internally in our own lives and externally in the cosmos in terms of its teachings. As Baeck states: "… The word of the Bible was the ultimate measure of reality in history."[8]

Finally, the rabbis believed in interpretation without end, since for them "the potency of being was greater that the potency of thought." Indeed, any verse could be interpreted in many ways, since a single interpretation may only do justice to one dimension. So, we find in rabbinic commentaries such statements as "another interpretation" that can be the opposite of one interpretation with another; each one illustrating a part of the truth. Reality for the rabbis was multi-dimensional, and different people saw it according to their capacity.

Inwardness

The great sage Hillel was approached by a pagan asking to be taught the Torah while he stood on one leg. Hillel offered a brief response that has become central in Judaism: "What is hateful to you, do not do to your fellow human being; this is the essence, the rest is commentary; go and learn."

The statement is simple enough on the surface for even a child to understand—things s/he does not want others to do to them s/he should not do to others. Yet one wonders, what does this seemingly uncomplicated moral statement have to do with the vast compendium and code called the Torah, a body of profound and deep wisdom? The key lies in the latter part of the statement: "this is the essence, the rest is commentary; go and learn."

The fact is that everyone understands what is demanded of him but very few can actually do it. The task then is to go and learn how to do it. What will it take to deal with the inner struggle and attain the personal transformation that must take place so that one can develop the state of being wherein you can treat another exactly as you would want to be treated? We can wonder why we feel this imperative is obligatory, but we also realize that we can't reach that level unless we do our own soul-searching in order to change our own behavior. This great work leads us to inner reflection.

We act, and when we rationalize or justify our actions, we begin to understand that perhaps we should have or could have done otherwise. Why is this the case? Why is it that we know the better and want to be always treated well by others, and yet in our own actions often do not do to others what we would want to be done to us? This is a very important question, and the Jewish tradition tries to deal with it by making a significant distinction between knowing something and really understanding it.

Knowing something is to be aware of it in general and as it applies to others. Understanding something is recognizing it in particular as it applies to us as individual beings. This concept has much to do with the genuine comprehension of freedom. Freedom, I believe, can be best understood as knowledge of a situation vis-a-vis knowledge of oneself, and knowledge of oneself vis-a-vis the knowledge of the situation.

If we do not have sufficient self knowledge to be aware of how we will act in a particular situation, we are not genuinely free. The Bible makes this distinction clear in the encounter between the prophet Nathan and King David (II Sam. 12:1-15). David had taken Bathsheba, the wife of Uriah the Hittite, and then arranged for his death so he could marry her. Nathan went to David and told him a story about a rich man who had many ewe lambs and a poor man who had only one ewe lamb that he loved and cherished. One day, when the rich man received a guest, instead of using one of his many animals for the meal, he took the poor man's ewe lamb.

When David heard the story, he was furious and said, "That man deserves to die for he hath no pity." Then Nathan confronted David and said to him, "Thou art the man." David knew, abstractly, that it was wrong for a rich man to do what he did, but when the prophet came to him, he was given to understand that the very thing he condemned in the other he himself had done. An inner re-cognition had taken place. It is this re-cognition that is at the core of freedom.

The great Orthodox rabbi Joseph Soloveichik describes why Moses received the Torah twice. The first time, the Torah had been received publicly in front of the whole people, but Moses broke the tablets of the Ten Words when he saw the idolatry of the Israelites. The second time he came down with the Torah, the reception was a private receiving of the Torah anew—an internal acceptance of Torah by each individual.

The point Rabbi Soloveichik makes is that the Torah, the commands and teachings we receive openly in society, commandments that have been handed down to us through the ages, have not become a part of our inner being. These we inevitably break. Through our own personal struggle, we have to reintegrate and internalize each of the commandments through self-conscious transformation. Only when one understands the need for inwardness can one begin to understand Torah—the teaching, the guide—in a new and personal way.

The significance of inwardness is at the heart of the Jewish spiritual tradition and is expressed in one of the most famous Biblical passages in Leviticus. The injunction is one in a series of ethical commandments that include not standing idly by your neighbor's blood, not cursing the deaf, not putting a stumbling block before the blind, and most importantly that one should love one's fellow human being as oneself. A more accurate translation of love would be caring or tender concern for your fellow human being. The neighbor is like you. There is a common ground of humanity between you that must be respected.

There is more to this text. One can interpret it to mean: Be conscious of your fellow human being as you are conscious of yourself. The other also has an inward spiritual dimension as you have and you must strive to be aware of that as much as you are aware of your own inner self. Your relationship with another human being cannot be a subject-to-object relationship. It must be a subject-to-subject relationship—for another human being is not simply a means to your end. Judaism then can be described as the going from a subject-object relation to our fellow human beings to a subject-subject relation.

There are correlations between the way we live our lives, our thoughts, feelings and actions and the text of the Torah, as we have seen with Baalam. The Biblical stories are not simply the retelling of basic events in the lives of Jacob, Moses or Jonah, Sarah or Job. Rather, these narratives directly confront us with our own lives and our own actions. The legislation, the rules, the laws, are not only about external acts alone, they call us to inner reflection.

In the Covenant Code in Exodus (Exodus 21-23) it states that if one sees the animal of one's enemy fall under its burden, one should help him. There is a Midrash that tells of a man who witnessed this and felt good to see his enemy in trouble. But then he looked into the Torah and realized that it was incumbent upon him to help his fellow man—even his enemy—and he went and helped his enemy.

Jewish tradition is fully aware of the discrepancy between what we know is the right thing to do and is painfully aware of our failure to do it. This is why the Bible is full of questions calling us to reflect on what we have done and who we are.

In Genesis, God calls upon Adam and Eve to reflect on their actions. He calls on Cain to explain himself. From the first, even in the Garden of Eden, the lesson was one of introspection, of being responsible. Eve first blamed the snake for what she did, and then Adam blamed Eve. Neither took responsibility for what they had done. The same was true of Cain.

"And the Lord God called unto the man, and said unto him, 'Where art thou?'" (Gen. 3:9)

"And the Lord God said unto the woman: 'What is this thou hast done?'" (Gen. 3:13)

"And the Lord said unto Cain, 'Where is Abel thy brother?' And he said, 'I know not: am I my brother's keeper?' And He said, 'What hast thou done?'" (Gen. 4: 9-10)

The question here is not whether God knows where Adam and Eve are or what Cain has done. The question is do they know? The answer to these queries and the answers Adam, Eve and Cain give have serious consequences, for taking or not taking responsibility for ourselves is a key to who we are.

What is it that we personally have actually experienced? The question is addressed to us personally and even the redemption has to be understood inwardly.

This is why when God describes bringing the Israelites from Egypt, the statement reads in the singular form: "For I am the Lord that brought you (in the singular) up out of the land of Egypt, to be your God: ye shall therefore be holy, for I am holy." (2 Lev. 11:45). Every individual came out of Egypt—not just "the people." One then is forced to ask what is freedom and how have I been liberated?

In the Passover service, wherein the liberation from Egypt is described, we recite the story in the context of what was done for each of us as an individual, as it states: "And thou shalt relate to thy son that day, saying, 'this is on account of what the Eternal did for me, when I went forth from Egypt'…" (the Haggadah). The Hebrew word *Mitzraim*, the translation of Egypt, means a double restriction—meaning that our slavery was two-fold—spiritual as well as physical.

This connotes the element of inwardness, that one can ignore or probe. If it is probed, one can begin to ask the questions that prompt reflection: In what way have I been in Egypt? How have I been enslaved? What is it that makes me a slave and what liberates me? It brings the realization that one significant understanding of God is that God is that Being that leads me to freedom. As the text states: "I am the Lord God who brought you out of the land of Egypt, out of the house of slavery."

Ethics

Judaism is an affirmation of the ethical as inseparable from the holy. The most significant result of ethical living is making it possible to be near God, to know God. This connection is what the rabbis mean by spirituality.

Rabbinic passages abound that stress the centrality of the ethical—for example, "All the precepts and ritual laws (of the Torah) put together cannot equal in importance one ethical principle of the Torah" (*Peah* 16D) or "a ritual precept or ceremonial law is strictly prohibited if it involves the disregarding of an ethical principle." (*Sukkot* 30A)

Religious ritual was created to foster closeness with God. But ritual without ethics is fruitless and ultimately idolatrous, since unethical behavior avows subservience to self-centered desires. Ritual is supposed to awaken in us a search for our true selves, the self that needs to be nourished and fulfilled.

You must ask yourself: "Are you aware that you are created in the Divine image? How are you expressing that in your own life? Are you squandering your life in worthless pursuits?" That is the first set of questions. And the second set of questions is, "Once you're clear about where you are, how about your brother? Where is he? And who is your brother? Is it just a person in your family, or is it one who is destitute and needy, in prison, in a home somewhere that no one goes to see or care for? Who indeed is your brother?"

On the Day of Atonement in the confession of sins, only moral sins are enumerated. Forgiveness from God and our nearness to Him are conditioned on reconciling ourselves with our neighbor. The services examine the promises we make, with the traditional liturgy rising to a crescendo in the *Neilah* (concluding) service that ends with the repetition of the affirmations of the true God's attributes as compassionate, gracious, patient, full of steadfast love and truth, with the realization that these attributes are not the only attributes of God, but that they are the means to bring us closer to Him.

Hermann Cohen said, "We look for God and we find man. We look for man and we find God." We look for and find God by imitating His attributes, but we can only do so in relation to our fellow human beings. After all, who can we be compassionate with, or gracious to, or patient with except for our fellow human beings? And when we look for man—not the self-centered, egotistic individual, but the inner being of a person as he or she strives and struggles to find meaning and truth, as we see the soul of the other, we find God, the soul of all souls. Thus the ethical is indissolubly connected to the religious and the spiritual.

The ethical makes a demand on us to bring about a more humane, genuinely compassionate and just order of things. This can only come about by human beings taking upon themselves the burden of ascent. It involves transforming the status quo in terms of an ideal. However, such transformation requires struggle and sacrifice and, often, intense suffering. The rabbis understood this as the noble and righteous taking upon themselves this burden.

The Midrash in confronting the suffering of the righteous specifically affirms that the righteous must suffer. Because it is only by the righteous taking upon themselves the burden of ascent that the Messianic age can be ushered in.

Why is it that ethical and spiritual teachings are so hard to carry out? We must investigate what it is that gets in the way of our doing what we know to be right and just.

The Good and the Evil Inclination

The rabbis interpreted the verse, "The imagination of the human heart is evil continually" by introducing the teaching as to the duality of man—the *Yetzer Tov*, the good inclination, and *Yetzer Harah*, the evil inclination.

It is important to keep in mind that one possible interpretation of the word *ra* (evil) in Hebrew can also mean excess. So, for example, in the 23rd Psalm, the statement, "Though I walk through the Valley of the Shadow of Death, I will fear no evil for Thou are with me," can also be translated, "I shall not be excessively afraid."

Similarly, in Isaiah, where it states: "I form light and create darkness, make peace and create evil (*ra*)," the prayer book changes it to "creates all things," implicitly accepting the translation to mean excess. This gives us a clue as to the meaning of *Yetzer Harah*. It is that inclination or more literarily that formatory power within us that wants excess, always more. It is that part of ourselves that is consumed with ambition and strives mightily to fulfill that ambition. Yet Judaism sees nothing wrong with ambition in and of itself or the desire to achieve something in one's life for oneself and those we love. It simply condemns the self-centered ambition realized at the expense of others.

Rabbi Nachman quotes the Bible where it says "And behold, it was very good," and notes this refers to the evil inclination. Then he asks, "How can the evil inclination be called good?" The answer is that the evil inclination is good because if one did not have an evil inclination, an inclination for achievement or excess, one wouldn't build a house or take a wife or beget a child or engage in business.

Why is that? His answer is that the labors and skills an individual has come from rivalry with one's neighbors. The evil inclination is the competitive element in each of us.

However, this element can easily become perverted.

Without the control of the good inclination, the evil inclination by itself can be very destructive. If it is allowed to express itself unchecked it can lead to great harm and devastation. Unchecked, uncontrolled, unregulated and unmanaged it leads to idolatry and death.

It is the dynamic force within us and has great strength. It makes us want to succeed at the expense of someone else. It is the part that makes us want to triumph over others. The evil inclination is the competitive self, the impulsive self;

the self-righteous impulse that immediately gets angry and hurt when anyone says the slightest thing that can be interpreted as an insult.

There are numerous Rabbinic comments to illustrate this: *Talmud Bavli Shabbos* 105b says: "Such is the art of the evil inclination: one day it bids a man, 'Do this'; the next day, 'Do that'; until finally it says to him, 'Go worship idols.' And he goes and worships them."

Talmud Bavli Bava Bathra 16a says: R. Simeon ben Lakish said: "Satan, the evil inclination and the Angel of Death—all three are the same thing." R. Simeon ben Lakish also said: "A man's evil inclination grows in strength from day to day and seeks to slay him as it is said, 'the wicked watches the righteous and seeks to slay him' (Psalm 37:32) and but for the Holy One who is his help, he could not withstand it, as it is said 'The Lord will not leave him in his hand.' (Psalm 37:33)"

It is important to understand that idolatry is misconceived if it is seen as simply the worship of wood and stones or images. Rather idolatry is the having of a false sense of the Holy.

It is the making sacred of all those things, objects, persons, institutions that have no right to be sacred. It is anything that makes you feel good for the wrong reason. It gives you a false sense of self and your place in the scheme of things. An idol is anything that frees you from what makes you responsible.

The Torah, in its ethical and ritual manifestations, enjoins us to continually guard ourselves against the temptation to attribute holiness to the projection of our fears and desires. An idol is a false hope. It is the taking of something that is finite, limited, and time bound and giving it the status of the ultimate and eternal.

That is why Judaism tells us not to worship other gods—that is gods that are other, that are foreign to our own welfare.

That is why Judaism tells us not to worship images—and it does not necessarily mean here sculptured images—but it means our own false image of ourselves that we worship.

The worst form of idolatry is the acting as if we are the center of the universe and that all is there to serve us and to cater to us as if we were Divine; it is the taking of ourselves and all extensions of ourselves as the true sacred without any consideration for the claims of others; it is not recognizing our proper place in the scheme of things. The proper understanding of idolatry and its rejection can be seen in the Talmud's definition of a Jew as "Whoever repudiates idolatry." (*Tractate Megillah* 13a).

On the other hand, the *Yetzer Tov*, the good inclination, is the formatory power for good—meaning completion. It is that part of oneself that seeks the truth about oneself and strives to be true to one's best self and live with integrity. The good inclination is the cooperative self. It's the cooperative impulse, that part of us that genuinely wants the best, not just for ourselves, but for everybody. It's that part of our self that is the loving, caring, giving part that doesn't worry about whether that caring or loving and giving is going to be recognized, but it is at the heart of what it means to be a human being according to Judaism: Yes, it's important for us to have this tremendous urge to succeed, but at what price? That is when the Biblical questions apply directly to us. "Where are you? What have you done with your life?" Because we so often fail to overcome the worst in ourselves, repentance takes a central role in Judaism.

It is one of the archetypal ideas established before the creation of the world and is the central focus of the holiest day of the year—Yom Kippur, the Day of Atonement. Baeck clearly indicates its importance in his classic work, *The Essence of Judaism* (p. 163); he states:

> *Man can 'return' to this freedom and purity, to God, the reality of his life, if he has sinned. He is always able to turn and to find his way back to the Holy, which is more than the earthly and beyond the limitations of his life: He can hallow and purify himself again; he can atone. He can always decide anew and begin anew. For man there is always the constant possibility of a new ethical beginning. The task of choice and realization, of freedom and deed, is never completed. 'Return'—thus does Judaism speak to men as long as they breathe; 'return'—but not as misunderstanding has interpreted it, "do penance" this return, this* teshuvah, *is the atonement of which man is never bereft and in which he is always able to renew his life.*

The teaching that the past can be redeemed, if it can be connected to a present that endeavors to redeem it, is at the heart of the Jewish teaching of repentance.

We need to repent every time we fall short of embodying the basic virtues of Judaism. There is a specific virtue for every relationship—and the proper virtue for the relationship between human beings is justice. The most important thing that you have to think about in terms of your relationship with your fellow human beings is the question of whether it is a just, fair relationship. When I do something, am I doing something that is just or something that is unjust? Am I lying? Am I deceiving myself and others, or am I acting justly?

The virtue for the relationship with oneself is Peace. Shalom. Now peace doesn't mean what the English word, which comes from the Latin *pacem* means—that externally it should be somehow calm but internally it can be a torrent and a torment—like, for example, the Pacific Ocean. Peace, in the true Hebrew meaning of the word means integrity and wholeness, a unification in ourselves, so that we are not at war within ourselves; we have a kind of integrity about ourselves. The rabbis said you can't have justice with your fellow man until you are at peace with yourself.

For until you are at peace with yourself, you're not going to relate to other human beings with any sense of integrity or peace, but you are always going to relate to the other person in terms of wanting something that your self lacks, that your self needs. And you want to manipulate and manage and rearrange the nature of that relationship in terms of the level of integration in yourself.

The fact of the matter is that if a person is not at peace with his/her self, the only relationships you can have with your fellow man is one of fear on the one hand or desire on the other. It is only when you are at peace with yourself that you don't ask for anything that you do not deserve, and you don't function out of need. You are not afraid. You can see your fellow human being as he or she truly is.

How does one come to peace with one's self? The rabbis say, strangely, that the only way you can be at peace with yourself is if you have the proper relationship to God. And the proper relationship to God is not justice, it is love.

Now, why is that? Because only if you love God and firmly strive to do the will of God, to imitate his attributes, then a new dimension will emerge wherein there is a correlation between the individual and God so as to produce an enhancement, a connection, that leads to peace.

Figuratively, we speak of this as God's loving us, but it is actually our love of God that melts the evil inclination in us. By loving God we understand that God creates us, that God nurtures us, renews us and melts the stony heart within us.

On the Day of Atonement, when we look at the worst elements in ourselves—listing all the sins that we may have committed, both individually and collectively—never once is there mentioned a doctrine that our beings are sinful.

We may do sinful acts, but we are not sinful beings. On the contrary, Judaism affirms that the soul that God gives to human beings is pure. And Judaism affirms that even as the soul is pure when entering upon its earthly career, so can man, through repentance, purify it and return it, in its pure form, to God.

We are here to do God's will. We are here to strive in the best possible way we know how to recognize and to overcome the worst in ourselves. As we have seen, Judaism is a way of facing the truth about ourselves, meaning that we honestly face the worst in ourselves and change what we do. By overcoming the worst in ourselves, we take upon ourselves the tasks and the burdens of ascent and make the world somehow a little better than we found it. Can God count on us to overcome our *Yetzer Harah*, to overcome our self-centered, self-righteous and competitive selves? Can we really find that peace within that comes from the love of God that enables us to be just and fair to our fellow man? And in doing that, can we bring real peace to the world?

The Calling

The love of God is central to Judaism, and this centrality is expressed in the Shema, the most significant and essential prayer of Judaism. It is the first prayer a child learns. It is said first thing upon arising in the morning, repeated in the morning and evening service during the day and repeated again at bedtime. It is inscribed in phylacteries (*tefillin*) and in the amulets (*mezuzot*) affixed to the doorposts of Jewish homes. They are the last words that escape from a man's or a woman's lips as s/he is ready to confront death.

"Hear O Israel, (that is Understand O Israel) God is our God, God is One.

"You should love the Lord your God with all your heart, with all your soul, and with all your might."

Why is this particular passage in the book of Deuteronomy so essential? Why is it seen as the creed of Judaism? Why is it the one-sentence definition of a Jew?

The rabbis picked this particular verse for a profound reason. The first thing that impresses us when we read those words and when we say these words is that we are not the center of the universe. God is the center of all Creation. If we are to love God with all of our very being, with all of our very might, and all of our very essence, we must accept that we are on the periphery and God is at the center. The rabbis were very wise psychologists, and they knew that human beings think they're at the center and everything else is on the periphery.

The love of God and the love of our fellow human beings are corollary. We love God through our fellow human beings and we love our fellow human beings by loving God.

In this volume you will find teachings of Judaism that touch on all of these matters. You will embark on a journey that describes the task of building the road to the Divine in one's life, in society and in the world. You will discover that this ancient road, this well-traveled road, is still under construction, and that many who came before have toiled mightily to bring us this far. We wayfarers join them in this task, in this responsibility, in the tradition that has been handed down from generation to generation.

Notes:

1   Danby, Herbert. *The Mishnah: Translated from the Hebrew with Introduction and Brief Explanatory Notes*, p. 388. Oxford: Oxford UP, 1933.

2   Herford, *My Amended Translation of Rabbi Jose*, p. 25.

3   "Pharisees and Other Essays," *Essays in Tradition in Judaism*, p. 53.

4   XVII Theropeia by Cushman.

5   Slonimsky, "Philosophy Implicit in the Midrash," *Essays*, p. 24.

6   Leo Baeck, *The Pharisees and Other Essays*, Schocken Books, NY, p. 57.

7   Max Brod, *Paganism, Christianity and Judaism*, University of Alabama Press, 1921, p. 87.

8   Baeck, op. cit., p. 59.

Jewish Imagery

Despite the tradition against the creation of images as expressed in the Ten Commandments, many Jewish artists and artisans express themselves in the plastic arts by exulting in the service and glorification of God. This will to express God's transcendant nature manifests itself in a continuous, evolving artistic narrative—from the mosaics of the ancient synagogues to the glass memorials at Yad Vashem.

Because this narrative has been constantly broken through the millennia, with confiscations of moveable property and the destruction of synagogues added to recurring persecutions and expulsions, very few objets d'art survive. But in those that do, the basic truths inherent and experienced by believing in God and living through Jewish history are reiterated. The works often depict rituals and ceremonies, or use Biblical texts and Hebrew characters as motifs. Much that did survive was not intended to be "art"—they are the adorned ritual objects that are nevertheless expressions of deep emotion and love of God.

And God descended awesome in might,

And God spoke the Ten Commandments to every Israelite,

Baruch Atoh Adonai, hamaariv aravim.

Beloved God, You make the day pass and bring in the night.

—Yosef the Lesser bar Shmuel, R. Yosef Tuv Elem

The soul of every living being shall bless Your Name, Lord, our God; the spirit of all flesh shall always glorify and exalt Your remembrance, our King. From this world to the World to Come, You are God, and other than You we have no king, redeemer or savior. Liberator, Rescuer, Sustainer and Merciful One in every time of distress and anguish, we have no king but You! God of the first and of the last, G-d of all creatures, Master of all generations, Who is extolled through a multitude of praises, Who guides His world with kindness and His creatures with mercy.

—from the Nishmat prayer, Sabbath and Holiday liturgy.

O Lord thou hast deceived me,

And I was deceived;

Thou art stronger than I,

And thou hast prevailed.

I have become a laughingstock all the day;

Everyone mocks me.

For whenever I speak, I cry out,

I shout "Violence and destruction!"

For the word of the Lord has become for me

A reproach and derision all day long.

If I say "I will not mention him,

Or speak anymore in his name,"

There is in my heart as it were a burning fire

Shut up in my bones,

And I am weary of holding it in and I cannot.

—Jeremiah 20:1-10

Salvation of the Lord

I called to the Lord, out of my distress,

And he answered me; out of the belly of Sheol I cried,

and thou didst hear my voice.

> *For thou didst cast me into the deep, into the heart of the seas, and the flood was round about me; all thy waves and thy billows passed over me.*

> *Then I said, 'I am cast out from thy presence; how shall I again look upon thy holy temple?'*

> *The waters closed in over me, the deep was round about me; weeds were wrapped about my head at the roots of the mountains.*

> *I went down to the land whose bars closed upon me for ever; yet thou didst bring up my life from the Pit, O Lord my God.*

> *When my soul fainted within me, I remembered the Lord; and my prayer came to thee,*

> *Into thy holy temple.*

> *Those who pay regard to vain idols forsake their true loyalty.*

> *But I with the voice of thanksgiving will sacrifice to thee; what I have vowed I will pay. Deliverance belongs to the Lord!*

> *—The Book of Jonah*

Jerusalem of Gold

The mountain air is clear as wine

And the scent of pines

Is carried on the breeze of twilight

With the sound of bells.

And in the slumber of tree and stone

Captured in her dream

The city that sits solitary

And in its midst is a wall.

Jerusalem of gold, and of bronze, and of light

Behold I am a violin for all your songs.

—Naomi Shemer

This Berlin synagogue in the Moorish style was dedicated one week before Hitler took power in 1933 and was set ablaze in the 1938 pogrom known as Kristallnacht. The local chief of police, Wilhelm Krützfeld, tried to save the magnificent structure and ordered the flames doused. As a result, he was rebuked and demoted. The building was left in ruins until 1987 when, as part of the 750th birthday of Berlin, the GDR restored the synagogue, which is now part of the Jewish Museum complex in the city.

Sound the great Shofar for our liberty,

And raise a banner to gather our exiles,

And gather us together

From the four corners of the Earth.

     —from the Amida,

      the Eighteen Benedictions in the daily liturgy

בָּרוּךְ אַתָּה יְיָ שׁוֹמֵעַ קוֹל

יִשְׂרָאֵל בְּרַחֲמִים

קִי

הָ

עוֹ

כְּ

עַ

אִם

רַחֲמֵינוּ כְּהַחֵם אָב עַל בָּנִים

Hear, Israel, the Lord is our God, the Lord is One.

Blessed be the Name of His glorious kingdom for ever and ever.

And you shall love the Lord your God with all your heart and with all your soul and with all your might. And these words that I command you today shall be in your heart. And you shall teach them diligently to your children, and you shall speak of them when you sit at home, and when you walk along the way, and when you lie down and when you rise up. And you shall bind them as a sign on your hand, and they shall be for frontlets between your eyes. And you shall write them on the doorposts of your house and on your gates.

—Deuteronomy 6:4–9, daily liturgy

•

CHAPTER ONE

Basics Concepts:
Jewish Thought and Tradition

Give ear, O my people, to my law:
incline your ears to the words of my mouth.
I will open my mouth in a parable:
I will utter dark sayings of old:
Which we have heard and known,
and our fathers have told us.
We will not hide them from their children,
shewing to the generation to come the praises of the Lord,
and his strength, and his wonderful works that he hath done.
For he established a testimony in Jacob,
and appointed a law in Israel, which he commanded our fathers,
that they should make them known to their children:
That the generation to come might know them,
even the children which should be born;
who should arise and declare them to their children:
That they might set their hope in God,
and not forget the works of God,
but keep his commandments.[1]

—Psalm 78:1-7

Parabola
Volume: 26.2
Light

On the First Day

Howard Schwartz

Everyone is familiar with the words of Genesis 1:3, "And God said, 'Let there be light,' and there was light." But the ancient rabbis, who scrutinized the words of the Bible for every hidden mystery, wondered what light this was. After all, God did not create the sun, the moon, and the stars until the fourth day. So what was the light of the first day?

In discussions scattered throughout rabbinic, kabbalistic, and Hasidic literature, the rabbis consider this question. They search for clues about this mysterious light in every book of the Bible, and find the clue they need in a prophecy of Isaiah. He speaks about what the world would be like in the messianic era: "Moreover, the light of the moon shall be as the light of the sun, and the light of the sun shall be sevenfold, as the light of the seven days" (Isaiah 30:26). Here a Biblical mystery is explicated right in the Bible: the light of the seven days of creation was seven times brighter than the sun.

Drawing on Isaiah's explanation, the rabbis conclude that the two lights—that of the first day and that of the fourth—are different. The light of the first day is a primordial light, what they call the *Or Haganuz*, or Hidden Light. This resolves the problem. But it also raises a whole series of new questions—what was the nature of that sacred light? Where did it come from, and where did it go?

These questions have been debated among the rabbis for many centuries, and they have arrived at a variety of explanations. But beneath the guise of exegesis, the rabbis wrestle with profound questions about God and the way in which God created the world. What is actually happening is that a Jewish myth is taking form, a very essential myth about the nature of the Divine and the mysteries of creation. Let us consider some of the primary permutations of this myth, which are often contradictory:

First of all, where did the light come from?

Some say it was the light of Paradise, which God brought into the world at the time of Creation. For the first three days and nights, the primordial light shone undiminished. Seven times brighter than the sun, it was so intense that no created thing could gaze upon it. In this light it was possible for Adam to see from one end of the universe to the other.

Yet others say that the light existed even before the Creation. When God said, "Let there be light," light came forth from the place in the universe where the Temple in Jerusalem would one day be built. Surrounded by that light, God completed the creation of the world.

How, then, did God bring the light into the world?

Some say that God wrapped himself in a prayer shawl of light, and the light cast from that prayer shawl suffused the world. Others say that God draped the six days of creation around Himself like a gown and dazzled the universe with His glory from one end to the other. Then there are those who say that God took the light and stretched it like a garment, and the heavens continued to expand until God said, "Enough!"

And where did the light go?

Some say that sacred light pervaded the world until the very moment that Adam and Eve tasted the forbidden fruit. Then the first thing they lost was that precious light, for losing it was one of the punishments of the Fall. Without it, the world grew dark around them, for the sun shone like a candle in comparison. Never again did they see the world in the splendor of that light, and that was the most painful punishment of all. Out of sympathy, God is said to have hidden a bit of that light inside a glowing stone and given it to Adam and Eve when they were expelled from the Garden, as a reminder of all that they had lost.

This stone, known as the *Tzohar*, is itself the subject of fabulous stories about how it was passed down from Adam, who slept in its light, to his son Seth, and from there to Enoch, Methuselah, and Lamech, until it reached Noah, who used it to illuminate the ark. Later, it was passed to Abraham, who is said to have worn it as an astrolabe around his neck, and eventually to the kings David and Solomon, who are said to have hung the glowing stone in the Temple in Jerusalem. After the destruction of the Temple, it disappeared.

By now, most of the questions have been addressed, but still unanswered is one of the most important: Did God create the primordial light or did it pre-exist? This question delves into mysteries of creation, about whether anything else existed before God created the world, whether God drew upon such preexisting elements or created everything anew, whether God had any assistance in creation, and even the unthinkable question of who created God. These are the kinds of questions that could undermine monotheism, the central pillar of Judaism. The advice of the Talmud is to avoid them: "Whoever gives his mind to four things, it would have been better if he had not been born—What is above? What is below? What came before? And what will come after?" Despite this warning, the Talmudic rabbis and all of their successors delve deeply into these questions, even when it brings them to the brink of what might be described as Jewish Gnosticism.

Take the light that existed in the place of the Temple, long before the Temple was built. What was it? It seems to have been some kind of primordial force existing in the universe, which God drew upon in creation. God chose to place the earth there because of that light. For the same reason, the site of the Temple in Jerusalem was at the very source of that light. The myth goes on to say that this holy light continued to emanate even after the Temple was built in that place. Its source was in the Holy of Holies, and it lit up the Temple and shone forth through the windows—for there were windows in the Temple, but instead of light coming into them, it went out of them. Indeed, the windows were built for this purpose, narrow on the inside and broad on the outside, in order to send forth light into the world. The light that shone forth from the Temple filled the Holy Land, and all basked in its presence.

According to this version of the myth, the primordial light continued to exist, at least until the Temple was destroyed. This differs from other versions which insist that God removed the light from the world and hid it somewhere; that is why it is known as the Hidden Light. Most say

God hid it in the world to come. That is where the souls of the righteous are said to go when they take leave of this life, where the rewards of Paradise—such as studying Torah with the Patriarchs—await them. But in the thirteenth century the Zohar, the central text of Jewish mysticism, offered a hint that the light might have been hidden somewhere else: "Whenever the Torah is studied at night, a single ray comes from the hidden light and stretches out to those who study." Drawing on this clue in the eighteenth century, the Ba'al Shem Tov, founder of Hasidism, proposed that God had hidden the primordial light in the Torah. For those who immerse themselves in the study of the Torah, the light would shine forth, and they would experience the revelation of the Hidden Light.

Rabbi Nachman of Bratslav, the greatest Jewish storyteller—who also happened to be the great-grandson of the Ba'al Shem Tov—agreed with his great-grandfather's explanation of where the light was hidden. But he added that it was hidden in the stories of the Torah. Rabbi Nachman truly loved *stories* and found them full of hidden light.

That might have been the end of the story, but it's not. Another nineteenth-century rabbi, Rabbi Menachem Mendel of Riminov, insisted that the primordial light had never been hidden after all and was still present, but only the truly righteous could see it. It is invisible to everyone else.

Jewish myths have continued to evolve even into the present. The many explanations of the meaning and fate of the hidden light are part of a continuing dialogue that has gone on for more than two thousand years. Rabbi Nachman of Bratslav said of this dialogue: "Two men who live in different places, or even in different generations, may still converse. For one may raise a question, and the other who is far away in time or in space may make a comment or ask a question that answers it. So they converse, but no one knows it save the Lord."

Thus the Bible begins with a mysterious light—distinct from that of the fourth day of creation—which God brings into the world as a sacred, primordial light, cast from God's garment. In some versions of the myth God removes the light and saves it for the righteous in the world to come. In others, God hides it in the Torah, where it is waiting to be found. In still others, it has been here all along, for those who are capable of seeing it.

Parabola
Volume: 14.2
Tradition and
Transmission

AFTER THE BRIGHT LIGHT OF REVELATION

Interview with Rabbi Adin Steinsaltz

Rabbi Adin Steinsaltz has published many books on the Talmud, Jewish mysticism, religious thought, and related topics. He has also translated many ancient Hebrew and Aramaic texts of the Talmud and their later commentaries into modern Hebrew and English, adding new commentary and extensive notes. Yehuda Hanegbi, a close friend and associate of Rabbi Steinsaltz, spoke to Rabbi Steinsaltz about the Jewish tradition.

Yehuda Hanegbi: *Since the Jewish tradition is one of the oldest in human history, it would be valuable to learn something of its origin and durability. Is it possible to ascertain the sources of this tradition? Are they specifically Jewish or are they not also drawn from a broad ancient pre-history, like the stories of Creation and the Flood, original monotheism, primitive worship of the heavenly bodies?*

Adin Steinsaltz: Even though much of the Biblical tradition relates to legends and events that occurred before the giving of the Torah, this total revelation at Mt. Sinai stands at the center of the world of Jewish consciousness. All the other sources that presumably preceded it, like certain stories of the Creation of the world, the origins of the laws and customs of ancient society and so on, did not reach Judaism independently, they passed through the great filtering of divine revelation at Sinai. The influences of the outer world, ancient legends and lore of the nations round about, certainly spread to the Jewish people of the time, but it was all cast into the melting pot of the Jewish tradition itself. The bright light of revelation of the Torah at Sinai fused it into a single entity. It was a process that was repeated in subsequent generations. To the extent that external influences did find their way into Judaism, they almost always appeared as subsidiary, not intrinsic to the core. And indeed there was a certain opposition to them: if they could not be merged, they were ultimately ejected. When they did melt into the Jewish tradition, they were so thoroughly integrated that it would be almost impossible to identify them as foreign.

YH: *What is the role of Divine revelation in Judaism, especially considering the preponderance of law and custom?*

AS: As we have said, theologically and not only theologically, the revelation at Mt. Sinai is the core of Judaism. And this not only because it is the beginning but because it is apprehended as a total and all-inclusive revelation. That is, this revelation is considered the opening point, the transition point between the higher essence and the lower essence (God and man). After this revelation there is actually no need for a new revelation because besides being the first or original of its kind, the Revelation is a one-time event that includes all the other revelatory events. It has been compared to the primordial act of the creation of the world, which was also a first and single act and included all that was and will be in the world. So too, the revelation at Mt. Sinai is such a unique event containing in it all that afterwards will ever be made known about the connection between God and man.

Therefore the Jewish tradition is full and complete—not because it relies only on an ancient single source, the Bible, but because it is open to additions. All the accumulated oral traditions are considered part of the original written Torah. Even details of the oral Torah, obviously belonging to a much later period, are considered to be continuations of the original revelation. It is all the same revelation, written or oral, and includes the ancient text and the ever-changing unwritten social form and custom.

In the *Pirkei Avot* book of the Talmud, the tradition is described as a *Shalshelet Kabbalah*, a chain of reception, a process of handing on, from one generation to the next: from Moses to Joshua and from Joshua to the elders and from the elders to the prophets, until the last of the Sages. This concept of a continuous chain is very central to the whole Jewish outlook on tradition. And it does not only go back to revelation: the very notion of the inspired person or persons who act as a link in the chain throughout the generations is a profound contribution to the revelation without necessarily changing it. The original revelation contained all that was eventually relevant to it. Those men who contributed to knowledge were in reality discoverers; they did not invent new ideas or theories, they merely uncovered truths that were already there.

YH: *What is the secret of the tenacity of the Jewish religion, outlasting persecution, dispersion, the fall of civilization, and even the influence of modernism?*

AS: There are certainly many reasons for the lasting existence of the Jewish religion. In a certain sense, it is one of the riddles, or permanent secrets, of the reality of things. As the philosopher Kant is believed to have said: There are two proofs of the existence of God: one is the stars in the sky, the other is the existence of the Jewish people. One may discern that there is a secret here, a hint of the dialectic interrelation between tradition and historic reality. Because when tradition is all-embracing, beyond the influence of time and place, it becomes that in which reality is contained. If and when a collision does occur between tradition and unanticipated aspects of changing realities, the individual person will reach out to find in his tradition those elements of coherence and certainty that are relevant to the new situation, whether it be a material or spiritual challenge. And the Jew has known a great number of such challenging confrontations: exile, servitude, harsh decrees, antagonistic opposing philosophies and oppressive circumstances. His return to tradition has taken many forms; it was never the mechanical restoration of a fixed structure. The tradition itself adjusted to the new situation. New responses were elicited. Because the Jewish tradition is not an inert inheritance, it is like a living organism able to react and respond to a variety of changing circumstances.

YH: *How does the concept of* Knesset Yisrael *function in the preservation of the tradition? Is it as a mystique of the national ego or as a mystique of egolessness (contained in the concept of the* Shekhinah, *or spirit of God) which is its counterpart?*

AS: In many respects, tradition in Judaism is called "Torah." And this is one of the words that have no exact translation: the accepted translation, "Law," is certainly incorrect. "Torah," even in its verbal meaning, includes the Bible as well as the law, philosophy, dream, legend, and everything else that constitutes human life. The one word, Torah, signifies that which instructs and enlightens: it is much more broad and dynamic a concept than simply the teaching. And the subject of Torah, that which carries it, or the medium through which it manifests, is Knesset Yisrael. The translated concept is "the assembly of Israel," but it is not at all a statistical totality or a numerical sum of a particular group of people; it is that which one may loosely call the soul of the people. Most important is its function as the bearer of the Torah. In many ways its life and actions are themselves among the creative forces of Torah, of tradition. The Jewish community keeps determining *Halacha*, doctrine and custom, at every crossroads. The decision is made by consulting the Torah and then itself becomes Torah. So that Knesset Yisrael is not the passive bearer of a yoke of Torah and law that has been thrust upon it; it is an active component of the Torah. Its entire being is a constant merging of life and Torah and the result is the essence of Jewish tradition. Not in vain has the relation between God and Knesset Yisrael been likened to that between man and wife. From which it may be understood that the interaction, besides the love and respect between them, has a great depth of intimacy and potency. In order for something to be born, for anything to happen, the role of Knesset Yisrael is that of the bearer, the means, or the vehicle. As such Knesset Yisrael is the many-sided subject and instrument of Torah and Jewish tradition.

YH: *Can one say that Judaism has a special relation to time, enabling it to transcend the natural forces of decay?*

AS: The problem of the relation to time is indeed intrinsic to the tradition, but not in the sense of a fossil, of something petrified. Time itself is an entity within the tradition. The image is generally that of a tall tree, a living organism; as more time passes, the taller it grows. The tradition thus does not undergo drastic changes; its essence remains the same. Like certain trees, thousands of years old, that live as a biological unity, the tradition creates from within itself the parts that renew its intrinsic form. The factor of time, as a process of decay, has relatively little influence on its basic essence. It can be uprooted only by some massive upheaval, but not because it has reached a certain point in time. Unlike anything fabricated, or man-made, it has the capacity of restoring itself by division and multiplication and growth, and by a stubborn retention of essence.

YH: *What are the modes of transmitting the tradition? Is it mainly through written works like the Bible and the Talmud? Or are other factors, such as custom, holidays, and oral transmission, more important?*

AS: When the tradition is vital and active within the community, it carries on almost without words, without saying anything. It is transmitted because the Jewish tradition is not only a verbal deposit, it is a very inclusive message that relates to the whole of life and not only to religion or to the historic past. Therefore it is passed on via almost all the channels of daily life. The written past of the tradition lives within the details of contemporary work and food and blessings. One may even define the tradition as being composed of two elements: One is that of life—habits, speech, manners, from the preparation of food and the choice of garments to the various rituals of passage and the facial expressions of the people: the other is that which is transmitted by written texts and verbal teachings. The relation between these two aspects of the tradition is, on one hand, a very conscious application and carrying out of the inherited legacy: on the other hand, it is an unspoken belonging to the written Torah. That which is not articulated is not less important. The conscious and the unconscious transmission proceed together to create the wholeness of living tradition. And wherever there is a crisis in any one aspect of transmission (if the conscious community connections are severed or if there is a break in the educational conveyance of the past), the tradition tends to become atrophied into some kind of mask of itself or else it becomes excessively vulnerable to outside influences without even knowing what is happening.

In a community that manages to live in some sort of integrated wholeness, there is a dynamically proportional relation which is not the same for all the members of the community. The functions are divided. For certain people the conscious component is greater, for others it is much less. For all of them, however, there is a need to combine the two components, the conscious and the unconscious, so that the society finds itself automatically structured by them. There is an ordering of functions, as in a living body. The brain, which consists of the more intellectual and learned part of the community, has to be maintained at a high level. The rest of the body, whose level of consciousness is different, divides itself, and each part relates with great plasticity to the rest of the being. To be sure, it is impossible for any part not to have some degree of consciousness or connection with consciousness. At the same time, there is no part without its relatively unconscious physical elements of existence, blood vessels and bones and flesh. The whole is what makes each part function.

YH: *As far as the documentary evidence shows, the Kabbalah was never a prominent feature in the life of the people, yet there can be little doubt as to its profound influence on the religion, customs, folklore. What was its place in the past, what is its role today?*

AS: The Kabbalah was never a conspicuous part of the daily life of the Jewish people. To be more precise, we would say that the Kabbalah as a conscious study was restricted to a small elite. This was usually a closed circle of people who could devote themselves to it—not only because of the intellectual complexities of the Kabbalah, but because, more than in any other field of Jewish tradition, a very great moral purity was required of the student. Such a high level of moral and spiritual experience could scarcely be expected of an ordinary person. In any case, by its very nature, the pursuit of esoteric wisdom is limited to a chosen few.

Nevertheless, the Kabbalah has had such a profound influence on the tradition that one may even see it as the theology of Judaism. This is especially true of the last 500 years or so—in spite of the fact that in our own time the Kabbalah is just beginning to emerge from the obscurity into which it was thrust by "enlightened" rationalism.

What is apparent, however, is the influence of the Kabbalah on almost all the features of daily life, from ancient times to the present. True, not everyone is aware of it, but almost every Jewish custom is likely to have some Kabbalistic significance or at least to have been fashioned by some such influence.

This means that the practical Kabbalah—not in its crude magic and miracle-making folk expressions, but in its deep penetration into the action, rituals and prayers, the laws, language and customs of the people—is still existent. There is a core of those few who have made the Kabbalah a source of inner transformation and esoteric knowledge. But there are widening circles, whose authority was never significant, but whose influence manages to be felt somehow.

To be sure, only the inner circle is likely to know the meaning of many of the old expressions and actions. In the further circles, people simply know that this is the way things are done; certain words are said, ritual actions are performed without comprehending why or how they came into being. From this point of view, the Kabbalah is still very much present—even if unknown to the majority of the people. Most Jews would probably angrily reject the notion that many of their traditional modes of expression are "kabbalistic."

YH: *What lies behind the various legendary versions of the carriers of the tradition in every generation, such as, for example, those mentioned in* Pirkei Avot, *or, in another sense entirely, the thirty-six hidden* tzadikim *(wise men) whose existence sustains the world?*

AS: As we said, the tradition of the *Shalshelet haKabbalah*, the Chain of Receiving, is basically the tradition of Jewish leadership. It is a listing of a certain number of the more prominent persons who were bearers of the light of knowledge; it does not deny that there were others who also carried it. The point of the chain is that there was a continuity, an uninterrupted flow.

We also have the concept of the thirty-six *tzadikim* whose existence sustains the world from one generation to another. In this age-old tradition, it is not a body of people who are in touch with one another; each one is alone and for the most part does not have any idea about himself or the others. They simply do not know who they are or what they're doing.

The important thing is that, from the point of view of divine justice, the world cannot continue to exist except if there be a certain number of persons who justify its existence. As an archetype, we have the story of Abraham and the destruction of Sodom and Gomorrah. The question is: Why should any place that is full of wickedness be allowed to perpetuate itself? And the answer is that a minimal number of righteous persons can compensate for the evil of the many and check the course of retribution. Thus, if there were not a certain number of *Tzadikim* who justify the continued existence of the world, the world would be destroyed like Sodom, like the world at the time of the Flood. Therefore there is the tradition of the thirty-six saintly persons whose existence on earth in every generation, whether they know it or not, keeps the world from being annihilated.

YH: *Can there be said to be a definite Jewish body that carries the tradition, whether national, racial, or social?*

AS: Even in the distant past, there was probably no single body that one could point to as the sole bearer of Jewish tradition; but let us return to the analogy of the body. Generally, we can claim that the center of consciousness is in the brain. But at many periods of time during the day or the night, the point of consciousness moves to different centers; sometimes it's at the speech center, sometimes it is concentrated in the eyes or some other organ of perception. The movement of consciousness seems to be one of the signs of life and one could almost imagine light bulbs going on and off all over the body to indicate where awareness is being focused.

Every part of the organic wholeness, which is both the mystical and the material body, has a special function which is his and only his. His role is vital to this body and no one else can fill it. And the way a person fills his role is significant, not only for himself but for the entire body. What is more, just as a person cannot be sick only in his little finger and just as any sickness of a part imperils the well-being of the whole body, so too is there a vital interrelationship between the individual and the community. The way the individual Jew assumes his rightful place in the organism determines the shape of his life and the life of the whole.

Historically, too, there is such a movement of the center of Jewish consciousness, from country to country, from place to place. Of course there have been occasions when the center was not in any one particular place or country but could be seen as scattered, or existing simultaneously in a number of places.

YH: *How much of the tradition can you guess has been lost?*

AS: From the very nature of things, it is very difficult to know the quality and the value of whatever got lost. In those instances where fragments have remained we can only surmise what had once been there, like the stump of a tree. But even less than that can we know anything about human traditions that have left no mark. And this is true of every realm of human life—law, custom, mysticism, art.

In recent generations especially, the wanderings (and changes) of the Jews have been characterized by a brutality and swiftness that are almost unprecedented. We can observe how, before our very eyes, the inability to permit adequate transition and acclimatization of well-established structures (education, religion, social services) and of life patterns in the family, has entailed the loss of thousands upon thousands of details.

In spite of efforts to save some fragments of the tradition, most of it is irretrievably gone, and it does not matter whether it's old songs or ancient wisdom or the food preparations of a millennium. A large part of the Jewish tradition is thus continually being lost; and it's not only that most of the old ways and social forms and institutions are being swallowed up by more modern methods, it's the tone and inner unity that go.

To follow the simile of the tree, one would say that the whole or branches of the tree had been cut off by a combination of many outside forces. But there is always the hope that when circumstances will change, some of the buds that have always remained will grow again—with the renewal of those branches the form and the content will be complete.

In the large scheme of history, it may be observed that the Jewish people, which grew up and reached a certain maturity in its own land, was in exile for hundreds of years. And this meant the loss of much more than national sovereignty: whole areas of tradition were abandoned and only vague hints survived in memory. One can hardly reconstruct the richness of this tradition from the written evidence. To a degree, the temple, the legal and social structure, the schools and synagogues, can be pieced together in some fashion or other. The mystical traditions are far more elusive to the modern researcher. Most of them have been totally wiped out by time, such as the schools of the prophets. We have nothing resembling such schools, either in Israel or in the Diaspora. In fact, there have been attempts to make such a restoration by pasting scattered indications together. Some of this material has survived only in written form; most of it is considered irretrievably lost. Nevertheless, the dream or hope of restitution has remained. In the days to come, a regeneration is possible, if the right stimulant will appear. This anticipation is possible because, as in every organic entity, the code of the whole is contained in the fragments, so that from the little that has come down to us it may be possible to reconstruct a semblance of the ancient tradition.

YH: *Can you point to something definite that has been learned by the Jews that would help other traditions now in danger of extinction?*

AS: There is at least one thing that other traditions can learn from the Jewish experience, and that is that a tradition in itself—even if it is almost hermetically sealed, something that doesn't exist any more—cannot continue to exist only by the force of inertia. A tradition cannot leave things in a state of unchanging status quo. In the Jewish experience this factor has been very prominent; the group awareness was always alive to whatever threatened it and ready to invest energy to guard the tradition and to maintain it—not necessarily to freeze it. Whenever the group was unwilling to pit itself against imminent change by investing thought and effort, the change was destructive to the tradition.

The question here is not the value of the resilience of the tradition, but the fact that any social form that does not keep reinvesting energy into its continuation will tend to die out. The efforts required are always very great. True, many traditions have survived in conditions of relative isolation. But today, folk cultures are being destroyed by no more than superficial contact with some outer influence. And this is because the people involved are without adequate consciousness of themselves or without the will to do anything about it. They are not prepared to invest the enormous effort required to meet the challenge of the contact with alien forces. But this has to be learned—and sometimes it comes too late.

The Jewish world has almost always been intensely aware of the problem. And over the centuries, a very great deal has been poured into education, in the preparation of spiritual guides and teachers of all sorts and in the maintenance of the general framework of the tradition. In many places it amounted to one third or even more of the general expenditure of the local or national body. This was one of the main factors that helped keep the tradition going in spite of very difficult external conditions. Therefore, one can say that any group or tradition that is willing and able to invest considerable effort in maintaining its existence is that much more able to withstand the process of decay from within and destruction from without.

Parabola
Volume: 17.3
Oral Tradition

ETHICS OF THE FATHERS

Translated by Philip Birnbaum

Moses received the Torah at Sinai and handed it down to Joshua; Joshua to the elders; the elders to the prophets; and the prophets handed it down to the men of the Great Assembly. The latter said three things: Be patient in the administration of justice; develop many students; and make a fence for the Torah.

Simeon the Just was one of the last survivors of the Great Assembly. He used to say: The world is based on three principles: Torah, worship, and kindliness.

Antigonus of Sokho received the oral tradition from Simeon the Just. He used to say: Be not like servants who serve the master for the sake of receiving a reward, but be like servants who serve the master without the expectation of receiving a reward; and let the fear of Heaven be upon you.

Yose' ben Yo'ezer of Zeredah and Yose' ben Yohanan of Jerusalem received the oral tradition from the preceding. Yose' ben Yo'ezer said: Let your house be a meeting place for scholars; sit at their feet in the dust, and drink in their words thirstingly.

Yose' ben Yohanan of Jerusalem said: Let your house be wide open [to strangers]; treat the poor as members of your own family; and do not gossip with women. This has been said even with regard to one's own wife, how much more does it apply to another man's wife. Hence the sages say: Whoever gossips with women brings harm to himself, for he neglects the study of the Torah and will in the end inherit *Gehinnom*.

Joshua ben Perahyah and Nittai of Arbel received the oral tradition from the preceding. Joshua ben Perahyah said: Provide yourself with a teacher; get yourself a companion; and judge all men favorably.

Nittai of Arbel said: Keep aloof from a bad neighbor; do not associate with an evil man; and do not give up the belief in retribution [wickedness will not succeed in the end].

Judah ben Tabbai and Simeon ben Shatah received the oral tradition from the preceding. Judah ben Tabbai said: Do not [as a judge] play the part of a counselor; when the parties in a lawsuit are standing before you, regard them both as guilty; but when they go away from you, after having submitted to the judgment, regard them both as innocent.

Simeon ben Shatah said: Examine the witnesses thoroughly; be careful with your words, lest through them the witnesses learn to give false testimony.

Shemayah and Avtalyon received the oral tradition from the preceding. Shemayah said: Love work; hate the holding of public office; and do not be intimate with the ruling authorities.

Avtaylon said: Scholars, be careful with your words! You may incur the penalty of exile and be banished to a place of evil waters [heretical teachings], and the disciples who follow you into exile are likely to drink of them and die [a spiritual death], with the result that the name of Heaven would be profaned.

Hillel and Shammai received the oral tradition from the preceding. Hillel said: Be of the disciples of Aaron, loving peace and pursuing peace; be one who loves his fellow men and draws them near to the Torah.

He used to say: He who seeks greater reputation loses his reputation; he who does not increase his knowledge decreases it; he who does not study deserves death; he who makes unworthy use of the crown [of learning] shall perish.

He used to say: If I am not for myself, who is for me? If I care only for myself, what am I? If not now, when?

Shammai said: Make your study of the Torah a regular habit; say little but do much; and receive all men cheerfully.

Rabban Gamaliel said: Provide yourself with a teacher and avoid doubt; and do not make a habit of giving tithes by guesswork.

Simeon his son said: All my life I have been brought up among the sages, and I have found nothing better for a person than silence; study is not the most important thing but practice; and whoever talks too much brings about sin.

Rabban Simeon ben Gamaliel said: The world is established on three principles: truth, justice, and peace, as it is said: "You shall administer truth, justice and peace within your gates" (Zechariah 8:16)

Rabbi Hananyah ben Akashyah said: The Holy One, blessed be he, desired to purify Israel; hence he gave them a Torah rich in rules of conduct, as it is said: "The Lord was pleased, for the sake of [Israel's] righteousness, to render the Torah great and glorious" (Isaiah 42:21).

From *Ethics of the Fathers*, Philip Birnbaum, tr. Reprinted by permission of the publishers, Hebrew Publishing Co., PO Box 157, Rockaway Beach, NY, 11693. Copyright © 1977. All rights reserved.

Parabola
Volume: 15.3
Liberation

LIVING LIBERATION AT A PASSOVER SEDER

Rabbi Philip Bentley

In each generation a person is obligated to see himself as though he had gone out of Egypt. As it says in the Torah: "And you shall explain to your child on that day, 'It is because of what the Lord did for me when I came forth out of Egypt'" (Exodus 13:8). For not only did God redeem our ancestors from Egypt, but we were redeemed along with them.

—The Passover Haggadah

The exodus from Egypt is a basic archetype of Western political thought and culture, one which has been adopted by many of the world's peoples. For the Jewish people, however, it is the fundamental myth of both their religious and national origins. Being a part of that living myth is an essential element of every Jew's identity.

In order for each Jew to see himself as actually having been among those who were liberated from bondage in Egypt, it is not enough just to retell the story of the Exodus. No synagogue ritual could possibly achieve what is accomplished at the Passover Seder, a festival meal usually held at home. Through rituals, symbols, readings, songs, discussions—and even games—the experience of going from slavery to freedom is reenacted at the family table.

All of this is based on a slender book called the Haggadah, which means "telling" in Hebrew, though there is much more here than a story. The Haggadah is a manual which guides the participants through every aspect of the Seder. No book in all of Jewish literature exists in so many versions and forms: there are said to be over a thousand editions in existence. Some feature the work of an artist interpreting the story and rituals, some include commentaries, some are versions especially written to respond to a particular need, and some are simple little pamphlets providing the text and a translation.

This book is actually a sophisticated pedagogical device. It contains elements which are meant to appeal to every temperament, every age, every intellectual capacity. Of special interest to children are the hide-and-seek game with a piece of Matzah, the description of the moment when the door of the house must be opened to admit the Biblical prophet Elijah, and the recitation of the Four Questions which are meant to encourage everyone to ask many questions. On the other hand, there are sophisticated comments and observations meant to pique the interest of the most scholarly person at the table. As it says early in the Seder:

> *And even if all of us were wise, all of us intelligent, all of us learned in the Torah, it is still a commandment to tell about the Exodus from Egypt; and everyone who enlarges on the telling, behold this is praiseworthy.*

On the Seder table there are many symbols, most of which will actually be eaten. On a special plate in the center of the table there are six items:

> *1 -* Z'roa: *a lamb shank symbolizing the paschal lamb;*
> *2 -* Beytzah: *an egg, usually roasted, symbolizing renewal;*
> *3 -* Maror: *a bitter herb, usually horseradish, symbolizing the bitterness of slavery;*
> *4 -* Hazeret: *a second bitter herb, usually romaine lettuce;*
> *5 -* Karpas: *a green vegetable, usually parsley or celery, symbolizing Spring;*
> *6 -* Haroset: *a brown-colored condiment which is a reminder of the mortar used in the work of the slaves in Egypt.*

Near the Seder plate is a covered plate with the unleavened bread called Matzah. By each place there is a wine cup which will be filled four times during the Seder. Also on the table are dishes of salt water into which the green vegetable will be dipped. The brine is a reminder of the tears of slavery. Finally there is a special wine cup set for the prophet Elijah who, according to tradition, visits every Seder and who will someday come to announce the ultimate liberation of the whole world under the Messiah.

The story of the Exodus is not told in a straightforward way. In fact it is begun twice and interrupted twice before it is told at all. Each time the humility of Jewish beginnings is emphasized: "We were slaves to Pharaoh in Egypt." In Hebrew the word for "Egypt" is *Mitzrayim*, a word which is understood to come from the word *tzar*, which means "narrow." To be in slavery is to be in a tight spot.

After a rather lengthy interruption, the story begins again: "Our ancestors were idol-worshippers." This emphasizes that if Jews have become special, it is because of what they have done, not because of any innate superiority.

After another interruption, the story really begins: "Go forth and learn what Laban the Aramean sought to do to our father Jacob." The Jewish people were slaves and idolaters and fugitives, yet were liberated. At the Seder they remember not only the liberation, but also the humble beginnings and sufferings which preceded it. This is very much in tune with the Torah's reminding its readers no less than thirty-six times not to mistreat strangers and foreigners because they themselves were strangers and foreigners in Egypt. In eighteenth century Poland, Rabbi Jacob Joshua Falk asked why the Torah says "Proclaim liberty throughout the land unto ALL the inhabitants thereof" (Leviticus 25:10). The "all" is not superfluous, because in any state where anyone is not free, no one is free.

The telling of the story itself is not a simple narrative but a running commentary on a brief retelling of the story which is part of a ritual described in Deuteronomy (26:5-9). Moses is not the hero: he is only mentioned once. God, Israel, and Egypt are the only important "characters" in this story, which is part of what gives the Exodus, as experienced at the Seder table, its timeless mythic quality. The telling is bracketed by passages which emphasize the present factor of liberation. Before the telling, we read:

This promise has held true for our ancestors and for us. It is not one only who has stood against us, but in every generation there are those who stand against us seeking to destroy us and God saves us from their hand.

After the telling comes the passage with which this article began. The rituals of the Seder thus encompass liberation in the past, in the present, and in the future.

Two of the symbols on the table are especially potent in teaching us about liberation: Matzah and wine.

Near the beginning of the ritual, the leader lifts up the Matzah plate and recites:

This is the bread of affliction which our ancestors ate in the land of Egypt. Let anyone who is hungry come and eat. Let anyone who is in need come and celebrate Passover. This year we are here; next year may we be in the Land of Israel. This year we are slaves; next year may we be free.

Through most of the telling of the story the Matzahs are left uncovered so as to act as witness to the Exodus. At the end of the telling, before the actual meal, the major symbols on the table are pointed out and explained:

Why do we eat this Matzah? Because the dough of our ancestors did not have time to rise before God was revealed and redeemed them. ...

"The bread of affliction" has now become a reminder of liberation. How can it be both? Part of the answer may lie in a traditional explanation of why Jews are commanded to eat only unleavened bread during Passover: leavening is said to symbolize arrogance, being "puffed up." Truly free people do not try to lord it over others but are willing to share: "Let all who are hungry come and eat." The Talmud says, "One who has acquired a slave has acquired a master." To be truly free one must also be freed of the need to rule over others. Those who can give up leavening and limit themselves to unleavened bread and are, moreover, willing to share even that, can see the bread of affliction and poverty become the bread of liberation.

Four cups of wine are drunk at the Seder. These are said to correspond to four expressions of redemption found in the Torah (Exodus 6:6-7), as Rabbi Benzion Uziel has explained:

> *1 - "I will free you" – This refers to the physical removal of Israel from bondage in Egypt.*
> *2 - "and deliver you" – This refers to Liberation in preparation for Redemption. A slave will never be redeemed if he does not even recognize that he has been given liberation from bondage. Simply being taken out of slavery does not give a person freedom. Freedom only comes when slaves overcome their feelings of servitude.*
> *(3) "I will redeem you" – this alludes to ultimate Redemption,*
> *(4) "And I will take you" – The Israelites were not only redeemed from Egypt and its servitude, but were also promised to be lifted to a higher understanding of God's provenance, to create a just and compassionate society and to live their lives on a high level of holiness.*
>
> —*As quoted by Rabbi Marc Angel in*
> A Sephardic Passover Haggadah, *p.85.*

A fifth cup is sometimes poured to symbolize future redemption. The last part of the Seder looks to the future. The blessing for the fourth cup of wine is a prayer for a return to the Land of Israel in peace and prosperity. The end of the ritual is punctuated by singing out, "Next year in Jerusalem!" The evening ends with a series of songs whose texts are alphabetic acrostics and number games. Each of them ends on a note of hope for future redemption. The most poplar and famous of these, "An Only Kid," is a game song (much like "The Farmer in the Dell" or "The House That Jack Built") which is said to retell the story of the people of Israel (symbolized by the kid), who have suffered under one power after another but will, in the end, be redeemed by God, who will conquer even death.

Jews for many generations and in many lands, under all kinds of circumstances, have celebrated liberation at the Passover Seder. Those living under the most horrible persecutions celebrate the freedom that is theirs because they serve God, and not any human power, first of all. Those living in more comfortable circumstances, even in lands of political liberty, say, "Now we are slaves," remembering not only that once they were indeed slaves, but that they share something with all of the enslaved of the world.

All of us are slaves and need to free ourselves; and no matter what is imposed on us, all of us are free.

Parabola
Volume: 9.4
Food

Manna and Wisdom

From the Zohar

YHVH said to Moses
"I am about to rain down for you bread from heaven."…
Moses said to Aaron
"Say to the whole assemblage of the children of Israel:
'Approach *YHVH*, for He has heard your grumbling.'"
As Aaron spoke to the whole assemblage of the
  Children of Israel,
they turned to face the desert,
for there, the Presence of *YHVH* had appeared in the
  cloud. …
That evening, the quail rose and covered the camp.
In the morning, there was a fall of dew around the camp.
The fall of dew rose,
and there, on the face of the desert,
a fine coating, as fine as frost on the ground.
The Children of Israel saw.
They said to one another, "What is it?"
for they did not know what it was.
Moses said to them
"It is the bread that *YHVH* has given you to eat."
  —*(Exodus 16: 4, 9-10, 13-15)*

Come and see:
Every single day, dew trickles down
from the Holy Ancient One to the Impatient One,

and the Orchard of Holy Apple Trees is blessed.
Some of the dew flows to those below;
holy angels are nourished by it,
each according to his diet,
as it is written:
"A human ate angel bread"
(Psalms 78:25).
Israel ate of that food in the desert.

Rabbi Shim'on said
"Some people are nourished by it even now!
Who are they?
The Comrades, who engage Torah day and night.
Do you think they are nourished by that very food?
No, by something like that very food;
two balancing one.

Come and see:
When Israel entered and joined themselves to the Holy King
by uncovering the holy marking,
they were pure enough to eat another kind of bread,
higher than at first.
At first, when Israel went out of Egypt,
they went into the bread called *Mazzah*.
Now they were purer;
they went in to eat higher bread from a high sphere,
as it is written:
'I am about to rain down for you bread from heaven,'
literally: from Heaven!
It was then that Israel discovered the taste of this sphere.
Comrades engaging Torah are nourished from an even higher sphere.
Which is that?
That which is written:
'Wisdom gives life to those who have it'
(Ecclesiastes 7:12),
a very high sphere."

Rabbi El'azar said to him
"If so, why are they weaker than other human beings?
Other human beings are stronger and more powerful;
the Comrades should be the stronger ones."

He said to him, "A good question!
Come and see:
All human food comes from above.
The food that comes from heaven and earth is for the whole world.
It is food for all; it is coarse and dense.
The food that comes from higher above is finer food,
coming from the sphere where Judgment is found.
This is the food that Israel ate when they went out of Egypt.

The food found by Israel that time in the desert,
from the higher sphere called Heaven—
it is an even finer food,
entering deepest of all into the soul,
detached from the body,
called angel bread.

The highest food of all is the food of the Comrades,
those who engage in Torah.
For they eat food of the spirit and the soul-breath;
they eat no food for the body at all.
Rather, from a high sphere, precious beyond all: Wisdom.
That is why a Comrade's body is weaker than a normal body:
they do not eat food for the body at all.
They eat food for the spirit and the soul-breath
from someplace far beyond, most precious of all.
So their food is finest of the fine, finest of all.

Happy is their portion!
As it is written:
'Wisdom gives life to those who have it.'
Happy is the body that can nourish itself on food of the soul!"

Rabbi El'azar said to him, "Certainly that is true.
But how can such food be found now?"

He answered, "Certainly a good question!
Come and see:
This is the clarity of the word. ...
The food of the Comrades engaging Torah is most precious of all.
This food flows from Wisdom on high.
Why from this sphere?
Because Torah derives from Wisdom on high,
and those who engage Torah enter the source of her roots;
so their food flows down from that high and holy sphere."

Rabbi El'azar came and kissed his hands.
He said, "Happy is my portion! I understand these words!
Happy is the portion of the righteous!
Engaging Torah day and night
entitles them to this world and the world that is coming,
as it is written:
'That is your life and the expanse of your days.'"

Parabola
Volume: 17.3
Oral Tradition

THE UNWRITTEN TORAH

Lawrence Fine

Since Judaism is founded on an unending structure of
written texts, as one author has aptly put it, like an inverted
pyramid with the Torah at the base, we might imagine
that there is little room for oral tradition there. Doesn't
the Torah itself leave us with the impression that the
awesome theophany in the wilderness of Sinai resulted in
a *fully formed* revelation, the utterly complete and perfect
word of God, rather than a story with a recognizable past,
or one in need of oral revision and embellishment? And
doesn't the post-Biblical tradition, with its thousands of
written sacred texts, its virtual requirement of literacy for
devotees, and its veneration of the written word, rule out
a prominent place for oral transmission? Nothing could
be further from the truth. On the contrary, as with every
living culture, every organic community, oral tradition has
played a crucial role in the long life of the Jewish people.

Despite the long-standing view that the Torah is a
divinely-authored revelation, "carved in stone" so to
speak, contemporary Biblical scholarship suggests to us
in increasingly sophisticated ways the complex processes
by which this literature evolved and took shape. Behind
the literary artistry of Biblical myth makers, historians,
storytellers, lawmakers, teachers of wisdom, and poets,
we can discern centuries of oral traditions. What else

would we expect from a literature so varied and so rich, one whose development took place over hundreds of years?

The phenomenon of oral tradition in Jewish culture assumes a more overt and self-conscious character, however, in the years following the Biblical era, as captured in the Hebrew expression *Torah she-be'al peh*, that is, "Oral Torah" or perhaps "Torah by memory." One of the earliest attestations of this conception is found in the writings of the first-century Jewish historian Josephus, who tells us that the Pharisees possessed ancient tradition which they had received from earlier generations. Another early reference to the existence of oral tradition surfaces in a well-known story said to originate in the time of Hillel and Shammai (first century BCE—first century CE). The great teacher Shammai, responding to the question of a prospective proselyte concerning how many Torahs exist, asserts that there are "Two, one that is written and one that is oral" (*Avot de-Rabbi Nathan*, 15; Babylonian Talmud, tractate *Shabbat* 31a). The proselyte, unconvinced by this response, turns to Hillel, Shammai's contemporary, and asks the question once again. Writing letters from the Hebrew alphabet Hillel points to the first letter (an *aleph*) and asks:

> "What is this?" "Aleph." "That is not aleph but bet (the second letter)! And what is this?" "Bet." "No, it is not bet but gimel!" Then he (Hillel) added: "How do we know that this is aleph and this bet and this gimel, except for the fact that our ancestors have handed down by tradition that this is aleph and this bet and this gimel? Just as you have firmly accepted this [teaching], so accept that [of the oral Torah] as well."

What came to be widely known in the early centuries of the common era among the sages of the Talmud as *Torah she-be'al peh* was the result of extra-Biblical customs and traditions which had evolved naturally over a period of time among the Jewish people of the land of Israel, along with teachings which grew out of more deliberate, self-conscious efforts to elucidate and interpret the meaning of scripture, that is, the *written* Torah. Both of these types of traditions go back at least as far as the period of the Second Temple (second–third centuries BCE), and both of them were taught and transmitted *orally*, in part to preserve the distinction between them and the written Torah.

Between 50 BCE and 200 CE, as these oral teachings began to proliferate, scholars took up the task of carefully memorizing what they had learned from their teachers and, in turn, meticulously transmitting them to their disciples. In fact, these early rabbis (as they were called after 70 CE) were also known as *tanna'im*, literally, "repeaters" of tradition. They were *living repositories* of orally preserved teachings, divided into "schools" which differed somewhat from one another in that they possessed varying chains of tradition. To be a student of Torah in late antiquity meant, then, to have studied at the feet of a master, to have imbibed his teachings, and eventually to pass on what you had learned to your disciples:

> *Rabbi Bizna ben (son of) Zabda taught in the name of Rabbi Akiba, who learned it from Rabbi Panda who had learned it from Rabbi Nathan, who had received it from Rabbi Biryam …*
> *Rabbi Idi ben Abin taught in the name of Rabbi Amram citing Rabbi Nahman who had received it from Samuel …*

Around the year 200 CE a sage by the name of Judah ha-Nasi succeeded in editing a selected corpus of (mostly legal) oral teachings, which comes down to us as the Mishnah. But even this edited corpus was preserved *orally* for a considerable period of time. Rabbis, both in the land of Israel and in Babylonia beginning in the third century, furthered the process of oral tradition by devoting themselves to systematic study of the Mishnah, resulting in the voluminous Aramaic compendium known as the Gemara. Together, Mishnah and Gemara (which was edited between the fourth and sixth centuries) came to be known popularly as Talmud. Importantly, even though these great bodies of interpretation and exegesis were finally committed to writing, they continue even today to be regarded as "oral tradition."

Once established, what was the standing of these oral traditions in the minds of the people? Those familiar with rabbinic tradition are well aware that the rabbis made a critical and extravagant claim in which they endowed their oral teachings with the status of divine *revelation*. They successfully contended that they were in possession of traditions and rules of interpretation that go back to Sinai itself! God had revealed *two* Torahs to Moses; while one was passed down as a written legacy the other was transmitted from one generation to another orally. Thus, for example, when Rabbi Akiba's students asked him what the authority for his teachings was, he could reply: "It is a teaching given to Moses at Sinai."

According to the astonishing narrative in which this account is given, Moses asks God why he is adding certain decorative flourishes to particular letters of the Torah. God informs Moses that in a future generation a man by the name of Akiba will be able to deduce a great deal of meaning from these decorative signs. At God's suggestion, Moses turns around and finds himself seated in the back of Akiba's classroom but is unable to understand what Akiba is teaching! Nevertheless, when he hears what Akiba is telling his students concerning the authority behind his knowledge, he is delighted. To put this another way, the Written Torah is pregnant with meaning; the sage who combines knowledge of his teacher's tradition with intellectual acumen and spiritual insight is himself able to help give birth to what appears to be "new" Torah, but which is actually as old as the event at Sinai. Thus the Written and Oral Torahs constitute the *whole* Torah, the former ever in need of the latter so that every generation is able, by itself, to discover the meaning of *kedushah*, holiness. As the Babylonian Talmud teaches us: "Even the *questions* that some bright student will ask his teacher in the future were given at Sinai."

There is much for us to learn from this, regardless of the tradition we call our own. The sacred traditions which our ancestors have bequeathed are still grist for sacred conversation. They *invite*, even obligate us to engage in dialogue with them, to take our place in a vast and endless dialectical discourse. To study "Torah" turns out to be less a matter of having answers than it is one of wrestling with tradition on the basis of our questions. Study, in Judaism, is a sacred *rite*, a devotional act informed by creativity and imagination, ideally practiced with others who are committed to listening to the past and to one another, and in the process adding their voice. From this dialogical conversation—with texts, with other people, with our teachers, with our students—we too become repositories of Oral Torah, we too becomes rabbis.

In the medieval mystical tradition of Kabbalah, which began in Provence and Spain in the late twelfth and early thirteenth centuries, oral tradition played a pivotal role. A contention among some of the earliest kabbalists was that authentic esoteric tradition is one which has been personally transmitted orally from teacher to disciple. One of the outstanding representatives of such a view was Rabbi Moses ben Nachman, or Nachmanides (1194-1270), the most prominent teacher and communal leader of thirteenth-century Spanish Jewry. Concerning the question of reliable kabbalistic teaching, Nachmanides has the following to say:

> *This matter contains a great secret of the secrets of the Torah, which cannot be comprehended by the understanding of a thinker, but [only] by a man who gains them, learning [them] from the mouth of a teacher, going back to Moses our Master, from the mouth of the Lord, blessed be He.*[1]

The most prominent kabbalist of the sixteenth century, Isaac Luria (1534-72), also denied the legitimacy of mere reason as a way of fathoming the inner mysteries of Torah. Along with personal transmission from teacher to disciple, however, Luria included revelatory experiences of various types as a reliable source of mystical truth. In the words of his chief disciple, Hayyim Vital:

> *... there is no doubt that these matters [i.e., esoteric knowledge] cannot be apprehended by means of human intellect, but only through Kabbalah, from one individual [directly] to another, or directly from Elijah, may his memory be a blessing, or directly from those souls which reveal themselves in each and every generation to those who are qualified to receive them.*[2]

Vital provides us with Luria's views regarding the history of kabbalistic transmission. Kabbalistic mysteries were taught openly and publicly until the death of Rabbi Shimon bar Yohai, to whom tradition ascribes authorship of the seminal work of Spanish Kabbalah, the Zohar. Ever since Shimon bar Yohai's death "wisdom has departed from this earth" (Zohar I, 217). All of the sages who have borne kabbalistic wisdom since that time have done so in great concealment, each disclosing his knowledge to a single disciple. What is more, even to these select disciples kabbalistic masters taught in generalizations only, revealing but a portion of their knowledge. In such a fragmented and fragmentary way kabbalistic wisdom was passed from one generation to the next until the time of Nachmanides. Luria's role in this process, according to Hayyim Vital, was that he represented nothing less than the first and only appearance of truly authentic kabbalistic knowledge since Nachmanides. Even more, his knowledge may be compared solely to that of Shimon bar Yohai himself. We know that Isaac Luria gathered around him a circle of about thirty disciples, whom he taught both as a group and individually. At a time when kabbalistic teachings were becoming more and more widespread, Luria's circle sought to preserve the centrality of direct, unmediated oral transmission from mystical master to disciple. It was only after Luria's death that his teachings became widely circulated.

Today, in an age enamored with quick and easy solutions to every problem, this view serves to remind us that serious spiritual life, like serious athletic or musical training, is hard won, requiring time, patience, and perseverance. We risk losing much if we forget that spiritual life is *cultivated* through a process which evolves, slowly, and it is nourished by *personal relationships* with teachers who can show us a path through their words and deeds.

There is also an important role for the oral tradition in Hasidism, the great mystical-pietistic movement that flourished in the towns and villages of Eastern Europe beginning in the eighteenth century, and which survives to this day in such diverse sacred centers as Crown Heights in Brooklyn, and Jerusalem. The founder of Hasidism, the Ba'al Shem Tov (1700-60), disclosed his message largely in the form of tales and parables, which he conveyed to his disciples orally.[3] Similarly, tales *about* the wondrous powers of the Ba'al Shem Tov began to flourish, providing a model for generations of future *hasidim* to celebrate their own rebbes, or teachers, through stories told orally in Yiddish. Storytelling became one of the quintessential elements in Hasidic piety and community, and various ritualized occasions evolved to accommodate such activity.

The *oral* nature of storytelling is so critical in Hasidism that many rebbes caution their disciples to resist reading *printed* tales as they may be false. Rather, they encourage their disciples to listen only to the rebbe, who received the tale from his father who had received it from his father, or at least from someone who stands in a reliable chain of transmission. Authenticity is encoded in a story by including the name of the rebbe concerned, and usually the name of the disciple who heard the tale and passed it on: "I heard this story from a man, Shimon of Kalish in Poland. He was a *hasid* by the grandfather [Rabbi Yehuda Leib] of the present Gerer Rebbe ..."

It is told of the Stoliner Rebbe that he always seated a certain elderly *hasid* at the head of the table because this person had been in the presence of the Stoliner's father. Of this man the Stoliner used to say: "Blessed are the eyes that looked at the eyes of a *tsaddik* (a master)."

In Hasidism, then, stories passed orally from one generation to the next are tantamount to "Torah," and they must be transmitted with the perfect accuracy with which Torah is taught. The Hasidic oral tradition is Torah fashioned out of the fertile ground of living community, thick with power and vitality.

Notes:

1   Moshe Idel, "We Have No Kabbalistic Tradition on This," in *Rabbi Moses Nachmanides (Ramban): Explorations of His Religious and Literary Virtuosity*, Isadore Twersky, ed. (Cambridge, MA: Harvard University Press, 1983), p. 59.

2   Lawrence Fine, "The Art of Metoposcopy: A Study in Isaac Luria's Charismatic Knowledge," *AJS Review*, Vol. XI, No.1, Spring 1986, p. 94.

3   Concerning this subject, see Jerome Mintz, *Legends of the Hasidim* (Chicago and London: The University of Chicago Press, 1968).

Parabola
Volume: 9.2
Theft

BIRTHRIGHT

Rabbi Jonathan Omer-Man

My name is Esau. This is my home, this is where I live, on Mount Se'ir, the hairy mountain. My line has prospered and grown strong here; powerful kings and princes have sprung from my loins. We are a warrior nation, and we seek the high road to God. We have had our defeats, but we do not complain. In our calling we take risks.

No one visits me now; I no longer await the arrival of my brother. Once he said that he would visit me up here on Mount Se'ir, but he found another way to complete what he had to complete. At any rate, when we last met, at our father's funeral, he made no mention of the matter. Our paths are separate now. For years they were intertwined, and we could do nothing without reference to the other. Now we no longer need each other. My brother no longer needs me. Do I feel used? Well, I was used. We are all used by our brothers, but I am no longer angry, I am not bitter. Even when he tricked me and stole from me, I did not remain angry for long. True, the second time he outwitted me, I did scream and roar that he was a cheap thief, and that I wanted to kill him, but that passed. Some of his descendents tell strange stories about me, about the diabolic Esau, but they do not understand. They follow after my brother, but they do not comprehend the significance of the story of Esau and his brother.

Even in our mother's womb, we struggled. Even in there, twins in the belly of the matriarch, our limbs entangled, we were two individuals, two nations bound together and yet destined to tread different, divergent paths. Our mother had waited a long time for the pregnancy, and when it occurred, she felt that she could not live with all the jostling and pushing and wrestling within her. Most women forget the pangs of pregnancy, but she remembered. When we were small children and were making too much noise fighting over some toy, she liked to tell us how she had gone to complain to the Lord about the inner commotion, what we were doing inside her, and what God had told her:

Two nations are in thy womb,
And two nations shall be separated from thy bowels;
And the one people shall be stronger than the other people;
And the elder shall serve the younger.

You know, for years I was tormented by that prophecy. I would brood over it, turning it over and over in my mind. Its significance seemed to change, to shimmer before me. Would the separation be just one brother from the other, or also one son from the parents? Who would serve whom? Would it be the stronger? I seemed to be stronger. And after my brother tricked me out of the birthright of the first-born, did I then become the younger? It was so unclear! For a long time that prophecy was the touchstone of my life. My brother's too, but for him it was different. You see, I thought that it was a challenge, that it meant that everything was open, that both of us had a chance; but he thought that it meant that everything was foreordained, that he was the chosen son. I was willing to fight for it, to strive for it, to risk my world on a single cast of the die, to win in glory or to lose in ignominy. But my brother was different: he didn't want to have to fight for the birthright, he wanted to be the first-born. When he stole something, and he stole a lot, he truly believed that it belonged to him. When he took my father's blessing from me, he thought that he was just correcting an accident of nature, a minor accident of chronology, the fact that he arrived in this dark world a few minutes after me.

When I was a child, I would accompany my father when each evening he went into the fields to pray. He used to stand motionless, mouthing words that I could not hear, gazing intently at a bush or a boulder or a lizard. It was then that I began to look at things, at the details. Later, as a lad, I used to go out into the fields and the forests alone to bring back game for the family. Whenever I caught a deer, I would prepare venison, which my father loved; we would all sit together and study, and he would favor and praise me. We were an odd family. My mother loved my brother, my father loved me. My brother stayed at home a great deal, and he learned the occult arts of the tent dwellers. I became a hunter, and I learned a different wisdom. I had to discover the limits of my powers: how fast I could run, how far I could throw, how long I could stand motionless. I learned to watch, to read the signs and to know the lore of the field. I learned patience and precision. I became a cunning person. But still my brother outwitted me!

I shall tell you what happened that first time. We must have been fifteen years old. I had been out hunting for more than a week, tracking a small flock of mountain goats. There were seven or eight of them. Each time I approached, they would climb higher into the crags. At last I surprised them, and I killed a young male with a long sling shot across a crevasse; but when I lowered the carcass down a cliff face, I tore a muscle in my right thigh. The way back was difficult and took me longer than usual, as I was limping badly. A few hours' trek from home, I saw a hyena in my path. It had been tracking me, and now it was blocking the trail. It didn't attack me, but it was waiting for me to falter. It stayed out of stone's throw. I was too tired to fight, and I had to abandon my winnings to the meanest of scavengers. As soon as it started devouring the carcass, I hobbled off to our encampment. So I came home with nothing, exhausted, injured, and hungry. When I saw my brother squatting outside our tent, making some red lentil pottage, I wanted to cry. I told him that I had lost everything, but he continued with his cooking without looking up at me. I told him about the hunt and the climb, and still he was silent. I told him about my hurts, and about the hyena, and he continued to cook, stirring and adding herbs. Then I told him that I was faint, and I asked him for some of his bloody red lentil stew, and he said, "Sell me first your birthright." Then I wept, for I realized that he was a better hunter than I. "Take it," I told him, "I have no use for it."

Later I learned that on that very day grandfather had bequeathed his powers to our father, who had thereby become great high priest; either my brother or I was to be his sole heir. Let them not say that Esau despised the birthright! He did not; he honored and revered it and fought hard for it, but he lost it in a game he didn't understand.

My father had married when he was forty, and at that age I took two Hittite women, Judith and Basemath, as wives. My father and mother hated them, for the Hittites worshiped a different way. But a man cannot dally forever. When my whoring days were over, I knew it was time to marry, and promptly. Later my brother was to work for years to win his brides, which I cannot understand.

My father and I grew closer again when his eyes began to fail. I would sit at his side and tell him stories of the hunt, and he loved every detail. He wanted to hear more, and so I began to invent adventures to please him. Sometimes when I was sitting with him, relating some improbable tale of the chase, I would hear my mother clucking in disapproval from her side of their tent. She thought that I was dishonestly trying to win his heart. I began to understand my father more in those days, especially after he told me about that awesome journey he made with his father to Mount Moriah. Perhaps he saw in me someone who would have refused to comply, who would have fought. Perhaps he saw in me all the attributes that he had lost. He certainly saw in me the future of his line. But by then his vision was seriously impaired.

One day he called me.

"My son," he said.

"Here I am," I answered.

"Behold now," he said. "I am old, and I know not the day of my death. Now therefore take, I pray thee, thy weapons, thy quiver and thy bow, and go out to the field, and take me venison; and make me savory food, such as I love, and bring it to me, that I may eat; that my soul may bless thee before I die."

O how my soul wept when I heard those words! What man can remain unmoved to hear the parting blessing of his poor old blind and dying father! I choked upon my tears and ran to do his will, happy like a child who knows that he is loved, and despondent like a lad who knows that to gain his treasured prize he must lose so much. My heart was overfilled with emotions as I left his tent, and I was not attentive to what was happening around me. The truth is, I wanted that love of his too much.

The rest is documented history. I came back and prepared my father his food. I brought the meal into his tent in mock ceremony, and playfully announced like a herald:

"Let my father arise and eat of his son's venison, that his soul may bless me."

My father looked perplexed. "Who are you?" he asked.

I thought he too was jesting, and answered: "I am thy son, they first-born, Esau."

He became very agitated, as together we began to understand what had happened.

"Who was it then," he asked, "who prepared me venison, and brought it to me, and I ate it, all this before you came? Whom have I blessed? For whomsoever have I blessed, he alone shall be blessed."

I was hurt and angry and bitter. I screamed and roared and sobbed. I asked my father for the impossible: "Bless me, please bless me," I implored. But the blessing he had given my smooth and slippery brother was unique: it was the transmission of a power that cannot be divided.

"Your brother came with cunning," he said. "He has taken your blessing."

"Have you not a blessing for me?" I begged.

His answer was more than I could bear. "Behold, I have made him thy master; I have given him his brothers for servants; I have sustained him with corn and wine; what then shall I do for thee, my son?"

"Do you not have even one blessing for me?" I asked, and I wept.

Well, he did give me a blessing. It was not that which I desired, but I learned to live with it:

> Behold, of the fat places of the earth shall be thy dwelling
> And of the dew of heaven from above;
> And by thy sword shalt thou live, and thou shalt
>   serve thy brother.
> And it shall come to pass when thou shalt break loose,
> That thou shalt shake his yoke from off thy neck.

My brother and I separated after that. I spent several days fuming and muttering that I was going to kill him, and with my mother's help he escaped to Uncle Laban in Haran. When I saw him again at Yabbok, my blessing had come to fruition; I was free of him, and he still had work to do. I had learned that it is not the fruits of victory that make a true warrior, but steadfastness in battle. And my brother was learning not to fear my strength.

You ask me if I still think that my brother was a thief. Well, he took things that did not belong to him. But no, he was not a thief. You see, my brother was not a man like you or me. His mind was different. He appeared to be devious, but he went straight to what he knew. He didn't think or speculate, he knew. My brother never doubted. The fact that he contradicted the law was irrelevant to him. He saw how things were meant to be, and how they would be in the future. And he was right. The birthright and the blessing probably did belong to him. I wanted too much to win, and losing them was my teaching. But I warn any lesser man not to try to imitate Jacob! We punish thieves harshly here on Se'ir.

Parabola
Volume: 7.4
Holy War

The Wisdom of Jewish Mystics

Dov Baer, the Maggid of Mezeritch, said to his disciple the holy Rabbi Zusya that in the service of God he should learn three things from a child and seven things from a thief.

From a child he should learn
(1) always to be happy;
(2) never to sit idle;
(3) to cry for everything one wants.

From a thief he should learn
(1) to work at night;
(2) if one cannot gain what one wants in one night to try again the next night;
(3) to love one's co-workers just as thieves love each other;
(4) to be willing to risk one's life even for a little thing;
(5) not to attach too much value to things, even though one has risked one's life for them, just as a thief will re-sell a stolen article at a fraction of its real value;
(6) to withstand all kinds of beatings and tortures but to remain what you are;
(7) to believe your work is worth while, and not to be willing to change it.

•

CHAPTER TWO

THE INNER SELF:
DISCOVERING THE PURPOSE AND MEANING OF THE INDIVIDUAL

When you speak, think that the
World of Speech is at work within you,
for without that presence,
you would not be able to speak at all.
Similarly, you would not think at all were it not
for the World of Thought within you
Man is like a ram's horn;
the only sound he makes is
that which is blown through him.
Were there no one blowing into the horn,
there would be no sound at all.[1]

—Maggid Devaraw Le-Ya'aqov

Parabola
Volume: 21.2
The Soul

THROUGH A DARK PASSAGE

Rabbi Eliezer Shore

The path of the soul is not simple; it travels a tortuous route in this world—twisting and turning in the course of life, moving from unity to dissolution before reaching the final destination of wholeness. But in the process, it gains a depth and fullness that it never would have attained had it not initially set out.

The soul begins in unity. Prior to entering this world, it exists in a state of attachment to the Divine. It gazes in a light that shines across creation and learns a supernal wisdom. However, at the moment of birth, this original connection is lost. As the soul descends into the world, it becomes fragmented and broken, splintered into millions of pieces and scattered across creation. Like rain upon the fields, the soul seeps deeply into all things animate and inanimate. It is these drops of soul, embedded within the objects of this world, that give life and vitality to existence.

Thus, while the soul is focused in the body, its influence does not end there. Hasidic texts explain that elements of a person's soul can be found in all of his belongings. Soul extends even further, beyond one's immediate realm, to touch those things that are not yet in one's possession. Thus, the crops of the field, the fish in the sea, all grow and develop due to the far-flung sparks of human soul within them. Because their life-source is derived from a particular individual, these things will, over time, re-enter his domain. It is at that moment they can be uplifted, for the path of spiritual growth lies in collecting these soul-fragments and reintegrating them into the being.

This means to say that all of life is a gathering up of soul. In every encounter with the physical world, in the food one eats, the clothing one wears, lost fragments of soul are being regained. All of them must be collected, for if even a fraction of the soul were to be missing, a person would have to travel across the world to retrieve it. However, physical objects do not yield up their soul so easily. More often than not, material desires will pull a person down, engulfing any level of spirituality that has been attained. Soul is elicited from the things of this world by using them in a *sacred* way. Judaism regards the human being's role as that of a fulcrum for creation, with the power to uplift reality and invest the world with holiness. At the heart of Jewish spirituality is the practice of the *mitzvot*, the commandments, whose primary concern is the sanctification of the physical world. Every *mitzvah*, explains the Kabbalah, releases another aspect of soul from its imprisonment in the physical.

From another perspective, we can say that the pursuit of soul manifests itself in the consciousness as the search for *meaning* in life—that essential quality that lies beneath the surface of the world. Like soul, the search for meaning can propel an individual to the most distant places on earth. Seen in these terms, the Torah presents itself as an all-encompassing system that seeks to align reality within a vast meaning-framework. The Torah is the "blueprint" of creation, in the words of the Midrash. There is nothing so mundane that it stands outside its realm of concern. In this, the Torah invests all life with the ultimate meaning that is born out of the relationship with God.

Sparks of soul are not just scattered throughout the physical world, they are embedded in the consciousness as well. Within the daily flood of ideas and emotions, fragments of soul—thoughts of holiness and longing for God—can be found. These too must be sought after and gathered up. Spiritual work must always address the whole person—the inner dimension as well as the outer. In Jewish spirituality, the path of *mitzvot* is accompanied by that of prayer and Torah study—the service of the heart and of the mind. These bring all facets of the being into relationship with the Divine, and all of life into the structure of meaning.

The search for soul can lead a person across the world, and into the innermost recesses of the being. There are times when the presence of soul shines forth brightly; at other times, it remains completely hidden. Kabbalah teaches that in the soul's initial descent to this world, the highest sparks invariably fall to the lowest levels—the dark side of human nature. This means that the encounter with evil is a crucial element in the process of reintegration. Only by entering the dark places of the being—moments of anger, depression, or despair—can one redeem the sparks of soul that are trapped there. Without a willingness to confront this negative side of the personality, the individual will forever remain incomplete.

Thus, Judaism understands the most important spiritual work to occur precisely in times of darkness, in the depths of personal exile. "From the bowels of hell I cried out, and You heard my voice" (Jonah 2). Only by maintaining faith and hope in the moment of crisis can the fallen fragments of soul be redeemed, so that out of greatest dissolution, the greatest wholeness can be formed; for soul is born out of its very opposite. Likewise, the need to find meaning in the face of mortal suffering is one of the most intrinsic aspects of being human. As anyone who has encountered personal tragedy knows, it is precisely through the struggle with hopelessness and despair that the greatest levels of integration and spiritual awareness can emerge.

The passage of the soul, from original unity, through darkness and dissolution, to final integration, is paralleled in the cosmos by the universal redemptive process.

Kabbalah teaches that at the birth of creation, sparks of Divine Presence—the soul of the world—were scattered throughout existence. By means of exile and redemption these sparks are collected. "Know that your descendants shall be foreigners in a land that is not their own," God told Abraham. "They shall be afflicted … and afterwards, they shall come out with great wealth" (Genesis 15). For when all these pieces have been gathered, the soul of the world will be complete, and the presence of God will be revealed in creation.

Thus, the history of the world is the history of soul, the history of humanity's search for meaning. Just as an individual must confront suffering in order to redeem the most precious elements of his being, so must all of humanity. In doing so, it can emerge "with great wealth." Mystical sources explain that in the age of the future redemption, it will be revealed that the darkest moments of history were actually the times that held the greatest light—a truth that is impossible for us now to comprehend. "Behold, there is a place by Me," said God to Moses, "I will put you in a cleft of the rock, and will cover you with My hand while I pass by: and I will remove My hand and you shall see My back, but My face shall not be seen" (Exodus 33). Only looking back will we see how God was present in the places He had previously been concealed, and how soul was made manifest in the face of the greatest despair.

Parabola
Volume: 13.3
Questions

Heart Searching

Martin Buber

Rabbi Shneur Zalman, the *Rav*[1] of Northern White
Russia (died 1813), was put in jail in Petersburg, because
the *mitnagdim*[2] had denounced his principles and his way
of living to the government. He was awaiting trial when
the chief of the gendarmes entered his cell. The majestic
and quiet face of the rav, who was so deep in meditation
that he did not at first notice his visitor, suggested to the
chief, a thoughtful person, what manner of man he had
before him. He began to converse with his prisoner and
brought up a number of questions which had occurred
to him in reading the Scriptures. Finally he asked: "How
are we to understand that God, the all-knowing, said to
Adam: 'Where art thou?'"

"Do you believe," answered the rav, "that the Scriptures are eternal and that every era, every generation and
every man is included in them?"

"I believe this," said the other.

"Well, then," said the *zaddik*,[3] "in every era, God calls
to every man: 'Where are you in your world? So many
years and days of those allotted to you have passed, and
how far have you gotten in your world?' God says something like this: 'You have lived forty-six years. How far
along are you?'"

When the chief of the gendarmes heard his age mentioned, he pulled himself together, laid his hand on the rav's shoulder, and cried: "Bravo!" But his heart trembled.

What happens in this tale?

At first sight, it reminds us of certain Talmudic stories in which a Roman or some other heathen questions a Jewish sage about a Biblical passage with a view to exposing an alleged contradiction in Jewish religious doctrine, and receives a reply which either explains that there is no such contradiction or refutes the questioner's arguments in some other way; sometimes, a personal admonition is added to the actual reply. But we soon perceive an important difference between those Talmudic stories and this Hasidic one, though at first the difference appears greater than it actually is. It consists in the fact that in the Hasidic story the reply is given on a different plane from that on which the question is asked.

The chief wants to expose an alleged contradiction in Jewish doctrine. The Jews profess to believe in God as the all-knowing, but the Bible makes him ask questions as they are asked by someone who wants to learn something he does not know. God seeks Adam, who has hidden himself. He calls into the garden, asking where he is: it would thus seem that he does not know it, that it is possible to hide from him, and consequently, that he is not all-knowing. Now, instead of explaining the passage and solving the seeming contradiction, the rabbi takes the text merely as a starting-point from where he proceeds to reproach the chief with his past life, his lack of seriousness, his thoughtlessness and irresponsibility. An impersonal question which, however seriously it may be meant in the present instance, is in fact no genuine question but merely a form of controversy, calls forth a personal reply, or rather, a personal admonition in lieu of a reply. It thus seems as if nothing had remained of those Talmudic answers but the admonition which sometimes accompanied them.

But let us examine the story more closely. The chief inquires about a passage from the Biblical story of Adam's sin. The rabbi's answer means, in effect: "You yourself are Adam, you are the man whom God asks: 'Where art thou?'" It would thus seem that the answer gives no explanation of the passage as such. In fact, however, it illuminates both the situation of the Biblical Adam and that of every man in every time and in every place. For as soon as the chief hears and understands that the Biblical question is addressed to him, he is bound to realize what it means when God asks:

"Where art thou?", whether the question be addressed to Adam or to some other man. In so asking, God does not expect to learn something he does not know; what he wants is to produce an effect in man which can only be produced by just such a question, provided that it reaches man's heart—that man allows it to reach his heart.

Adam hides himself to avoid rendering accounts, to escape responsibility for his way of living. Every man hides for this purpose, for every man is Adam and finds himself in Adam's situation. *To escape responsibility for his life, he turns existence into a system of hideouts.* And in thus hiding again and again "from the face of God," he enmeshes himself more and more deeply in perversity. A new situation thus arises, which becomes more and more questionable with every day, with every new hideout. This situation can be precisely defined as follows: Man cannot escape the eye of God, but in trying to hide from him, he is hiding from himself. True, in him too there is something that seeks him, but he makes it harder and harder for that "something" to find him. This is the situation into which God's question falls. This question is designed to awaken man and destroy his system of hideouts; it is to show man to what pass he has come and to awake in him the great will to get out of it.

Everything now depends on whether man faces the question. Of course, every man's heart, like that of the chief in the story, will tremble when he hears it. But his system of hideouts will help him to overcome this emotion. For the Voice does not come in a thunderstorm which threatens man's very existence; it is a "still small voice," and easy to drown. So long as this is done, man's life will not become a *way*. Whatever success and enjoyment he may achieve, whatever power he may attain and whatever deeds he may do, his life will remain way-less, so long as he does not face the Voice. Adam faces the Voice, perceives his enmeshment, and avows: "I hid myself"; this is the beginning of man's way. The decisive heart-searching is the beginning of the way in man's life: it is, again and again, the beginning of a human way. But heart-searching is decisive only if it leads to the way. For there is a sterile kind of heart-searching, which leads to nothing but self-torture, despair and still deeper enmeshment. When the Rabbi of Ger,[4] in expounding the Scriptures, came to the words which Jacob addresses to his servant: "When Esau my brother meets thee, and asks thee, saying, Whose art thou? and whither goest thou? and whose are these before thee?", he would say to his disciples: "Mark well how similar Esau's questions are to the saying of our sages: 'Consider three things. Know whence you came, whither you are going, and to whom you will have to render accounts.' Be very careful, for great caution should be exercised by him who considers these three things: lest Esau ask in him. For Esau, too, may ask these questions and bring man into a state of gloom."

There is a demonic question, a spurious question, which apes God's question, the question of Truth. Its characteristic is that it does not stop at: "Where art thou?", but continues: "From where you have got to, there is no way out." This is the wrong kind of heart-searching, which does not prompt man to turn, and put him on the way, but, by representing turning as hopeless, drives him to a point where it appears to have become entirely impossible and man can go on living only by demonic pride, the pride of perversity.

Notes:

1   Rabbi.

2   Adversaries of Hasidism.

3   One proved true; so the leaders of the Hasidic communities are called.

4   Gora Kalwarya near Warsaw.

Parabola
Volume: 19.1
The Call

THE RELUCTANT PROPHET

Mordechai Beck

Recently I met the prophet Jonah, son of Amitai, again. Of course, I had known Jonah's fanciful tale since childhood—his supreme chutzpah in defying God's apparently absolute command to turn the willful inhabitants of Ninevah to repentance. I had shuddered at the thought of his punishment in the dark belly of the giant fish for three days and nights, and puzzled at his rage against God's manifest benevolence—both for his forgiveness of Nineveh's evil and for the smaller mercy of providing a shady gourd for the suicidal prophet.

I used to wonder why the rabbis in their ancient wisdom yoked this enigmatic tale to Yom Kippur, the most sacred day in the Jewish calendar. Only lately have I glimpsed a deeper and more disturbing truth beneath this apparently naïve tale of fish-eats-man.

Jonah revealed himself to me as an individual who had good reason to show defiance toward the Deity. He wanted to be his own person, not part of some cosmic plan, however Divine it might be. He wanted to explore the innermost reaches of his own being, wherever that might take him. So he ran away from God, towards far-off, utopian Tarshish.

In fleeing, Jonah discovered himself, and possibly, he started to understand why God had chosen him to do His work in the first place. Jonah had talent. He could excite people's interest in spiritual truths—without even trying. But Jonah ran more—this time from himself. So God called him again—with the exact same call—but this time it was after Jonah's world had been encapsulated inside the belly of the divinely prepared fish, and he had begun to see things differently.

Jonah ran into what is a modern crisis. If the Book of Job is echoed in the sealed-off, isolated anguish of Auschwitz, Jonah reappears in the concerns of a generation torn by a search for meaning and independence. Numerous references in recent books, poems, stories, and illustrations connect us to this slim tale, among them the works of Nobel prize-winner Shmuel Agnon, Israeli poet Yehuda Amichai, artists Nahum Gutman and Jacob Steinhardt. It seems that Jonah's strange story has now taken on a more profound shading for us, and the themes carried by the narrative are suddenly meaningful to modern people.

A key that guided the preparation for a representation of the story in etchings was the Hebrew word for "big," which appears thirteen times in the original text. Jonah feels overwhelmed by the bigness of everything—including his own potential. God's response to His prophet's low self-image is reassuring, if tentative. Yes, you can do what seems impossible, even crazy, you have the power. Even if you made a mess of it the first time around, you're being given a second chance.

The message spoke reams to me. Any one of us could receive a second call. We just have to pray we're worthy of the task when it is laid upon us.

An exhibition featuring *Maftir Yonah, Book of Jonah*, with etchings by Mordechai Beck and calligraphy by David Moss, ran from September through December 1993 at Yeshiva University Museum in New York City.

Parabola
Volume: 15.3
Liberation

RETHINKING JONAH: THE DYNAMICS OF SURRENDER

James L. Bull

The Biblical story of Jonah is a mythic tale of deep human meaning with which we can all identify. Taken metaphorically, it tells of spiritual purpose denied and resisted, followed by surrender, shelter, and rebirth.

The narrative as presented in Chapters 1 and 2 of the Book of Jonah (to which I will limit myself in this discussion) is straightforward. God gives the prophet Jonah a destination to which to go to deliver his message, but Jonah decides to go elsewhere instead. A great storm comes up as a result, and Jonah attempts to avoid this by going to sleep in the bottom of the boat. The sailors consult an oracle and conclude that Jonah is to blame. When he is awakened by the captain and asked to identify himself and his part in the mounting calamity, he not only acknowledges his responsibility for the storm, but advises the crew that they must sacrifice him if they are to survive. They attempt to disregard this advice, rowing harder than ever, but this strategy fails, and they throw him overboard. The storm subsides, and the sailors experience a religious conversion upon witnessing the miracle. Jonah, meanwhile, is swallowed by a great fish which delivers him to dry land three days later.

Jonah is thus given a mission in life. His life journey is represented in the Biblical account by a geographical assignment. It is clear that he is aware of this calling, as he chooses a destination in the opposite direction "to flee from the presence of the Lord." The storm which arises is the perfect metaphor for the inner turmoil we all experience when we separate ourselves from our inner nature, from the Spirit within us. As with all such experiences, in Jonah's case, the longer he denies it, the worse it gets. Jonah does what we usually do to escape distress—he goes to sleep, and as far away as possible, in the bottom of the boat. Up to now, he has displayed some fairly typical human behavior. Then Jonah is awakened by the captain of the boat—an important and wonderful figure who comes as a messenger. He is the external counterpart of Jonah's own spirit, and the one who resonates to that part of Jonah which is capable of waking up.

In responding to the captain's call, Jonah now shows himself to be a person of rather extraordinary courage: he arises, identifies himself, acknowledges his responsibility for the growing storm, and offers himself as a sacrifice, so that by his death others might continue to live. At this point, Jonah has leapt ahead of the others in his consciousness; they are, as it were, still asleep, and do not awake fully to the reality of the situation until after the storm has subsided. Moreover, Jonah engages the *community* in the solution. He could have, upon waking and recognizing his responsibility, simply leapt into the sea to solve the problem. In that scenario, the only relationship that would count would be between Jonah and the Lord. By calling on the others to throw him into the sea, he makes them a part of the process; he forces them to become involved. There is an important difference between suicide and communal sacrifice. By their participation and recognition of the consequences, the sailors have their own consciousness raised as well, so that they also in a sense wake up. Jonah leaves behind a greatly solidified community who think him dead but who have themselves come to life. The parallel to Christian sacrifice and community is striking.

Jonah, meanwhile, falls into a mysterious timeless period in the sea, the unpredictable blessing that follows his surrender and leap of faith, for we never know what the consequences of surrender will be. He falls deeper and deeper into the dark wetness of the sea, into a space between life and death, between death and rebirth, having delivered himself to his own spirit for resolution. Something wonderful happens: he is provided with a safe place of transition, a place that is dark, enclosed, protected, and secure—a kind of womb. It is from this womb that he is reborn to carry out the activities described in the last two chapters of the book.

This is the key event in the entire Jonah account: Jonah awakens; he regains consciousness and takes responsibility for his actions. To sleep is to lose consciousness. Sleep and waking provide wonderfully vivid metaphors for what happens when we shift to a new level of consciousness. Jonah completes both halves of the process of coming to life: he regains consciousness, and he acts on that new awareness. The action is the natural consequence of the shift and the evidence that it has occurred, not only for the world, but for the self as well.

In order to appreciate the process of awakening or coming to life (sleep and death being so closely related), it is first necessary to understand the shutting-down process which avoids it. Up to this point, Jonah was multiple; he was divided within himself; he was attempting to ignore the presence of the spirit within himself. His account at this point bears an interesting resemblance to the parable of the prodigal son, where a man wastes his resources and ends up in what would be the equivalent of skid row in contemporary society—at the very bottom. Then we read, "he came to himself" and decided to change his life and recover his self. To do so he, like Jonah, acknowledged his actions and took responsibility for them. To "come to oneself" is a significant phrase, for it implies a reuniting of previously severed parts. It is like coming home: the part that has been away or outcast is welcomed by the part that never left. In this case inner reunion corresponds to family reunion, and the man's father correctly recognizes the event as cause for celebration.

To be split and divided against ourselves corresponds to what is known today in psychology as being "in denial." What this means is that we relate to an important part of ourselves as though it did not exist, and then fashion our behavior accordingly so that others may support us in our deception. Being grouchy and then denying the grouchiness is a small but familiar example.

Because this process causes distress and consumes a great deal of energy, we may use a variety of escapes to assist us in maintaining our unconsciousness, our sleep. But what is really being denied is our integrity—our completeness.

Although there are hundreds of ways to go to sleep in the bottom of the boat, one way which figures prominently in contemporary society involves the use of alcohol, which functions well in this regard as it is a powerful anesthetic and sedative drug which masquerades as a popular beverage. Many people use alcohol to kill pain—especially emotional pain—to relieve stress, and to release inhibitions.

If we hold to the concept of separation from Spirit as the essential characteristic of denial—that it is our own deepest nature that is being denied—then the use of alcohol or any other way of escaping our situation can be seen in its accurate context. The behaviors connected with suppressed material aren't necessarily nice, as they frequently flow from injury and frustration. The deeper and more essential the suppressed impulse or desire, the greater the sense of separation. The monster, or the playful child, may turn out to be a precious part of ourselves, and the suitable recipient of our compassion rather than of our rage and condemnation.

It is important to recognize that the process of waking or coming to oneself is by no means automatic; indeed, it may be uncommon. Kierkegaard writes:

> *And this is the pitiful thing to one who contemplates human life, that so many live on in a quiet state of perdition; they outlive themselves, not in the sense that the content of life is successively unfolding and is now possessed in this expanded state, but they live their lives, as it were, outside of themselves, they vanish like shadows, their immortal soul is blown away, and they are not alarmed by the problem of its immortality, for they are already in a state of dissolution before they die.*[1]

Their loss is compounded: they have lost the ability to recognize that they are lost. Their entrapment is internal, not external. They are not trapped by circumstances, but by not being aware of being trapped. Put positively, an expanded vision would allow them to perceive new opportunities. This is why only radical change will save them—because they are unaware of their true location, doing more of the same does no good. If adversity arises, they may, like the sailors on Jonah's boat, row harder, but this kind of effort will not bring the right *kind* of change. It is like words spoken in the wrong language. Kierkegaard notes that such a person "learns to imitate the other men, noting how they manage to live, and so he too lives after a sort, ... but a self he was not and a self he did not become."[2]

The metaphor of a picture frame is useful here. The frame provides a visual separation between the pattern of the picture and whatever pattern exists in the surrounding wall surface. More importantly, the frame draws our attention to what's inside it. The more fixed we become in our internal frame of consciousness, with its anxieties, excitements and especially its unspoken assumptions, the less likely we are to recognize our true location and transcend the frame:

> *No statement made from within a given frame of reference can at the same time step outside the frame, so to speak, and negate itself. This is the dilemma of the dreamer caught in a nightmare: nothing he tries to do in his dream will be of any avail. He can escape his nightmare only by waking up, which is by stepping outside the dream. But waking is not part of the dream, it is a different frame altogether; it is nondream, as it were. Theoretically, the nightmare could go on forever, as some schizophrenic nightmares obviously do,* for nothing inside the frame has the power to negate the frame.[3]

We come back to the metaphor of sleep and waking, and this time with a question: If realms of consciousness, and especially addictive ones, are self-contained and self-perpetuating, then how is radical change possible? The answer to the question of transformative change lies in the part of us that never went to sleep. Remember Jonah, and remember that we are not singular, but multiple. God's message to Jonah remained exactly where it was received—in his deep self, in that part of his unconsciousness which moves ahead in time and across frame boundaries. There remained in Jonah a self which was capable of responding to the captain. We, like Jonah, can communicate with our deep self, but these communications are intuitive, non-linear and non-verbal.

This, then, is what it means to "come to oneself": like cosmic gas and dust that gathers itself centripetally to form a star, we form ourselves, and having done so we achieve a reflexivity and self-awareness that did not previously exist—we can name and claim ourselves. Up until now all the choices were of externals, and they were trivial by comparison; they were choices of things—pleasures, commodities, fancies. Once we have chosen ourselves in earnest, we have a new possibility to remember who we are.

How does this happen? First, an incongruity exists between inner spirit and outward behavior and lifestyle; this incongruity generates tension and *may* lead to a crisis of despair. If this happens—if all the excuses are exhausted and we are forced to come to grips with ourselves—a breakdown of resistance occurs and the first expressions of true self appear, like young shoots.

Any shift to what may be the beginning of a new life is necessarily what Kierkegaard terms a leap of faith, and is therefore not entirely rational. It must be undertaken without knowing the outcome. It is like launching a boat with no assurance that the new land will be found. It is the epitome of anxiety met by courage.

Action is necessary to validate conviction; the boat must be launched. But because the world in which action takes place is a new world, all actions are new, and extremely uncertain. They are baby actions, taking their first steps.

The greatest struggles take place within the self. The world provides the setting where we can act it all out and grow by it—a grand projection, as it were. Often, we transform inner anxieties into objective fears to better deal with them and in the process wrongly attribute the source of the difficulty. When this happens, we believe the world to be the source of the difficulty. When this happens, we believe the world to be the source of our problems. It is not. As the poet Rilke writes:

> We have no reason to mistrust our world, for it is not against us. Has it terrors, they are *our* terrors; has it abysses, those abysses belong to us; are dangers at hand, we must try to love them. And if only we arrange our life according to that principle which counsels us that we must always hold to the difficult, then that which now still seems to us the most alien will become what we most trust and find most faithful. How should we be able to forget those ancient myths that are at the beginning of all peoples, the myths about dragons that at the last moment turn into princesses; perhaps all the dragons of our lives are princesses who are only waiting to see us once beautiful and brave.

Perhaps everything terrible is in the deepest being something helpless that wants help from us.[4]

The key phrase here is *holding to the difficult.* This means not going to sleep in the bottom of the boat. It means being alert, and staying alert to our inner voice which keeps us centered. It means having the courage to go on living, to wake up, to stay awake, and to not allow ourselves to be consumed along the way. It means to be true to ourselves, and this in turn means to believe that at our center there is something believable and good. It is as though Kierkegaard were writing about Jonah when he described the choice, and the action:

> *Therefore, it requires courage for a man to choose himself; for at the very time when it seems that he isolates himself most thoroughly he is most thoroughly absorbed in the root by which he is connected with the whole. He chooses himself and fights for the possession of this object as he would for his eternal blessedness; and it is his eternal blessedness.*[5]

Notes:

1   Søren Kierkegaard, *Either/Or* (Princeton: Princeton University Press, 1959). vol. 2, p. 172; translated by Walter Lowrie.

2   Søren Kierkegaard, *The Sickness Unto Death* (Princeton: Princeton University Press, 1954), p. 186; translated by Walter Lowrie.

3   P. Watzlawick, J. B. Beaven, and D. D. Jackson, *Pragmatics of Human Communication* (New York: W. W. Norton, 1967), pp. 204-205 (italics added).

4   Rainer Maria Rilke, *Letters to a Young Poet* (New York: W. W. Norton , 1954), p. 69; translated by M.D. Herter Norton.

5   Kierkegaard, *Either/Or*, p. 220.

Parabola
Volume: 24.4
Evil

THE RUNG OF EVIL

Martin Buber

Question: *The Talmud says that the child in the womb of his mother looks from one end of the world to the other and knows all the teachings, but that the instant he comes in contact with the air of earth an angel strikes him on the mouth, and he forgets everything. I do not understand why this should be: why first know everything and then forget it?*

Answer: A trace is left behind in man through which he can reacquire the knowledge of the world and the teachings, and do God's service.

Question: *But why must the angel strike man? If he did not, there would be no evil.*

Answer: But if there were no evil, there would be no good, for good is the counterpart of evil. Everlasting delight is no delight. That is how we must interpret what we are taught: that the creation of the world took place for the good of its creatures. And that is why it is written: "It is not good that the man"—that is to say the primal man God created—"should be alone," that is, without the countereffect and the hindrance of the Evil Inclination, as was the case before the creation of the world. For there is no good unless its counterpart exists. And further on we read: "I will make him a help meet for him"—the fact that evil confronts good gives man the possibility of victory: of rejecting evil and choosing good. Only then does the good exist truly and perfectly.

In the story of the Creation we read: "... and behold, it was very good." But, in the passage where Moses reproves Israel, the verse says, "See, I have set before thee this day life and good, and death and evil." Where did the evil come from?

Evil too is good. It is the lowest rung of perfect goodness. If you do good deeds, even evil will become good; but if you sin, evil will really become evil.

The Divine Presence comprises all worlds, all creatures, good and evil. It is true unity. How then can it contain good and evil, which are self-contradictory? But actually there is no contradiction, for evil is the throne of good.

Just as all worlds, the good and the evil, are comprised in the Divine Presence, so they were comprised in Moses. When God spoke to Moses for the first time, he did not answer: "Here I am," because he was stricken with wonder: how can unification come to pass? For when God revealed himself in the thorn-bush, that is to say, in evil, in the lowest rung, all the wells of fire gushed forth from the summit down to the depths—yet the thorn-bush did not burn; evil was not consumed. How could this be? But God called a second time: "Moses!" And then the lowest and the highest rung linked within Moses himself, and he said: "Here I am."

God's relationship to the wicked may be compared to that of a prince who, besides his magnificent palaces, owns all manner of little houses hidden away in the woods and in villages, and visits them occasionally to hunt or to rest. The dignity of a palace is no greater than that of such a temporary abode, for the two are not alike, and what the lesser accomplishes the greater cannot. It is the same with the righteous man. Though his value and service may be great, he cannot accomplish what the wicked man accomplishes in the hour when he prays or does something to honor God, and God who is watching the worlds of confusion rejoices in him. That is why the righteous man should not consider himself better than the wicked.

It is written: "Am I a God near at hand … and not a God afar off?" "Afar off" refers to the wicked. "Near at hand" refers to the righteous. God says: "Do I want him who is already close to me, do I want the righteous? Why, I also want him who is afar off, I want him who is wicked!"

Question: *It is written: "… for the Lord regardeth the way of the righteous; but the way of the wicked shall perish." The two parts of this sentence do not seem to belong together.*

Answer: The righteous have many and devious ways, and the wicked have also many and devious ways. But the Lord knows the ways of the righteous, because they are all one way and that is the way. But the ways of the wicked are numerous and manifold, for they are nothing but many ways of losing the one way. And in the end they themselves realize that each is losing his way and all ways, as when someone is walking through a wood and keeping to a certain way, though he does not know why he has taken that particular way rather than another. Day and night he keeps walking until he comes to a tall beech standing at the end; and, at that point the way is lost. The man cannot go forward and he does not dare go back, for he has lost the way.

It is written: "Let the wicked forsake his way." Does the wicked have a way? What he has is a mire, not a way. Now what is meant is this: let the wicked leave his "way," that is, his illusion of having a way.

It is God's will that there be freedom of choice. That is why he has waited until this day. For, in the days of the Temple, they had the death penalty and whipping, and so there was no freedom of choice. Afterwards, Israel had penal codes, so there was still no freedom of choice. But now everyone can sin openly and without shame, and live and prosper. And so, whoever leads a good life today is worthy in the eyes of God, and it is he who will bring about salvation.

The Evil Inclination is like one who runs about the world keeping his hand closed. Nobody knows what he has inside of it. He goes up to everyone and asks: "What do you suppose I have in my hand?" And every person thinks that just what he wants most of all is hidden there. And everyone runs after the Evil Inclination. Then he opens his hand, and it is empty.

He who harbors an Evil Inclination has a great advantage, for he can serve God with it. He can gather all his passion and warmth and pour them into the service of God. He who has no Evil Inclination at all cannot give perfect service. What counts is to restrain the blaze in the hour of desire and let it flow into the hours of prayer and service.

It is written: "... of every man whose heart maketh him willing ye shall take My offering." Every man should take the goodness with which he is to serve God out of all his heart's promptings, out of his cravings and desires, out of all his urge's drivings. If he is seized with love or fear, let him take this love or fear and use it to love and to fear God. Had Esau gone in the way of the teachings, his service would have been better than Jacob's, for he would have lifted all his evil passions up to God. In the righteous the Evil Inclination changes into a holy angel, into a being that yields power and destiny.

It is written: "Let us take our journey, and let us go, and I will go before thee." That is what the Evil Inclination says to a man secretly. For it is an inclination to become good and wants to become good by driving man to overcome it, and to make it good. And this is the secret request the Evil Inclination makes to the man he is trying to seduce: "Let us leave this disgraceful state and take service with the Creator, so that I too may go and mount with you rung by rung, although I seem to oppose, to disturb, and hinder you."

Excerpted from *Ten Rungs: Hasidic Sayings*, collected and edited by Martin Buber (New York: Schocken Books, 1962), pp.89-96. Copyright © 1947, 1995 Estate of Martin Buber. Reprinted by permission.

Parabola
Volume: 5.4
Women

The Wife of Jonah

Barbara Rohde

You do not know my name. Nor could you guess it by looking at me. You would guess, Leah, I think, the "weary one." Or Miriam. It would not be fair to call me merely Jonah's wife (though most of you do call me Jonah's wife), for that is not a name.

I will tell you then. I am Shoshannah. "The graceful lily." You see why you would not have guessed. My thighs are heavy now, my skin no longer fair. There are moments when I feel within me a great gift that I call *grace*, but I cannot walk it now. I cannot dance it. Now and then I sing it under my breath as I am grinding the grain or bathing in the river. Jonah looks at me then in a way that reminds me that I am Shoshannah. In the river I am graceful. I try to imagine how it would be to move always as I move in the river.

When I think about that, I think I better understand what Jonah used to try to tell me about his Voice, how, when he was alone in the wilderness, far from the noise of people and the cares of dailiness, the Voice was clear within him. But when he began to walk back into the noise and dailiness, the Voice became fainter and fainter. He said the fact that he could hear it at all was what made him a prophet. But the fact the Voice grew quieter, as the voice of the singing mother when her child slips into sleep, is what made him a bumbling prophet.

"Oh Shoshannah," he said to me once in the middle of the night, "it is a terrible thing to be a prophet." I did not say anything because I did not have anything to say. I knew mine was not the voice he was listening for. But I held him in the dark and stroked him, and in the morning I asked him to hold Aaron for me while I made the fire, for I have learned that the weight of a small child against one's body is as soothing as honey in the throat. I saw him smile at Aaron's small hands.

Once I asked Jonah, "Why can't I hear the Voice?"

"God needs you for other things," he said. "You bring forth the sons and daughters, you keep them from the wildness, you nourish them, you comfort them. Without you, God's world would become a barren rock."

I laughed. The idea that God needed me, or even Jonah, seemed absurd. My father and my father's father had taught me that we are the ones who need Yahweh.

Jonah did not like my laughter. He scowled a little. "God has no belly Shoshannah, to hold the little ones. God has no hands to plant the grain or to harvest. He has no tongue. That is why His word sounds in my head. You must understand, Shoshannah—we are the belly and the tongue."

I do not know whether it was what he said, or the way he said it, his voice soft but very firm, but I felt a sudden cool clarity, the way one does when one is alone in the desert at night and sees a star fall. I saw Jonah in a new way, a strange way. It was for a moment hard to remember that this was the man who lay with me at night, whose back I had washed in the river, whose own water I had seen arc from his body to the hot sand. I remembered the time as a child when I had stood in our village while the drummers sat beating their drums and suddenly the sound was not coming from the drums but seemed to be sounding in my whole body.

Jonah's words sounded through me like that long ago drum-beat and deep within me I felt an answering "yes." In that moment I believed that Jonah was God's tongue.

But later, after one of those long times when Jonah was with me but was not really with me, when he sat brooding for hours at a time and never looked at me but seemed to be looking at something far beyond me, when he did not smile at Aaron's new words, nor at the food I placed before him, nor at my own body, when he did not notice my moments of great tiredness at the end of the day and let me struggle alone with the water jugs and the animals—it was then I asked the question I never should have asked. Later I came to understand that the question I asked so innocently was the same terrible question that has haunted Jonah from the first moment he had heard his Voice.

"How do you know that it is the voice of God?"

When I asked that question, he heard me. He looked at me, truly seeing me. "I know the same way you know that the tiny movement within your belly is a child that will on a particular day be forced from your body and be cut from you forever and grow and become a man."

I thought about that. I thought I understood. But then I could not be sure I truly understood. I remembered the woman in the next village whose belly had grown as mine had grown with Aaron, who sang as I had sung with the joy of the child that was to come. And then she had fallen in death, and the people said it had not been a child within her but a sickness, that she had been walking through her days with death growing within her, not life. That was a terrible thing that made me shudder. I remembered it and wanted to ask Jonah about it, but I did not. I kept it in my own head where most of the time it lay asleep, but sometimes it awoke with me in the middle of the night and urged me to ask that question that never came out in the sunlight, "Is Jonah a prophet or is he mad?"

But what you want to know is the story of Jonah and the fish—that silly story that people keep telling over and over again and seem to want to believe.

It began this way. Jonah could not sleep well when he came back from one of his long journeys into the wilderness. He lay awake most of the night and only toward morning did sleep finally seize him, and then he slept late into the day, and I had to struggle to shade his eyes from the light and to keep Aaron from running to him.

"What is wrong with you, Jonah?" I would ask, but he told me nothing. He groaned sometimes, unaware, I think that he had done so. He lay staring into the dark. He spent long hours at prayer, but when he rose from his knees, there was no peace in him. He paced back and forth beside the fire and spat into it so that the flames shifted. Finally, after days of this, he took my hands in both of his and spoke with a kind of agony, "I must go to Nineveh."

I could not believe what he was saying. Nineveh is a city far to the north of us, a great city, the capital of the Assyrian empire. We had heard tales of its great size but more of its great wickedness. I felt fear enter me. Nineveh would not open its arms in welcome to the son of Ammitai.

"Why must you go to Nineveh, Jonah?"

"I must warn them of God's anger. I must ask them to repent."

Jonah spoke with strength, but I knew it was not a strength that came from the depth of him, but one he had put on like a splint on a weak leg. I knew he was as afraid as I was.

"Are you afraid?" I asked. I have learned one becomes stronger as one faces one's weakness.

"I am afraid, Shoshannah. They will not listen to my preaching, or if they listen, they will laugh, or if they do not laugh, their anger will seize them. They will curse me or stone me. They may put me to death in their anger."

Jonah's fear and my fear huddled together in the silence for a while. I knew the only way to end my fear was to end Jonah's fear but how could I do that?

"And will God not protect you from your enemies?" I asked.

Jonah looked at me strangely. I knew he had been thinking about this question. He spoke quietly then. "But, Shoshannah, what if it is only the sight of my mangled body that will bring them to repentance? What if I must be a sacrificed lamb?"

We stood in the silence again, our hands still clasped. Then he pulled his hands away angrily and turned his back and cried out in a kind of defiant pain, "No, I will not go."

A blackness was in him, as if the death he feared in Nineveh had found him out here. His eyes grew empty. He sat for long hours saying nothing, not even moving. I tried to bring him into the light again. I offered him fruit. I sang his favorite songs very softly while I was at my work. I asked Aaron to show him the small flower he had found blooming beside the wall. But the fruit withered before Jonah ate, and the songs caught in my throat and sounded even to me like the mourner's lament and Aaron became shy, afraid of Jonah's blackness and the heaviness of the silence.

Finally one morning I felt his hand on my shoulder, and I roused from my sleep and saw that he had prepared for a journey. I did not beg him to stay. I did not even ask where he was going. I thought it was to Nineveh. I kissed him and waited until he was out of sight to let my tears fall.

Now I must tell you of the day that Jonah returned. There were many who told me that Jonah would never return. Some said that they had heard he had been put to death in Nineveh, others that he had been seen at the docks of Joppa setting sail in a great ship going to the edges of the world. There were those who claimed that ship had gone down in a storm. Still I believed he would return.

Each morning when I awoke, I believed it would be the day of his return. Each evening I would say, "Maybe tomorrow." And then one day it was the day. I looked up from mixing the bread and saw a speck in the distance growing larger and larger, and soon I could tell that it was he. I did not even wipe my hands. I ran toward him, laughing and crying at the same time, not even heeding Aaron's calling after me as he ran far behind. And we met, Jonah and I, and then we stepped apart and stared at each other, trying to read in each other's faces what had happened since last we were together.

I knew the blackness had gone out of Jonah. His eyes were filled with love, though I do not think it was love only for me. I had the sense his eyes would have held love for whatever they looked upon at that moment. He looked older, somehow, and seemed at once both stronger and more gentle, the way a woman does after she has brought forth her firstborn—full of a deep knowledge of the marriage of pain and joy. We walked back together and when we met Aaron, Jonah lifted him onto his shoulders, and Aaron shrieked with delight and held onto Jonah's hair as if it were the mane of an animal and my heart was full of thanksgiving.

We lay awake late into the night while Jonah told me his story. I will try to remember his words to me and tell you, for they are very different from the story you have heard, about the fish.

"When I left you, Shoshannah, it was as if I were fleeing from myself, or from the eye of God. That was the madness in me. I had told myself that it was not God's voice sending me to Nineveh, but at the same time I knew it was God's voice. I thought if I sailed far away, far from our own country, as far as Tarshish, which is the edge of our world, and then beyond Tarshish, into the unknown waters, then the Voice could not follow me, nor God's eye see me, and I would find peace.

"So I walked to Joppa and went from ship to ship, looking for one setting sail for Tarshish that would take me aboard, and finally I found one and we sailed toward the place where the sun disappears. They were strange men on that ship, men who did not know our God at all but spoke of other gods who seemed like silly little men. When we sailed into a storm, they said their gods were angry and the only way to appease them was to throw the sailor into the sea who had offended the gods. They did not consider why the gods were offended nor try to discover what the offense might be with the skills of their own minds. They decided to draw lots to see which of them should be cast overboard.

"You may find this hard to believe, Shoshannah, for even now I find it hard to believe about myself, but in that moment I wanted to die. There was an emptiness within me as if someone had taken a knife and carved a great hole from my very center and the pain was so terrible I would do anything to end it, even if it meant ending my life. So I asked the sailors to throw me into the sea.

"They were afraid to do that—to follow *my* word rather than the word of Fate, but I told them I knew I had offended my God and surely it was my God that had sent the storm, and finally they did as I asked. There were two who seized my arms, and two my feet, and they swung me and threw me from the ship and I fell into the blackness of the water from which I thought I never would arise again.

"There was no fish, Shoshannah, no fish that swallowed me. Somehow, in a daze I clung to a log and was washed ashore, far from any village. I was bruised and cut and out of my mind, and I lay on the shore for a very long time, still in the depths of despair. The God that I had sought to escape was right there, within me.

"It is strange how when one seeks death and does not find it, the pain of life becomes even more unbearable. And I felt a great guilt for my longing toward death, the death of my body, the death of my spirit. Something deep within me knew that in hiding from God's judgment I hid also from his love, and that was the terrible emptiness I felt in my belly.

"But finally, I begged God to look at me. I felt I was so far in the depth I could sink no lower, so instead of hiding any longer, I begged God to *see* me—frail man—beaten, confused, corrupted, abandoned, lost—and in that moment I had the sense that God came into the depths of my Hell and whispered in my ear.

"I heard the sound of my own heart beating—the heartbeat of life. I turned over on the sand and looked up toward the blinding sun. I closed my eyes against its power but at the same time let its power caress me and heal me. I looked toward the sea, which seemed so gentle now, tender as a mother. The waves lapped at the shore. I walked down and bathed myself in those waters, and then I started walking along the edge of the sea until I found a small village. I must have looked very strange, my clothes in shreds, my body bruised. 'You must have come from the bottom of the sea,' the people said. 'Or the belly of a whale,' I said, laughing at my own inventiveness. Perhaps they believed me. Then I found the small ship that brought me back to Joppa and to you."

We lived simply and contentedly for a time, everything filled with a quiet joy. The simple acts of eating and bathing and singing to Aaron and lying down together at the end of the day of work had a kind of gleam to them. Jonah no longer seemed tormented nor troubled. His heart was not divided.

Still the story that he had been swallowed by a fish persisted. At first he tried to correct the story. "No," he would say, "I was not in the belly of a whale for three days. I was not vomited out upon the shore. I don't know where you got that idea." But the more he denied the story, the more it seemed to spread. Finally, he just gave up. "What does it matter?" he asked me. I think he enjoyed the fame a little, the way people looked at him when he walked in the market. There had been a miracle and Jonah had been at the center of it.

Perhaps it was partly the persistence of that tale that caused the change in him. I began to notice it after he had been home for a while. It is hard to describe exactly, but I had the sense that he was beginning to turn things upside down.

What became important to him was not that he heard God's voice but that *he* had heard God's voice. For some reason he began to think that God had chosen him not because God needed a man to be his messenger upon the earth but because he, Jonah, was so great in God's eyes—so eloquent, so strong, so faithful.

A strange arrogance came over him and often I found I was angry. Even the way Jonah was with me had changed. Where once I thought of myself as God's servant who had been called to help Jonah protect his gifts of prophecy, now Jonah made me feel like Jonah's servant. It frightened me as well as angered me because I feared that Jonah's head would become so filled with the sound of his own words that he would no longer be able to hear his Voice.

When Jonah told me that he had decided that he would go to Nineveh, that this time he would truly go, that he would dare the wrath of the people, that he would rebuke them for their dreadful wickedness and warn them of the punishment of the Just One, I was frightened by his fervor. I did not say much, but I tried to remind him of how he had felt, lying in the sun on the shore of the sea after he had been thrown from the ship. I tried to recall to him the serenity of God's love. He did not want to remember. He was too filled with his sense of mission. He had reached that place where he could no longer tell the difference between righteousness and self-righteousness.

And yet the long solitary journey that he took to Nineveh must have opened him a little. By the time he reached Nineveh, I suspect he spoke with a double voice—his own voice, the voice of a small and arrogant man, but deep within that voice another Voice, the Voice that held the truth of God. If that had not been so, the Ninevites would never have turned their faces in a new direction. If all they had heard had been the words of a little self-satisfied man, fat with the sense of his own importance, they could have laughed them off, or ignored them with a defensive outrage. There must have been something in what Jonah had to say or in the way that he said it that made them lie awake at night and wonder, and when they arose in the morning, made them see each other and themselves in a new way.

Never before had such a thing happened—a whole city felt the foolishness of its past. I wish I had been there to talk to those people. It is hard for me to imagine what it had been like. Yet, I suppose if the king himself takes off his rich robes and dresses as simply as a herdsman, if the king himself laughs at all the absurd past pretensions of his reign, the emptiness of his longing for power, then it is easier for the people. Jonah prophesied that Nineveh would be destroyed in forty days. At the end of forty days, Nineveh was still there, but it was a different Nineveh.

I thought Jonah would come home rejoicing, but he came home angry with an anger that turned into despair. He sat in silence, not showing any life in his eyes. It all seemed very strange to me.

"What is wrong with you, Jonah?" I would ask, but he only stared at the earth and said nothing.

The temptation for me was to become angry myself, or to withdraw so that I would not have to feel the pain of that silence. But I sat with him in his blackness and tried to understand what had happened to him in Nineveh. When Aaron was asleep, I would go off by myself and stare at the patterns of the clouds or the patterns in the sand, and little by little I began to think things I had not thought before.

Finally I went to Jonah. I sat down before him and looked into his face.

"You are a prophet, Jonah," I said, "not a fortune-teller."

I saw his face turning red. I knew anger toward me was rising within him. He was not used to hearing the voice of Shoshannah commenting upon his work.

Still, I continued. While I had been staring at the sand and skies, I had remembered the day Aaron was born, how hard it had been to let go of my Self long enough to get the task done, how long it had taken me to learn to ride with the pain rather than to try to control it. And I remembered that other thing, that sense of how something had used me to bring forth this child. At the moment of his cry I had shouted exultantly, "I've done it," and for a moment felt a strong pride, but then, in an instant, my attention was upon Aaron and my pride was for Aaron, our son.

I tried to speak all this to Jonah, though it was difficult to speak these things, to find the words and the courage. His anger made his eyes look hard and made the skin around his lips turn white.

"Don't you remember, Jonah, how much joy we felt when all the people came to see our son? We did not want them to look at us. We did not want praise for my labor. We wanted them to see the beauty of Aaron, to joy with us in our joy. Don't you remember, Jonah?"

Jonah lifted his hand and for a moment I thought he would strike me, but instead he held his hand in the air for a long time and finally touched my cheek with it, very gently, and started to laugh.

"Oh, Shoshannah," he said. "Oh, Shoshannah. My graceful lily."

Even now, there are times when Jonah and I are in the market square and we see one person nudge another and whisper and we know they are saying, "There is Jonah, the one who was swallowed by the fish." Jonah has stopped trying to deny or to explain.

"Let them have their miracles," he says. In his older years he has become much mellower. I am the one who wants to remind them of the real miracles—of our son, Aaron, and of our daughter, Rebecca, and of Aaron's son, but most of all of the miracle of Nineveh, the city that for some reason had ears to hear and overnight regained its sanity.

"It never happened before," I say. "It may never happen again."

"It will happen again," Jonah says. "Everything is possible. Meanwhile people would rather hear stories of fish swallowing men and vomiting them up again than stories of men learning to love."

I suppose Jonah is right. Still, I have never liked the story of Jonah and that fish. That is the reason I am telling you the story of Jonah's wife.

Parabola
Volume: 6.4
Demons

DEMONS BY CHOICE

Interview with Isaac Bashevis Singer

When Parabola first began discussing an issue on demons, one of the people we wanted to interview was Isaac Bashevis Singer. Certainly no writer in our time has described a world so filled with devils in fancy dress, demonic beings who fly through the air, dybbuks *taking up residence with the innocent, imps who play dastardly tricks, ugly old witches, or human beings, like the Magician of Lublin, so possessed. And certainly no one else has done so with such intelligence, grace, and compassion.*

We spoke to Singer in New York in the midst of a 95-degree heat wave. He had just finished an exhausting lecture tour and a series of book-signings, and was beleaguered by a bad toothache. But he gave of himself once more—because, he said, the subject of demons "interests me." Does Singer believe in the devil? Do demons exist as a separate reality? After reading the novels, the stories, the memoirs, after talking with the man himself, one is left with what may be the greatest gift of the very great storytellers: a richly etched, deeply felt portrait of our condition; no easy answers; and a million more questions that will enrich us and actively engage us in a search that Singer himself pursues with such benefit for us all.

> *Only on rare occasions did Rabbi Benish*
> *cross the threshold of his house. He would*
> *glance about him, and inquire of a passing*
> *porter or school boy:*
> *"How will it end?"*
> *"What does God want?"*
> —Satan In Goray

Parabola: *Do you think we need demons?*

Isaac Bashevis Singer: Do you mean do we need them in life?

P: *Yes.*

IS: It's a good question. I think it would be necessary. Because if people would never see anything of the supernatural, if we would never have any contact with other entities, we would live out our life with the feeling that this is it: our so-called reality is the only thing which exists. And that would make the human spirit much smaller than it is.

P: *Do you feel that the demons we deal with are as you say in* Gimpel the Fool *like "shoulders and burdens" from God?*

IS: If they exist, they certainly are from God. There is nothing in the universe which is not from God. If a person believes in nature, everything is from nature, which is again everything. There is a unity in the creation. We cannot believe in anything else.

P: *But does everything have a dark side, an "other" side?*

IS: I think that everything might have God knows how many sides! We don't know ourselves how many. Because if you take a pebble, you can look at this pebble from a chemical point of view, from a gravitational point of view—from many other points of view. According to Spinoza, the number of attributes of God are endless. And even if you believe in nature, you can say the same thing: that this pebble still can be seen from very many points of view.

P: *One of the things that seems very strong in your work is an idea that the demons are put here to test us …*

IS: I would say that behind all my ideas, the strongest idea of mine is conveyed in my thinking, even more than in my writing, is the freedom of choice. I feel that the freedom of choice is the very essence of life. Although the gifts which God has given us are small in comparison to the gifts which He has given maybe to the angels or to the stars, we have one great gift—and this is to choose. And we always indulge in choosing. If we pay attention to one thing, we have chosen to pay attention to it. If we love somebody, we have chosen this person for love. This is in every act of humanity. To me, God is freedom. And nature, to me, is necessity. Everything in nature is necessity. In God—who I think can overrule nature, is above nature—everything is free.

P: *But what about a situation like the one situation you describe in* Satan of Goray? *Would it make a difference if we acted differently? Or is it inevitable that we must encounter demons?*

IS: No, no … it makes all the difference. When people leave free choice, the demons appear. The demons are in a way the dark side of nature which we choose. If we stop completely believing in our power, then other powers can come upon us. In other words, the demon to me is a negative side of free choice. But we have free choice in every time of our life, in every minute of our day, so we can always choose. Even if we have a bad choice to make, there is always something which is better than the other.

P: *Can we be* easily *possessed by demons?*

IS: I don't think they can take us over so quickly. They only come when people resign almost from everything. When people say to themselves, "I'm not going to make any choices anymore. I will just let the powers work for themselves." It is then that the demon is bound to appear.

P: *Do you think we are in a time similar to the one you painted in* Satan in Goray *where the Evil One is triumphing again?*

IS: I would say we are always in such a time. If not the whole of humanity … you look what's going on, let's say, in this country with crime: how really wherever you go—if you go to a court where there should be justice, there is the very opposite—people who you can buy for money … I would say human life is one big crisis. The moment you have conquered one crisis, there is already another one lurking.

P: *But is that a part of what "moves" us?*

IS: I think it is a part of being alive, of choosing. In other words, the danger is always there: the danger of turning love into hatred, of turning justice into injustice, of turning talent into non-talent, and so on and so on …

P: *Do you think that your God would fight for us? Is God at war?*

IS: *I will tell you: He doesn't fight for us. Since He gave us free choice, He gave us a great gift, and we have to use it or misuse it. In other words, when it comes to choosing, we must rely mostly on ourselves. In this respect Judaism is a little different from Christianity. Where the Christians believe that once you belong to the Christian religion, the powers are resolved: When Jesus died, all the others should be redeemed forever. We believe the opposite: That the crisis is always there, the danger is always there—like a medical doctor who will tell you that the microbes are always there in your mouth and in your stomach, and if you become weak, they begin to multiply and become strong.*

P: *And if we lose out control, the microbes, or the demons, can take over.*

IS: Of course. Nothing which one man did, no matter how great he was, can really redeem you or guarantee you redemption forever.

P: *And in your story, "The Mirror," it seems that you are suggesting that everyone has a demon in the mirror.*

IS: Of course. Just as we are medically surrounded by dangerous microbes, so our spirit has always to fight melancholy and disbelief and viciousness and cruelty and all kinds of things.

P: *But in some of your stories, even in "Cunegunde," your demons have a kind of melancholy …*

IS: Oh, but the very essence of demons is melancholy. Because it's the very opposite of hope.

P: *So you have some sympathy …*

IS: Of course, I have sympathy for everyone who suffers and lives. Because we are all living in a great, great struggle, whether we realize it or not. Sometimes we realize it. This is a very difficult thing—we very often say how difficult life is.

P: *Do you think we learn from our encounters with the demons, from facing those demons?*

IS: We learn all the time, even if we don't use all the time what we have learned—because just as you learn all the time, we also forget all the time. There is a permanent amnesia planted in us, which just as we keep on forgetting our dreams, we sometimes keep on forgetting our reality. You see a certain thing; you think you have learned. And then you make the same mistake again, which shows that you didn't learn.

P: *So, is there any hope for us?*

IS: I will tell you: we have to go through this kind of struggle. In a way, the hope is that life does not last forever, the crisis does not last forever, and behind all this crisis, behind all this darkness, there is a great light. We have to struggle, but we are not lost, because the powers which have created us are actually great and benign powers.

P: *And you think we have the equipment to fight back?*

IS: We have the equipment. The only thing is we should not let it rust, we should not forget about it, we should not put it away, and say, where is it? We must be very much aware all the time—on the watch. This is true in science, it's true in literature ... If you don't all the time watch what you are doing, you're bound to make mistakes. In my own life, I feel it all the time. It's true in love, it's true in everything.

P: *You don't really feel that "evil" is a separate force?*

IS: It's a part of what we call life. I don't think that the rocks have free choice, or the meteors. They live in the world of necessity—which is again a different kind of war. What can you call it? A higher war? But we are, so to say, soldiers. We have to fight.

Our life doesn't last forever. The moment we leave this world, the great struggle is over—at least for a time. In a way, death is not such a curse, but it's a time of resting. People are afraid of death because they were created so, to be afraid, because, if not, they would mishandle the body. Actually death is in a way a great resting after the struggle.

All the powers work so that you should come to a bad ending, but our soul works for the opposite—that the ending should be good. Actually, the ending is always good.

Parabola
Volume: 11.4
Memory and
Forgetting

"At the Moment ..."

From the Qabbalah

At the moment of the creation of the child God ordains that the seed of the future human being shall be brought before Him, whereupon He decides what its soul shall become: man or woman, sage or simpleton, rich or poor. Only one thing He leaves undecided namely, whether he shall be righteous, for, as it is written "all things are in the hand of the Lord, except the fear of the Lord. ..." Thereupon God orders the angel in charge of the souls living in the Beyond to initiate this soul into all the mysteries of that other world, through Paradise and Hell. ... At the moment of birth, however, when the soul comes to earth, the angel extinguishes the light of knowledge burning above it, and the soul, enclosed in its earthly envelope, enters this world, having forgotten its lofty wisdom, but always seeking to regain it.

Parabola
Volume: 20.1
Earth Air Fire Water

A River Went out of Eden

Irving Friedman

In the ancient Middle East, the elements appeared in the guise of gods governing the universe. The mother of them all, the waters of the sea, was an unruly but prolific abyss. To impose order on it, heaven and earth were created out of the watery chaos. They emerged from it locked in union, and gave rise to their progeny, the air. This same air separated them, to allow space for life to breathe and grow.

The Hebrew god, his breath-spirit moving over the dark surface of the watery deep, first divided light from the darkness. Then He divided the waters into upper and lower, masculine heaven and feminine earth.

Still, the waters had to be contained, as they constantly threatened to re-engulf the domains wrested from them in the creation. The Hebrew god is depicted as subduing the monsters of the deep. He kept them under control with the winds upon whose wings He rode (Psalms 18:10, II Samuel 22:11).[1] Their golden figures hovered above the ark of the covenant which occupied the inner chamber of the temple.

The entire universe was regarded as a whirlwind resting on the arm of God. He impelled the winds to drive the waters that brought the great flood. He parted the waters of the Red Sea for Israel's escape from Egypt, and He opened a path through the Jordan River for Israel to enter the Promised Land.

In the ancient Hebrew temple a huge bronze vessel called the "Molten Sea" symbolized containment of the waters. Erected in the outer court, its waters were used by the priests for washing.

The control of the waters and the avoidance of flood also depended on a balance between the masculine waters which tended to flow down from heaven and the feminine waters which tended to rise from below the earth. Legend relates that the potential joining of the two waters was prevented by the opening and closing of the foundation stone in the floor of the temple. This stone was regarded as a jewel from the footstool of the divine throne,[2] which had been hurled into the watery abyss to form the navel of the earth and begin its creation.

These elements of the cosmos, symbolized in the temple, were also represented in the human body. *The Book of Creation* [*Sefer Yetsirah*, sixth century CE] depicts fire, water, and air as the three basic elements. Fire is embodied in heaven, but also in the head; water appears in the cosmos as earth, and in the abdomen; air forms the atmosphere in the universe and has its place in the chest.

Air possesses a special quality, balancing the two other elements both in the human being and the cosmos. This is derived from its direct descent, traced by *The Book of Creation*, from spiritual air called ether, which, in turn, is descended from the Divine Spirit. The special nature of air is echoed in the thirteenth-century *Kabbalistic* classic called Zohar, meaning radiance:

> *Though all sides are united, and bound up with one another, yet is air (spirit) superior to them all, without which nothing would live. The air comes between fire aloft and water on the surface of the earth and brings them together and they become one, and thus ends the conflict between fire and water.*[3]

This conflict is echoed in the human being between the head and the center of the body.

Many languages display the intimate relation between breath, wind, and spirit, for which Hebrew usually employs one term, *Ruach*. Life is seen to begin with the first breath at birth and to end when it ceases at death. The body's mouth is closed after breath's departure, and a window in the room is opened to facilitate its going out. The three traditional terms for "soul" were also based on respiration.[4]

The Biblical basis for the importance of breath is clear: The Divine breath-wind-spirit was breathing upon the waters at the creation; it was also breathed, as the breath of life, into the first mortal formed from the dust of the earth, creating a living soul.

At death, this process is reversed: "Then shall the dust return to the earth as it was; and the spirit shall return unto God who gave it" (Ecclesiastes 12:7).

It was reported that Elijah, Elisha, and Jesus were able to repeat this creative process, and bring the dead back to life by breathing into them, and a striking prophecy of the prophet Ezekiel forecasts rebirth for all of Israel:

> *Come from the four winds, O breath, and breathe upon these slain, that they may live ... and the breath came into them, and they lived, and stood up upon their feet (Ezekiel 37:9–10).*

This links rebirth to the breath coming from the cosmic wind, and is the earliest allusion to resurrection in Judaism.

In Ecclesiastes, it is stated that "All is vanity and vexation of spirit" (Ecclesiastes 1:14). However, the Zohar contends that the term translated as "vanity" should be rendered as "breath." With this striking change of mood, the aphorism now conveys that the whole world is based on breath. Here the term used for breath is *Hevel*, which emphasizes its fleeting character.

Air is a universal medium, permeable by all the other elements, as well as all the energies. It was therefore regarded as the primordial substance of the universe by the Greek Anaximenes. Its lightness and upward movement suggested spirituality and the migration of souls, as did the birds for which it was a haven.

Pythagoras proclaimed that the world inhales the "boundless breath" from outside the heavens. The Alexandrian Jewish philosopher Philo called the Divine Spirit a "fiery breath" which is exhaled into the human being and which is never separated from its higher source.

The physical traits of all the elements translate into psychic qualities. A flame burns upward, suggesting the same symbolism of ascent as does air. Rising from a black base, called in Judaism black light, or the "lamp of darkness," its crest is white light, suggesting vision, intelligence, and spirituality. The spectrum of intermediate colors expresses the heat of passion and the dynamic change of all energy.

Fire portrays the divine in appearance and activity. It can be protective as well as destructive: God spoke to Moses out of a bush afire, which "was not consumed" (Exodus 3:2), yet he could not approach and had to shield his face.

"His anger was kindled" against the complaining Israelites, "and the fire of the Lord … consumed them" (Numbers 11:1). The prayer of Moses was enough to quench the fire; the path of the Israelites was lit at night by a Divine column of fire.

The most spectacular display of Divine fire took place at the covenant on Mount Sinai. God "descended on it in fire: and the smoke thereof ascended as the smoke of a furnace" (Exodus 19:18). The populace had to be shielded; Moses alone could ascend into it. When he came back down, his face shone with such radiance that he had to be veiled to protect the people.

The power of sacred fire extended to the ancient temple, where the altar was kindled with a perpetual flame, believed to have originally descended from heaven. Furthermore, incense was burned so that it would form a cloud to mask the divine appearance.

But in a notorious Biblical incident, the two eldest sons of the high priest Aaron, brother of Moses, were devoured by fire inside the sanctuary. They had offered incense kindled with "strange or common fire," not from the perpetual flame. The Bible noted that more was demanded of them because of their high rank. Furthermore, the very destructiveness of fire could be purifying.

In the symbolism of sacrifice, there was a close relation between the offering on the altar and the Divine fire which descended to consume it. Some felt that the very soul of the sacrificer was at stake.

Prophets like Ezekiel had visions of heavenly energies which appeared as fire. These appearances became the basis of an early mystical school called "Riders of the Chariot" (*Yorde Merkavah*), which sought to come nearer to the heavenly throne in motion.[5] However, such inner attempts were regarded as being just as dangerous as an unsanctified approach to the ancient sanctuary had been.

In later worship, fire symbolized the inner fervor with which the devout sought to "cling" to God. Here again, the rabbis warned against excess. They asked how it was possible to cling to the Divine "devouring fire" without being consumed. Nevertheless, in certain circles, such efforts became a measure of the intensity of love for the Divine.

Fire symbolized the experience of energy on all levels, and each, even the infernal, had its own expression of the Divine. On the highest level, it appeared as the light of the Divine, who covers himself "with light as with a garment" (Psalms 104:2).

The Biblical creation of light was interpreted by the Kabbalists as the penetration of the inner light of God into the outer world of darkness. However, the vessels which transmit light cannot retain it, and they shatter. Sparks of the light scatter, and become trapped inside lower elements, like the kernel of a nut encased in its shell.

The human being is endowed with the moral responsibility for rescuing these imprisoned sparks of light and restoring them to their spiritual heritage. In this struggle, the elements of matter which act as the confining shells themselves become transformed.

There is another kind of light, according to the Zohar, which "is hidden and sown like a seed. Every single day, a ray of that light shines into the world and keeps everything alive ... renewing every day the act of Creation."[6]

The divine light was symbolized in the Temple by perpetual sacred lights, as well as by an annual ceremony of renewing the cosmic light. A golden candelabra with seven branches was prescribed in the Bible. The lights were likened to "the eyes of the Lord which run to and fro through the whole earth" (Zechariah 4:10).

Light, natural and Divine, makes our own faculty of vision possible. "In thy light shall we see light" (Psalms 36:9). Further, we ourselves are instruments for the retention of the higher energy of light. "The Master of Light, the man who all day has been cleaving to a consuming fire: Behold, Light abides with him."[7]

The element of water symbolizes the primordial ocean from which all fertility is derived and in which the formless takes shape. The female waters are the source of the potency from which Mother Earth receives her fruitfulness. Water satiates the thirst of all forms of life, irrigating the earth. It is then evaporated by the fire of the sun and completes its cycle by descending again, as dew, gentle rain, or torrential downpour.

Quenching the eternal thirst of the earth, it becomes a symbol for what satisfies spiritual thirst as well—called "fountains of living water." A source of fresh, running water symbolizes a source of life—physical or spiritual.

Flowing water also cleanses and purifies. Its hygienic effect broadens into a religious symbolism of purification. It includes the feminine bath known as the *mikveh*, but also washing and sprinkling to separate the sacred from the profane, and the living from the dead.

A Jewish tradition in the Middle Ages for transmission of the name of God from a master to his pupil required their prior immersion in water. "Then both must stand up to their ankles in water and the master must say: 'The voice of God is over the waters! ...'"[8]

Water's nature is to flow downward, and therefore it symbolizes the transmission of wisdom from a higher to a lower level. In Sumer and Egypt, one god was the lord of both water and wisdom. In Israel, the Torah was symbolized by both water and fire, and Wisdom was the right arm of the creator.

The fluidity of water allows it to merge with its medium, and therefore to symbolize intuition and feeling. We can see ourselves in quiet, limpid waters as in a mirror. But ordinary water may be bitter and require "sweetening." Moses was required to cast a special tree into it, and the prophet Elisha sweetened it with salt which was a symbol of permanence since it preserved food from putrefaction. It was employed to extract blood, whose consumption was forbidden, from "fowl and beast."

Earth, like its prototype the body, is relatively stable and permanent, in contrast to the volatility of the other elements. This allows it to receive and accumulate all the nutrients borne to it by the mobile elements. It can then bring forth life, which, in turn, makes the earth even more prolific.

After death, the bodily remains of living creatures are interred in the earth, enriching it. Cremation was not accepted in the orthodox Jewish tradition, possibly because the bodily dust mixed with the earth was to be available for a future resurrection.

Just as Adam and Eve were put "into the Garden of Eden to dress it and to keep it" (Genesis 2:15), so, during our lifetimes, we have a continuing obligation to take care of the earth, not merely to dominate it. Genesis has a continuous narrative of how the fertility of the earth suffered from the sins of Adam, Cain, and the pre-Noah generation. With the post-diluvian Noah, there was a divine covenant not to so imperil the survival of the earth again. This was attested to by the rainbow, a spectrum of light visible through the water-vapor, as a reminder of the Divine promise.

The descendants of Noah were enjoined not to pollute the earth by shedding blood upon it, as the earth "opened her mouth to receive" the blood of Adam's son Abel, killed by his brother Cain (Genesis 4:11). Furthermore, the fertility of the earth was to be protected by letting it lie fallow every seventh and fiftieth year, coincidental with the remission of debts and the freeing of slaves. The negative aspect of the stability of the earth is its inertia, the downward attraction of gravity. A solid structure on earth, even a living body, requires upward energy to move. It does not flow like water or air. When we stood erect on two legs rather than four, it was in defiance of Earth's gravity. The free legs became arms that could aspire upward, even to be raised in worship, attracted by a higher force.

The vertical structures we build are an extension of our own aspirations. But the upward thrust of the Tower of Babel was too remote from an earthly base, from gravitational support. It was interpreted Biblically as a threat to heaven: "Now nothing will be restrained from them, which they have imagined to do" (Genesis 11:6). But a temple was an earth-structure that could have stability, for it brought the upward pull of heaven down to earth. It was a balance born of a union of the two.

The strong contrasts between the elements are vital because they allow each to supplement the others. What would the world be like if everything floated like air, flowed like water, changed perpetually like fire, or were immobile like the earth? What if it were always hot or cold, wet or dry? The elements both energize and temper each other's extremes. Earth slows down the other three, while it absorbs their nutriment.

Combinations of opposing elements are conceivable only by their inclusion in a unity of opposites. The Zohar emphasizes that human beings have a role to play in this transformation of the elements of which they, as well as the universe, are composed. It regards them as having descended from an original unity, hidden but accessible to humans because they themselves belong to two worlds. "As the body is formed in this world from the combination of the four elements, so is the spirit formed ... from the combination of the four winds. The four elements are united with the four winds and all are one."[9]

"Fire, air, water, and earth are originally all united one with the other, and there is no separation between them. But when the earth dust began to generate, its products were no longer united."[10]

This original unity is symbolized by the single river flowing within the Garden of Eden. "A river went out of Eden to water the garden, and from thence it was parted, and became into four heads" (Genesis 2:10).

The divided branches which flowed out of the garden are viewed as the four separate elements "and the desires which they inspired."[11] Adam was detached from domination by these outer elements when he was placed in the garden. There he came under the influence of the "united river," which draws its sustenance directly from the "source of all life ... in the depth of the cistern."[12] If the human being conforms to this source, "he makes himself master of the four elements and becomes a river from which they are watered, and they obey him and he is their ruler."[13]

"When the Holy One created man, he breathed into him a Holy Breath ... whose superior energy allows him to apprehend and obey His precepts."[14]

The actions of a man who cares nothing for his soul dissipate into the lower world. But actions performed with a higher intention produce a breath which can both sustain the world and live on into the future.[15]

Notes:

1 All Biblical quotes are from the King James version. Zohar referenced in notes 2, 9–15 is translated by Harry Sperling and Maurice Simon (New York: Rebecca Bennet Publications, 1958); Zohar referenced in note 6 is translated by Daniel Matt (New York: Paulist Press, 1983).

2 Zohar, Vol. 4–222b.

3 Zohar, Vol. 3–24b.

4 *Nefesh, Ruach, Neshamah*

5   The term for "riders" can also mean descenders, implying an initial descent toward God. The term for "chariot" was also used figuratively for the Divine throne as it moves into the world of creation. See Leo Schaya, *Universal Meaning of the Kabbalah* (Secaucus, NJ: University Books, 1971), pp. 124–25.

6   Zohar, Vol. 1–32a., p. 52.

7   Zohar, Vol. 5–266a.

8   Gershom Scholem, *On the Kabbalah and Its Symbolism* (New York: Schocken Books 1965), p. 136.

9   Zohar, Vol. 3–23b.

10 Zohar, Vol. 3–24b.

11 Zohar, Vol. 1–27a., Shaya, *ibid*, p. 123.

12 Zohar, Vol. 3–63b.

13 Zohar, Vol. 1–27a, Shaya, *ibid*, p. 124.

14 Zohar, Vol. 4–182a.

15 Zohar, Vol. 4–182a-b, Vol. 3–59a.

●

CHAPTER THREE

The Higher Realm
The Nature of God and Man
Striving for Spiritual At-One-Ment

For each of us has come into this world as into a foreign city,
in which before our birth we had no part,
and in this city he does but sojourn,
until he has exhausted his appointed span of life.
And there is another lesson of wisdom that he teaches in these words,
even this—God alone is in the true sense a citizen,
and all created being is a sojourner and alien,
and those whom we call citizens
are so called only by a license of language.
But to the wise it is a sufficient bounty,
if when ranged beside God, the only citizen,
they are counted as aliens and sojourners,
since the fool can in no wise hold such a rank in the city of God,
but we see him an outcast from it and nothing more.[1]

—Philo: Philosophical Writings

Parabola
Volume: 30.1
Awakening

I Sleep, but my Heart is Awake

Interview with Rabbi Adin Steinsaltz

After Roger Lipsey spoke with Rabbi Steinsalz for Parabola, he commented: "Rabbi Adin Steinsaltz's voice is one that people of every faith and practice hear and value. He is, of all things, fun to be with. In his presence, one doesn't find oneself wondering what the great rabbis of ancient times or early Hasidic communities were like. They were surely something like this—profound yet earthy, learned but unassuming, utterly serious yet delighted by awareness."
—Roger Lipsey

Parabola: *Awakening is associated in the minds of many people with Buddhism rather than Judaism. Yet somehow one knows that every religious culture teaches awakening.*

Rabbi Adin Steinsaltz: In the Book of Isaiah you have it many a time. Wake up! Wake up! Wake up! Awakening is a combined metaphor there, because it's an awakening not only within a spiritual framework, but also within a social or national framework. There is another point: though most of us are confined to one particular culture, we are all human beings, and sometimes miraculously closer to each other than we could assume. Of course, all kinds of bizarre phenomena can belong to a particular culture or religion, but so many things are similar. Anything that is basic to human nature cannot be absent from a culture, even if some cultures lack the words to describe it.

P: *What is the essence of Judaism? I've asked myself this question, and two linked answers came to me. The essence is* adonai echod, *the one God, and then the prophet Micah's words: to do justice, love mercy, and walk humbly with thy God. Is it these things?*

AS: I met a youngish man who was a guru or spiritual teacher more or less in the Hindu tradition. He was Jewish—his name made that clear. We had a man-to-man discussion, and he told me about the teachers with whom he had studied, some well known in the West and some also in the East. And he said that he had left them. It wasn't because he had become discouraged. In fact, had he stayed, he said, he might have reached the top of ... whatever it is. But he had encountered a problem: some of these people were in one way highly spiritual, and he had no doubt that they had developed all kinds of powers, but most of them, he said, had deep moral and ethical failures, and he couldn't take it. I said to him, "That is the Jewishness in you speaking. Someone else might have felt that it was enough to possess a certain high spirituality. Someone else might have overlooked that their spirituality didn't interfere with all kinds of behavior about women and money and other things. But it troubled you that their spirituality was on one level, and their behavior on an entirely different level, and they didn't seem to feel that there is a connection. What you say is very typical of our times, in a way—a notion of spirituality that stands, *per se*, alone, without an ethical complement. But you felt that something is missing." And so, yes, Micah's words are one element in the essence of Judaism.

P: *How is the call of Isaiah—"Wake up!"—embodied in religious practice?*

AS: There is a point—you might call it a theological point—as follows: every child is born with a soul. The time of *bar mitzvah* is not just an occasion for celebration; celebrating is completely irrelevant. It is the time of the awakening of the soul. A sage in Jewish tradition has written that there are periods of life when an awakening occurs, and one such is the *bar mitzvah* age, basically the onset of puberty. Awakening at that time is both physical and spiritual. That special time can be misused and misspent because there are other, distracting forces moving within a person. It may then be another seven years or more until another opportunity to awaken—there is no rule, but it goes in jumps.

So there are periods of life when there can be an awakening. Everybody is called, as another author puts it, but most people don't hear. And among those who hear, only a part act. From time to time there is a knock on the door, but sometimes just the Lord will know it. And then it passes. It's an awakening, not a conversion, not a change of mind or sensibility. But another echo, an opening, comes to a person. At that point one has a choice to make.

I would say something about another Biblical text, but I suppose that the Bible is terra incognita for you.

P: *It's terra* demi-*cognita.*

AS: I see. The Song of Songs has always been understood in Jewish literature as a mystical song. It tells a story, up to a point, but it has always been understood that the Song serves mostly as a metaphor on two, three, or even four levels. Many years ago, I gave a speech on a very special occasion, the day of my wedding. Unfortunately, I didn't write down what I said, and I remember just pieces. One of the main points was that the Song is multidimensional, like a chain with many rings interconnected with each other. I quoted this passage (5:2-6):

> *I sleep, but my heart is awake.*
> *I hear my Beloved knocking.*
> *"Open to me, my sister, my love,*
> *my dove, my perfect one. ..."*

And she responds:

> *"I have taken off my tunic,*
> *am I to put it on again?*
> *I have washed my feet,*
> *Am I to dirty them again?"*

She resists. But then …

> *My Beloved thrust his hand*
> *through the hole in the door. …*

At last, trembling to the core of her being, she opens the door:

> *I opened to my Beloved,*
> *but he had turned his back and gone!*
> *My soul failed at his flight.*
> *I sought him but I did not find him,*
> *I called to him but he did not answer.*

This is quite a good description. I'm asleep, but my heart is some-how awake and there's a knock on the door. The Beloved is slipping in through the cracks, from the window and from the cracks. Knocking on the door. And sometimes I say that everything's all right and I'm just too snug in bed. Then it disappears and I have a total feeling of void. After that, I may try to chase it for a long time, but I don't find it.

This suggests something of the whole compass of awakening. When you are thirteen years old, it is one thing; at twenty or twenty-one, it is another. These are not exact times, but people sometimes experience a reawakening, hear another call. I hear the knock, and I know it—but I may not be ready. Later on I feel the void. What is it that I'm doing "in bed"? Writing a Ph.D. thesis? Creating a career for myself? Whatever it may be, after ignoring the call there will be a feeling of the void. Some people then set out on a long search, but it doesn't provide an answer. The call, the opportunity to awaken, doesn't happen every day. If I miss it, I can go on a quest. But I missed it, whatever it is, I missed it.

Certain things may happen only to a very particular, very small group of people. Such things are not a part of the common human experi-ence and common knowledge. But some things are universal. What I'm speaking of is universal—yet I may not hear the call. All the teachers say that sometimes a person hears only the last call.

P: *I wanted to ask you about that.*

AS: The last call, the last awakening is sacred. For those who can hear it, it lays to rest any notion of death as a horrible experience. It becomes just a completion. The notion is that whatever you couldn't achieve in your lifetime you now encounter.

P: *When you meet what you couldn't achieve in your lifetime at the last call, why isn't that a bitter disappointment rather than an awakening?*

AS: In a way it's a fulfillment, a reward. Through all these awakenings, you are not just kicked awake. You are awakened for a kind of meeting. Some people come to this at an early age, others at a more advanced age. Still others, at the time of the last meeting when they are dying, may encounter something they had sought throughout their lives but couldn't find, owing to external or internal problems. The body is in itself a confinement, because it is limited. It is limited not only physically, but also mentally. As a human being, there are certain things I can't do because I'm dependent on the machine, on the brain. The brain can do a certain amount and no more. So when I am leaving the body, the approach can become much fuller than it was in a lifetime in which I was confined by my abilities to do things. The last awakening is a meeting that you might call a unification—or an approach toward unification.

P: *What is the relation between faith and awakening? Is there a possibility for fulfillment that arises through an attitude of faith, which opens a terrain in front of us that would not open without some bizarre confidence that the terrain is already open and welcoming?*

AS: Awakening is not faith. Awakening doesn't include any notion of getting to a higher level of existence. It is, in a way, becoming aware of something. Awakening is not by itself a rising to a new dimension, but being aware that something is different. Faith can exist without awakening.

P: *Without awakening?*

AS: Yes. The question is beautifully taken up by Peter Berger in *A Rumor of Angels*, which is a personal book, though he is officially a sociologist of religion. The book deals with spirituality, faith, religion, and so on, but not from a sociological point of view. He writes there that, as children, faith is our only asset. As children, we take in a world without experience, without knowledge, but we take it on faith. In a certain way, faith can be depicted as a little child holding its mother's hand. That is faith. In a simple sense, that is faith. I hope I'm allowed to quote the Bible again …

P: *You're expected to quote the Bible.*

AS: Well, had I known I would possibly avoid it, just to be unexpected! I'm quoting the Bible because I think it's a very good book. Psalm 131, a very short psalm, says, "Like a little baby, weaned from its mother's breasts, so is my soul to Him." It's not the baby still suckling, but weaned, more separate yet completely trusting. So is my soul to Him. … This experience is universal among all human beings. Our first steps of consciousness are taken on faith. Faith is a capacity *there* in us.

I come from a city, Jerusalem, which is surrounded by dry land. And so I remember clearly the experience of learning to swim, which I happened to learn at a much older age than many people. You can strive when you are learning, but the more you strive the more you sink. You have to allow yourself to allow the water to carry you. When you allow the water to carry you, it seems you don't have to make any effort.

People say that babies can learn to swim even before they walk. Why? I'll put it in a way that verges on the mystical. Every creature is born a swimmer. We are born in water. Our basic environment is water. We tend to forget as time passes, but basically we are swimmers. And so it's not hard for us to swim.

We may be troubled, overburdened by a myriad of things. But if we would just allow ourselves the freedom of mentally relaxing, then faith comes to us. Because, you see, it is in us—in us as a part of our existence, and when we come to it, it should be an easy thing, not an effort. This kind of faith is not identical to mysticism or religion by any means. The point is, in a certain way, that as we grow up we learn, by teaching and experience, to be more and more suspicious. Trust comes harder and harder for us. You may be a child of five and experience betrayal or abuse. You may be five years old or four years old and experience such things. When that happens, it becomes harder to have this sense of trust. The root is suspicion, a kid of tenseness: "I am in a fight, and I have to make this tense sort of fight in order to. ...." When I lose that tension, things open for me. The ocean is not only *over there*, but always *here*. But you have to allow yourself to swim in it.

P: *Is there a distinction between enlightenment and awakening? Many people would say that, if not identical, they are closely related.*

AS: Awakening is, as I said, awareness—awareness of existence, awareness of reality, awareness of something that is calling me, "Come, come closer." In itself, enlightenment is no more than the enlightenment of becoming aware. When I speak about enlightenment, I'm thinking of the notion that there is *light*. Maimonides says that all of us are in darkness, utter darkness. Yet there are people to whom God gives the gift of light; they are the prophets. What does their light do? You are in front of the unknown, in an unknown place, in darkness. You don't know anything. Then there is a flash of lightning, and you can fix where you are. There is a hill beyond you, or the sea. Whatever it is, you now have a picture. So this enlightenment is exactly en*light*enment, not in the sense of a mystical experience, but in the sense that I see something. Something pulls my collar and says, "Well, see!"

I am awake. What do I do with it? I know more, I feel more than before. Enlightenment is the ability to have a context—a new context. There is the enlightenment that shows you how the angels are singing and the enlightenment that shows you how your life is going. I speak more of the latter.

P: *One of the most poignant images in the Bible is Moses touching the fringe of the Lord's garment. It's an image of the inevitable limitations of human awareness and possibility but also, in effect, a guarantee from ancient times that one can at least touch the fringe. So, the question is about limits—the limit on our human capacity for vertical awareness, the maturity to accept that limitedness, but also to experience it as ... the gate to the Garden of Eden, to something great.*

AS: The God that we can embrace very closely is possibly not God. I don't doubt that some people reach high spiritual levels, but they don't reach God. They reach different dimensions, possibly heaven. We have different windows to look through. We can see ourselves at different levels and there are, I believe, many and higher levels of human existence. But the notion that there is a window through which we can peep and see God. …Whatever kind of God it is, is a very small one. It's a human-sized miniature, not God.

Moses said, "I want to see the face of God." And God said, "You are not ready to see my face." "Please, can I see your face?" It cannot be. If you see the face, you have crossed over to the other side. And that's the end—not only the end of life but the end of that individual. Unless He gives me His hand, I won't be able to touch it. As high as I climb, the distance won't diminish. I may be very, very high compared to other people, but the distance won't diminish. The only way that I can have His touch is if He will give me His hand. To give me His hand is His ability, because the infinite includes the ability to cross the gap. Otherwise it's not possible. Let me return to an image we discussed earlier. You recall Freud's expression, the "oceanic feeling." There is the infinity of the sea. The sea is not unreachable. It is reachable—we can touch, so to speak, its fringes. When we stand at the seashore, we can touch only the little waves at the edge of that immensity, but there is nonetheless a recognition of immensity, of the infinite. We are aware of the presence, we are aware of it, but we are also aware of the distance.

Adin Steinsaltz on the Song of Songs

The Song of Songs is at one and the same time a private song and a general one; it is both carnal and spiritual. On the one hand it is certainly a love song between a man and a woman, lovers who admire one another greatly, who lose and find each other. On the other hand, it is also a song of love in the wider sense of the connection between Israel and her God; it is a song of love and devotion, of redemption and exile, of human error and repentance. And still another song may be found therein, and this too very personal, but definitely spiritual, concerning the relationship between the soul and the Divine, a song of yearning and neglect, of search and supplication. A fourth song is there too, which is a more general song about the rapport between the Creator and His creation, between the *Ein Sof* (Infinite) and the *Shekhinah* (the Divine Indwelling); it sings of the way the world comes and goes, disappears and gets hidden, only to return and merge with the creator. …

And just as the sensual poem is raised up by its being bound to the more spiritual songs, so too is the spiritual poem elevated and enhanced by virtue of the sensual poem. It is the sensual poem that gives the spiritual poetry its passion and vigor, involves it with the material world, with all its forms and colors. ...

Even when the lover, who represents the Divine, does not speak to us, and even when He himself seems to be at some unbridgeable distance, His love is steady and beyond doubt. The poignancy of the variations in feeling, of approaching and parting, of total devotion at one moment and of hesitant waiting for love to be stirred into desire at another moment, all belong to the beloved who is the human soul or the earthly form of the *Shekhinah, Knesset Yisrael.*

The dramatic description of the lover knocking on the door seeking entrance, while the beloved is not yet ready to receive him, idly hesitant about getting up and opening the door, is the classic description of the relation between *Knesset Yisrael,* the soul in particular, and the *Shekhinah* in general, to the call on high. The lazy heart, the inner reluctance to total commitment, even to any alteration of the comfortable existing situation, are common to both the people and the individual.

This great opportunity, that comes to nation and to person occasionally, is often missed. And afterward, the belated awakening of consciousness to the wonder of what was being offered urges one to run after and catch the missed opportunity, in spite of the difficulties, the dark night, and the cruel watchers of the wall. All this is an intrinsic part of the chronicles of Israel, just as they are intrinsic to the life of any human soul. They are universal depictions of the experience of the almost attained spiritual solution. ...

But a certain course is pointed out, how after the tormented searching, after the waiting and partings, there is fulfillment.

From Adin Steinsaltz, *On Being Free* (Lanham, MD: Jason Aronson, 1997), pp. 133-135, 141-143. Reprinted by permission of Jason Aronson, an imprint of Rowman & Littlefield Publishers, Inc., Lanham, Maryland.

Parabola
Volume: 23.2
Ecstasy

GOBLET OF GRACE

Martin Buber

Hitlahavut is "THE INFLAMING," the ardor of ecstasy. It is the goblet of grace and the eternal key.

A fiery sword guards the way to the tree of life. It scatters into sparks before the touch of *hitlahavut*, whose light finger is more powerful than it. To hitlahavut the path is open, and all bounds sink before its boundless step. The world is no longer its place: it is the place of the world.

Hitlahavut unlocks the meaning of life. Without it even heaven has no meaning and no being. "If a man has fulfilled the whole of the teaching and all the commandments but has not had the rapture and the inflaming, when he dies and passes beyond, paradise is opened to him but, because he has not felt rapture in the world, he also does not feel it in paradise."

Hitlahavut can appear at all places and at all times. Each hour is its footstool and each deed its throne. Nothing can stand against it, nothing hold it down; nothing can defend itself against its might, which raises everything corporeal to spirit. He who is in it is in holiness. "He can speak idle words with his mouth, yet the teaching of the Lord is in his heart at this hour; he can pray in a whisper, yet his heart cries out in his breast; he can sit in a community of men, yet he walks with God: mixing with the creatures yet secluded from the world." Each thing and each deed thus sanctified. "When a man attaches himself to God, he can allow his mouth to speak what it may speak and his ear to hear what it may hear, and he will bind the things to their higher root."

Repetition, the power which weakens and decolors so much in human life, is powerless before ecstasy, which catches fire again and again from precisely the most regular, most uniform events. Ecstasy overcame one zaddick in reciting the Scriptures, each time that he reached the words, "And God spoke." A Hasidic wise man who told this to his disciples added to it, "But I think also: if one speaks in truth and one receives in truth, then one word is enough to uplift the whole world and to purge the whole world from sin." To the man in ecstasy the habitual is eternally new. A zaddick stood at the window in the early morning light and trembling cried, "A few hours ago it was night and now it is day—God brings up the day!" And he was full of fear and trembling. He also said, "Every creature should be ashamed before the Creator; were he perfect, as he was destined to be, then he would be astonished and awakened and inflamed because of the renewal of the creature at each time and in each moment.

But hitlahavut is not a sudden sinking into eternity: it is an ascent to the infinite from rung to rung. To find God means to find the way without end. The Hasidim saw the "world to come" in the image of this way, and they never called that world a Beyond. One of the pious saw a dead master in a dream. The latter told him that from the hour of his death he went each day from world to world. And the world which yesterday was stretched out above his gaze as heaven is today the earth under his foot; and the heaven of today is the earth of tomorrow. And each world is purer and more beautiful and more profound than the one before.

The angel rests in God, but the holy spirits go forward in God. "The angel is one who stands, and the holy man is one who travels on. Therefore the holy man is higher than the angel."

Such is the way of ecstasy. If it appears to offer an end, an arriving, an attaining, an acquiring, it is only a final no, not a final yes; it is the end of constraint, the shaking off of the last chains, the detachment which is lifted above everything earthly. "When man moves from strength and ever upward and upward until he comes to the root of all teaching and all command, to the I of God, the simple unity and boundlessness—when he stands there, then all the wings of command and law sink down and are as if destroyed. For the evil impulse is destroyed since he stands above it."

"Above nature and above time and above thought"—thus is he called who is in ecstasy. He has cast off all sorrow and all that is oppressive. "Sweet suffering, I receive you in love," said a dying zaddick, and Rabbi Susya cried out amazed when his hand slipped out of the fire in which he had placed it, "How coarse Susya's body has become that it is afraid of fire." The man of ecstasy rules life, and no external happening that penetrates into his realm can disturb his inspiration. It is told of a zaddick that when the holy meal of the teaching prolonged itself till morning, he said to his disciples, "We have not stepped into the limits of the day, rather the day has stepped into our limits, and we need not give way before it."

In ecstasy all that is past and that is future draws near to the present. Time shrinks, the line between the eternities disappears, only the moment lives, and the moment is eternity. In its undivided light appears all that was and all that will be, simple and composed. It is there as a heartbeat is there and becomes manifest like it.

The Hasidic legend has much to tell of those wonderful ones who remembered their earlier forms of existence, who were aware of the future as of their own breath, who saw from one end of the earth to the other and felt all the changes that took place in the world as something that happened to their own bodies. All this is not yet that state in which hitlahavut has overcome the world of space and time. We can perhaps learn something of this latter state from two simple anecdotes which supplement each other. It is told of one master that he had to look at a clock during the hour of withdrawal in order to keep himself in this world; and of another that when he wished to observe individual things he had to put on spectacles in order to restrain his spiritual vision: "for otherwise he saw all the individual things of the world as one."

But the highest rung which is reported is that in which the withdrawn one transcends his own ecstasy. When a disciple once remarked that a zaddick had "grown cold" and censured him for it, he was instructed by another, "There is a very high holiness; if one enters it, one becomes detached from all being and can no longer become inflamed." Thus ecstasy completes itself in its own suspension.

At times it expresses itself in an action that it consecrates and fills with holy meaning. The purest form—that in which the whole body serves the aroused soul and in which each of the soul's risings and bendings creates a visible symbol corresponding to it, allowing one image of enraptured meaning to emerge out of a thousand waves of enraptured movement—is the dance. It is told of the dancing of one zaddick, "His foot was as light as that of a four-year-old child. And among all who saw his holy dancing, there was not one in whom the holy turning was not accomplished, for in the hearts of all who saw he worked both weeping and rapture in one." Or the soul lays hold of the voice of a man and makes it sing what the soul has experienced in the heights, and the voice does not know what it does. Thus one zaddick stood in prayer in the "Days of Awe" (New Year and the Day of Atonement) and sang new melodies, "wonder of wonder, that he had never heard and that no human ear had ever heard, and he did not know at all what he sang and in what way he sang, for he was bound to the upper world."

But the truest life of the man of ecstasy is not among men. It is said of one master that he behaved like a stranger, according to the words of David the King: A sojourner am I in the land. "Like a man who comes from afar, from the city of his birth. He does not think of honors nor of anything for his own welfare; he only thinks about returning home to the city of his birth. He can possess nothing, for he knows: That is alien, and I must go home." Many walk in solitude, in "the wandering." Rabbi Susya used to stride about in the woods and sing songs of praise with such great ardor "that one would almost say that he was out of his mind." Another was only to be found in the streets and gardens and groves. When his father-in-law reproved him for this, he answered with the parable of the hen who hatched out goose eggs, "And when she saw her children swimming about on the surface of the water, she ran up and down in consternation seeking help for the unfortunate ones; and did not understand that this was their whole life to them: to roam there on the surface of the water."

There are still more profoundly solitary ones whose hitlahavut, for all that, is not yet fulfilled. They become "unsettled and fugitive." They go into exile in order "to suffer exile with the *Shekina*." It is one of the basic conceptions of the Kabbala that the *Shekina*, the exiled glory of God, wanders endlessly, separated from her "Lord" and that she will be reunited with him only in the hour of redemption. So these men of ecstasy wander over the earth, dwelling in the silent distances of God's exile, companions of the universal and holy happening of existence. The man who is detached in this way is the friend of God, "as a stranger is the friend of another stranger on account of their strangeness on earth." There are moments in which he sees the *Shekina* face to face in human form, as that zaddick saw it in the holy land "in the shape of a woman who weeps and laments over the husband of her youth."

But not only in faces out of the dark and in the silence of wandering does God give Himself to the soul afire with Him. Rather out of all the things of the earth His eye looks into the eye of him who seeks, and every being is the fruit in which He offers Himself to the yearning soul. Being is unveiled in the hand of the holy man. "The soul of him who longs very much for a woman and regards her many-colored garment is not turned to its gorgeous material and its colors but to the splendor of the longed-for woman who is clothed in it. But the others see only the garment and no more. So he who in truth longs for and embraces God sees in all things of the world only the strength and the pride of the Creator who lives in the things. But he who is not on this rung sees the things as separate from God."

This is the earthly life of hitlahavut which soars beyond all limits. It enlarges the soul to the all. It narrows the all down to nothing. A Hasidic master speaks of it in words if mystery: "The creation of heaven and earth is the unfolding of something out of nothing, the descent of the higher into the lower. But the holy men who detach themselves from being and ever cleave to God see and comprehend Him in truth, as if in the nothing before creation. They turn the something back into nothing. And this is the more wonderful: to raise up what is beneath. As it is written in the Gemara: The last wonder is greater than the first."

From Martin Buber, *Hasidism and Modern Man*, edited and translated by Maurice Friedman, (New York: Harper and Row, 1966), pp. 74-82. Copyright © 1958, 1988 by Martin Buber. Reprinted by permission of the author's estate.

Parabola
Volume: 7.1
Sleep

From the Talmud

When God created Adam, the angels mistook him for a deity. ... But when God put him to sleep, they knew he was a mortal.

•

Parabola
Volume: 2.2
Creation

WORLDS OF DISCOURSE
Interview with Rabbi Zalman Schachter

*I met Reb Zalman Schachter at a conference on mysticism. My
first impression was of size and speed—a big man emanating
energy: a gown swirling with decisive rhythms, a tremendous
beard, shining brown eyes, a swift smile. He wore a remarkable series of hats, different each day: one, out of a Renaissance
portrait, of velvet and fur; a baseball cap; a yomulka that flew
off backwards with his vigorous movements, just as the other
head coverings threatened to be sent flying forward by a sudden gesture of rubbing the back of his head. Occasionally he
broke into a beautiful Hebrew song in a rich warm voice,
or a laugh followed by "… and that reminds me of a story!"
One morning during the conference a well-known academi-
cian logically examined the pros and cons of mysticism for the
whole period of time allowed for a dialogue between him and
Schachter; with three minutes left for his share, Reb Zalman
was reminded of a story by Kafka which ends: "You win!"
"Yes, but only in parable." "No, you win in fact; in parable,
you lose."*

*"Zalman Schachter has become something of a Jewish
guru," Philip Mandelkorn has written of him. "For by his*

●

eclectic methods, intuitive sensitivity and outright chutzpah, he has opened the doors of spiritual reawakening for literally thousands of thirsty souls in this time of Jewish renascence … He surely believes he has glimpsed a vision of a new age, now dawning, with Jews coming home to the faith, and the various religions weaving a harmonious pattern of holy brotherhood."

Reb Zalman was born in Poland in 1924. His youth and adolescence were spent in Austria, Belgium, and in an internment camp in France under the Vichy government. He was sixteen when he was released and came to the United States under the auspices of the Lubavitcher Chassidim, with whom he studied in Brooklyn and in 1949, at the age of twenty two, he was ordained a rabbi. For eight years he was a congregational rabbi in Massachusetts, but as time went on he became attracted to other spiritual ways and greatly interested in modern trends of thought, and his questioning led to a break with the Chassidic establishment. He followed his own path, studying, translating, and discovering his mission as friend and guide to Jews, young and old, who had lost—or never found—their way into the heart of their own tradition.

His methods are indeed eclectic, too much so for some tastes. He combines with Judaism the practices of Christianity, Zen, yoga, and Islam (he claims to be a Sufi sheikh of Pir Inayat Khan's sect as well as a Chassidic rabbi). His devotion is to humanity and to the G-d, as he would write it, of all religions. He is in the forefront of the ecumenical, charismatic movement which is kindling so much fervor today.

Rabbi Schachter's learning is as undeniable as his devotion. He has taught at Brandeis and Boston universities and was for ten years on the faculty of the University of Manitoba, heading the Department of Judaic Studies there. In 1975 he was appointed Professor of Religion in Jewish Mysticism at Temple University, where he had a tremendous schedule of lectures, classes and travels, talks and workshops, human relations and divine worship, with the joyous energy of the born ecstatic.

Among his many translations and publications is a book, Fragments of a Future Scroll: Hassidism for the Aquarian Age, *published by Leaves of Grass Press in Germantown, PA, and an album of two records with translations from Reb Nahman of Bratzlav who was one of his great sources of inspiration and the great grandson of the Ba'al Shem Tov, founder of Chassidism.*

—*D. M. Dooling*

D. M. Dooling: *I was very interested in your meetings last night, and I noticed how many of the people there were quite young. It is such an important aspect of life nowadays, this fact that young people are looking so hard for something. Would we agree that one thing they are looking for is a mystical approach to God? What would you say that there is for them now in Jewish mysticism especially?*

Zalman Schachter: I don't think that it is mysticism as we talked about it before the Second World War, or what Aldous Huxley and Frithjof Schuon had in mind. What young people today are looking for by and large is more of an empirical way of getting to God. It's not that they exhausted all the ways that traditional and spiritual-direction literature have prescribed, and come to the place where one has to "transcend the borders of the senses," to quote St. John of the Cross; but they found out that a lot of religious rhetoric was propaganda, was used to manipulate people, didn't deliver what it promised.

So the move has gone away from a contemplative mysticism that lost itself in the infinite, to a kind that is very blue jeans-like, that says: "If it works, it has got to work for me." So the stress now is all on how to do it; it isn't the mysticism of *what is it* or *how to love it,* but of *how to do it.*

The yogis and the swamis were saying, "We don't have a new religion to give you, what we have is a kind of science: a science of the spirit." That had an impact. And there has been a fantastic proliferation of how-to-do-it methods, from Arica to EST—and I don't want to say anything against them, because I've found that there are some people who do get through by the unlikeliest methods.

So, in this plethora of possibilities that are around today, what has Jewish mysticism got to offer to young people? Three or four things come to mind. Let me start with the hardest one: the mysticism that allows you to stay tuned to the infinite even in concentration camps. You can't quite do that with Hinduism, by saying *maya*, by wanting to move out of this space; it has nothing to say about how this world can be transformed. But the statement that *this* world can be transformed has a great deal to say to young people.

So the first idea that I would like to illustrate is that when people say *AUM* according to the Upanishads, one moves from the world of *A* to the world of *U* to the world of *M*, higher and higher and higher.

When you look at the Divine Name of Judaism: *Yod, He, Vav, He*, the movement is the other way—it is bringing the Divine *down*. It isn't possible to have one without the other, because they are parts of one system. So the open way that yoga manifests is in this movement up, openly; in the hidden way, it brings it down. That is the true esoteric part of yoga. In Judaism the open way is to bring God down; the esoteric way is to go up, so as to be able to bring Him down. So that which is hidden from view is the secret of the path. Our notion really is that on the manifest plane we want to bring the Divine down. We have become expert on how to be in touch despite bad conditions; that is a very heavy thing and it seems to me that with the problems the world has, this becomes really important. Transport yourself for a moment to eastern Europe and see someone like Tevye the milkman, who has a life that is pretty bitter, and yet gets into situations where he can still talk to God in this face-to-face way. That is one important thing.

Second, we know what to do with time. We don't have to escape to eternity in order to be able to find the spiritual; because for us the law of alternation works. The Sabbath is the alternation when we come up from the weekday situation. I used to say to parents who were upset about their children dropping out, "The reason they drop out completely is that they never saw you drop out on Sabbath." The Jewish way is that for six days you are square but you are a hippie for the seventh—which means you get into food in a really essential way, family life is very strongly emphasized, we are in touch with our senses; yet it is all vis-à-vis God—our sense life doesn't have to be separated from Him.

So we live more with time; and Professor Heschel was right when he said that the Jew lives less in space than he does in time. Shabbat is the punctuation of time, the signification of time. I haven't yet seen any other group of people that knows how to experience one day out of the week in such a way as to move so totally out of the everyday into the more mystical flight of the Sabbath. So I think that is a very important element that Judaism has to offer.

Next, since we mention the Torah: How do I discern God's will? How do I tap His wisdom? What is that pool of knowledge that flows down, in God's generosity, in teaching, in Torah? By not being dogmatic, allowing everyone to connect with the whole pool of this knowledge which is that mosaic which people connect with. So we have avoided the one-person syndrome: it isn't one Mohammed or one Jesus or one Paul or one Buddha who designates truth. Moses doesn't really play such a part, he is just one of so many. So we say that Jesus of Nazareth was one of so many people, including his martyrdom; Gautama was only one of the so many enlightened beings and avatars that have passed through our life; and to take one out of context and build the whole thing around him doesn't suit us too much.

On the other hand, we want to learn the material of this teaching and apply it, practically, to daily life, even to food and food packaging. This kind of concern about what God wants, even about such details, connects with the idea of how we can tap His wisdom, and shows that yes, one can, and one can make a blessing and get in touch with that wisdom, work on it, interact with it. So the word *covenant* is important. We talk about the covenant: "Are you in the covenant?"—which is a way of saying: "Are you in the reciprocal relation of Creator and creature?"

There are other things in Judaism, but I will leave it with these just now.

DD: *You were speaking of young people being more interested nowadays in the "how to do it," and I think that's very true. I suppose that always, not just in this generation, youth wants to "do," and certainly one of the favorite words today is "creativity." It's a word I'm very suspicious of, because it's one that people usually fool themselves with; yet surely there is some kind of creation that is possible, and maybe necessary, for human beings. What do you think is the real possibility of creativity for us?*

ZS: Torah and Shabbat make good connections with creativity. On Shabbat you don't go to the store, you don't go to work, not even work for God—even that should be playful, restful, relaxed. Worship is more fun on Shabbat. So creativity enters in this amazing idea of how to make routine exciting. Let's say you have to make the same soup week after week, but each time you put a different herb in it and it becomes a different soup. So creativity for the human being cannot be to make the substance, make the being itself, but comes into the form and shape and decoration one gives to it. We always are just the arrangers, not the composers, when it comes to creativity.

DD: *What about what you were speaking of last night, the service that man can perform for Torah: the constant renewing, the reanimation that his attention and energy bring to it?*

ZS: That is part of it! It has to do with the stress, you see? Everything that I am involved with has to have an element of consciousness. I touch the *mezuzah* when I walk out of the door of this room. It means I want to stop, just arrest my step for one moment as I leave the room, connect with the Ever-Abiding as best I can for that moment, and then move on. So on the outside nothing becomes visible except that gesture. Now it is also possible that this gesture becomes empty—as in most religions the gestures have a way of becoming empty. Then creativity is the way in which we constantly infuse the gesture with awareness, so that it shouldn't be empty.

For instance, the Sabbath comes; what do we do on the Sabbath? We have a custom here in this house that we write to each other Sabbath letters. Nowhere in Jewish spiritual-direction literature do you find anything like that. But somehow we found that living together, routine takes over in such a terrible way that we never tell each other how much we care to live with each other and how much we care for each other. So before the Sabbath we sit down and write each other love letters. When the sanctification of the wine and the bread is said, one of the children takes the letters around; and it feels really good to give and receive a warm letter that says "I care." Now, that is where creativity comes in and Torah gets renewed each time; because the next generation maybe in their Sabbath practice will say, "We received as tradition that on the Sabbath we must write a letter." So all those goodies that people invented along the way, which were produced by their eagerness to try to bring more of God into awareness and relation—that is where creativity comes in.

DD: *There is another angle which interests me. A number of creation myths suggest that God created man through some necessity of His. What could be this part man has to play? It seems you touch on it when you say that man maintains the life of Torah by—*

ZS: Embellishing it with consciousness.

DD: *Yes. But what really must he do? If God made man because He needed him, does man fulfill this need of God's willy-nilly, so to say? What is this need?*

ZS: I don't know if I can answer that without spelling out a kind of hermeneutics of reality. When we speak of Torah, it works the same way as the Divine Name with its four letters. Each letter represents another universe of discourse. So the lowest letter, *He*, represents the discourse of karma yoga, of action. The *V* is the world of *Yetzirah*, which means formation; the upper *He* is creation. The plane of formation, *Vav*, is the feeling plane; it has a new language, new laws, different from the laws of the plane below.

The upper *He* is the mental level, the world of *B'riyah*, where the contemplative is, where if I love God at all it is *amor Dei intellectualis*—I love Him with my intellect; whereas on the plane of *Vav* I love Him with my heart, and on that of the lower *He* I love Him with my action. So each plane has a different law.

You asked: on what plane does God need us? We can't say He needs us on the mental level; that is where all the "omni's" are—God is omnipotent, omniscient, omnipresent, all those superduper words. He doesn't need us. On the level of the lower *He*, if I feed God I am involved in idolatry; if I put real physical food before God, who can't eat it, I make a mistake. It is on this *Vav* plane (and it is here where most of Western language is deficient), the plane of heart, the plane of feeling, that God is hungry. So when the question is raised as to what is our input into the relation with the Divine which keeps the universe going, the answer is that we feed feeling into God.

The deep intuition feels that God is lonely: He is the only being of His kind—Its kind, Her kind; one can't find a decent pronoun that is personal but not masculine or feminine—and on that plane God is in solitary confinement in eternity. He can't get out and has no one to be with. For all the bliss that may be worth, it also creates a certain despair: will God ever be able to share with anyone? So what can we do? We can entertain God; God wants to be loved, He wants to be entertained. There is no purpose for this world on the plane were God is the Pleroma; there it is so full that nothing is needed. The lack that God needs to have filled comes on the plane of feeling, in this world of *Vav*, where one can say that God is hungry—hungry for that energy that comes from the heart.

Now how do we give heart energy to God? At one time we solved that with sacrifice. Mary had a little lamb, and everywhere that Mary went the lamb went too. Then Mary did something that separated her from God; she "sinned." The time came for her to get "at-oned," to get close to God again. So she took her lamb in which she had invested a lot of love and care and offered it as a sacrifice, saw it consumed in fire and with it all the pain that went along with the love that was offered. What does God get out of that? Something He can't get from any other being but man: relationship. Neither angels nor other beings have that which makes them capable of saying *no* to God; man can stand up in front of Him, sometimes even correct Him, say, "What You are doing is wrong." So when he says *yes* it becomes much more significant. That is considered to be the food of God.

The whole sacrificial element was bound up at first with the things that were offered; then the Temple was destroyed and we couldn't do it that way, and we tried to find the verbal formulae that would allow that feeling to be given to God. When someone says "I love you," it may not be new information; I told you that yesterday and the day before, so why say it again? The answer is that it is not for information, it is a vehicle for carrying feeling. And so all the worship and liturgy is a vehicle for feeling. We want to take the entire palette of feeling and offer it to God, including our despair, our sadness. If you look at the calendar you see that we have happy holidays and sad ones, we have mourning and lamentation days, because this entire range of feeling we want to give to God.

Now I think this is what our experience is, concerning loneliness, and concerning the possibility of transcending things whenever there are people around who are able to touch us. We can read books to keep the brain fed, we can do exercises to keep the body happy, but the feeling can't be happy in a vacuum. So the I-Thou relationship is in the conjunctive universe; and the conjunctive universe is in the *Vav*. That letter *Vav* is always used as a Hebrew conjunction; this *and* that, *haze v hazot*. It works the same way in the Upanishads, too, where the *U* world, which is between the *A* world and the *M* world, is a conjunctive. Now, the secret of that conjunctive is what one may say man provides. God makes the universe; people make those ligatures. Your work on *Parabola* is like that; your journal finds fragments of the human spirit all over the world and brings them together between two covers. That is one way of connecting those fragments so that the future's scroll will incorporate the whole works. These are ligatures that only people can provide. Take them out and you have a jumble; put them in and it makes sense. Those ligatures are a function that I call *signification*.

Reality is *so* vast, and nothing seems to connect, and then you bring someone with a mind and a soul who contemplates all that and says *Aha!* and each time he says *Aha!* it is as if another set of ligatures connected.

DD: *Then you see this function of man as being the connecting element not only with God but between all the different levels of life?*

ZS: Yes; he's a ladder. Let me show you how it works out. If I take those four letters of the Divine Name and draw them one on top of the other, they take on the appearance of head, shoulders and arms, spine, pelvis, and legs. And out comes something that says, "Man is made in the image of God."

Now how does God go about becoming Person, from the infinity of infinities? How does he focus into personhood? Isaac Luria, the sixteenth-century Kabbalist, teaches that the first flash God ever got on personality was something glorious: "Let there be person! Let there be this focus of awareness, of volition, of feeling—let there be that! And let us call it Adam Kadmon"—that stands for *maximus homo*, primal man. But between primal man and real man there is a lot that has to happen.

On the basis of the Zohar and other teachings (or, in more spiritual language, on the basis of revelations that he received), Luria realized that there is a level on which the Gnostics are right: this world is a calamity, it is a tragedy. All the stories of the Fall mean that we are in a post-calamity world; when we arrive on the scene, earth has already been ravaged. This calamity occurred at the time of the "breaking of the vessels"—this is the language used by the Kabbala. God started to work on his relationship with man with the whole range of colors of the palette, but the colors didn't mix. He began with love and then he put rigor into the world, but rigor and love didn't mix: the surface tension between them was so great that in order for rigor to develop, love had to be shattered—almost as if that early love got broken by the anger that was behind rigor. So what happened to all the pieces of love? There are fragments all over the universe that get lodged here and there, in high things and low things. A love poem, a psalm, a devotional song—all these are sparks of that original love.

But rigor doesn't give the world a way in which it can live; there isn't room to move. So God brings the next attribute, mercy; and that breaks through everything, and of course rigor shatters. And wherever there is a moment of awe of God, or that total rigor we have to pass through when we die, there is a spark of the original rigor. Compassionate mercy breaks rigor; but mercy is so good that sometimes it takes away initiative, and doesn't allow anyone to do anything. There can never be structure with mercy around, and God wants to have some structure; so mercy gets shattered. And wherever there is an act of pure grace, or where one person forgives another, it is the discovery of a spark of that original bit of mercy. So then there is structure; but structure becomes overweening, like the Tower of Babel: everything must obey the needs of structure; and it gets broken down by aesthetics, by beauty. *Netsah* gets broken by *Hod*. So there are fragments of structure around and sometimes we pick one up and make something work.

Then comes the next attribute, which is *Yesod*, communication. Because beauty can be hollow; sometimes it fails to convey anything, to communicate, so it gets broken for the sake of communication; and communication gets broken by that negation called *Malkhut*, which is the negation of all positives, the universal solvent. Everything gets dissolved again in Malkhut. Even Malkhut gets broken because God can't have life being constantly dissolved. But the fragments of Malkhut that are left allow for transformation; and what life is doing is picking up pieces of Malkhut in order to dissolve and recycle.

That world of calamities is called the world of *Tohu*, chaos; and man's task, says Luria, is to build the world of *Tikkun*, by fixing the world up. What happens is like making a stained-glass window, after those big sheets of glass, blue and red and all colors, are shattered; we put it together, and the lead that joins the pieces is our significance, as it were.

So in the end we put it so together that now there is another kind of rhyme and reason, and there is a blending possible among the various attributes. So says Luria: that is the purpose of the creation of man.

"All these are the things that God created in order to do." End of Chapter 1, Genesis. Read it not: "in order for God to do," but: "in order for man to do." He gives us a world which lacks just enough of perfection that we have got a lot of things we can do with it. So we get our significance out of living by trying to put things together. Each time we do it we ask: "Is that the way you want it, God?" and the answer comes, "No, not quite." So we take it apart and put it together again. So as history proceeds, each time we may put it together a little bit better, but we have as fallout a lot more problems—we see our activity creates a lot of junk. Up till now we thought we could throw the junk away, but now we see there is no place to throw it. So once more, we are learning about Malkhut—how to dissolve things, how to recycle, how to reconnect them.

Teilhard de Chardin sees the world like this: first there is this earth; there is no life. It begins like a vine, putting out creepers, and it fills itself with life, the biogenesis of life. Then this life gets conscious—

DD: *He doesn't explain how. That's where I stop; how can consciousness come from unconsciousness?*

ZS: It comes from someplace. Whereas the medieval people said God created the world out of nothing, the Kabbala said there isn't any such thing as nothing. Nothingness is negation of *something*. So if God creates, He can only make it out of Himself—because He fills it all, there is nothing that is devoid of Him. Even this table has to be God, having forgotten that it is God—imagining that it is a table and so acting as a table.

The rabbis teach how, when a child is conceived, an angel descends into the womb and teaches the child the Torah. Every time the baby kicks it is saying: "Oh, wow! What a neat insight that is!" and that is why the mother is so proud and says, "Look, look, how he's kicking!" So when the time comes for the child to be born, the angel is holding a light over his head but then he strikes him on the upper lip, on that little groove line under the nose, and the child forgets everything; so when it comes out into the world, the first scream means: "Oi, did I know so much, and look what I've forgotten!"

DD: *That's a different slant on the idea of the primal scream!*

ZS: From that moment the child sinks more and more into the body, which isn't capable yet of expressing that fullness, so it has to disappear into amnesia. But each time we learn something "new," or come to a "new" understanding, it is really a "reminder" of what the angel taught us. Maybe I should add that it is also said that the angel can't teach the new being the entire Torah, because pregnancy lasts only nine months and Torah requires a whole year; so each child only gets three quarters of it, and that is why we don't all remember the same parts of truth. And that is also why teachings that we didn't receive from the angel are not acceptable; they don't fit, and we reject them like a tissue reject. Sometimes we can't connect with a teaching that comes from our own tradition, and sometimes we need to take something from another teaching because it is closer to what we got from the angel.

DD: *But don't you think that people* do *accept teachings that don't fit them? You say all teachings are good; do you really think that? Don't you think that there are complete fakes and charlatans among the many gurus inhabiting our planet at the moment, and don't you think that they do harm people and spoil possibilities for them?*

ZS: Yes, I believe that. I agree with you. But sometimes the problem is in the application rather than in the teaching. Teachers can be of the body type or the head type or the heart. Moses was the former, Michelangelo's man of action. Buddha is usually depicted as a roly-poly viscerotonic, the heart type, and Jesus as the lean, Grunewald cerebrotonic, but I would rather see them the other way round; because for the Buddha, the answer is right or wrong knowing, and Jesus is very much the heart teacher. So if the guru is a heart person and someone comes to him with a head problem, if he is not a true, wise, universal, *big* guru he may give heart medicine for a head problem, and it will be poison. It may be true advice, but the person can't use it. Not everybody can be helped by being given a mantra; some people need to be put on a strict diet.

DD: *I am thinking of gurus who are neither of the heart nor the head, but only of the pocketbook!*

ZS: It is true that that is happening. It shows how great the need is, that people are willing to part with hard cash in inflationary times just to attend a weekend and be called asshole. The moment you franchise it, you put enlightenment out on the counter like McDonald's hamburgers. There isn't enough input. If a follower of Maharishi Mahesh gives me a mantra without sharing with me, without finding out anything about me, the mantra may turn out to be a monkey wrench in my machinery rather than the thing that will put me together.

DD: *What is to protect people—or how can they protect themselves?*

ZS: *Caveat emptor!* A little bit of common sense; doubt. Doubt is the best ally I have against sham. One of the things that caused my break from the system from which I came, Habad Chassidism, was that doubt was not permitted. I raised some very heavy questions, and when I was told they were bad questions and that I should put them out of my mind and submit again to a system, I felt it was time for me to graduate.

DD: *In connection with Chassidism, and with what are called the right-handed and the left-handed paths, where do you consider Jewish mysticism really to lie?*

ZS: The exoteric system will domesticate mystics provided they will be voices for the right-handed path. The right-handed path wants to make sure that the whole rational-legal establishment of religion will be supported rather than corroded. The left-handed path is the one that corrodes the legal-rational establishment's way by moving via the charismatic, the impetuous; so the Apollonian is the right-handed and the Dionysiac is the left-handed way of doing things, the way of charisma, of the child, of the fool. The left-handed path is so freaky, it throws one into such dangerous experiences, that one gets into great anxieties going in this way. By the right-handed path, I can't get back to the Garden of Eden except by going all the way around the globe; by the left-handed path, I can go directly to the Garden of Eden, but it turns out that there is this angel with a flaming sword who won't let me in; and I feel great anxiety the closer I get to the flaming sword, which has to do with ego-dissolution.

Part of the left-handed way has to do with sex. There's no greater metaphor than sexual union for the union between man and God; the Zohar and all the mystics of the past speak of being a lover of the Beloved, of shaping oneself reciprocally with the Lover. On the other hand, there is nothing that can so separate a person from God as sex—if it makes me feel that I am the god and there is no other, or that as long as we love one another that is all that matters. Sex that is a manifestation of ego is not kosher; but in that which says that God loves me through her, and her through me, and we both are melting in the pool of this divine love, the ego becomes transparent and consciousness becomes a threesome consciousness.

This is the way the teaching says it: the word for *man* is spelled *Aleph, Yod, Shin*; the word for woman is spelled *Aleph, Shin, He*. The two Alephs and the two Shins are the same for man and woman; the difference is that there is a Yod in the male and He in the female. Yod and He make the word *YA*, which is found in Hallelu*ia*, and which is one of the divine names and the beginning of the four-letter name (*YHVH*). If YA is taken out it leaves Aleph Shin, which is the word for fire; but when YA is left in, when God is there, man becomes a man and woman becomes woman. Without God all we can bring is just fire, which burns out and leaves ashes.

The left-handed path brings God into the things of life, into the bed and into food, for instance: if I enjoy food because it is there only for me to enjoy, then the ego becomes a barrier; but if I allow myself to become transparent I can lend God my palate; so whatever is delicious in the world, if I enjoy it as a transparent being I can enjoy it for Him.

Another meaning of sex, which is in Hinduism, in Sufism, and of course in the Kabbala, is that my real desire is for union with God, it is to make love to God; but God in His grace and wisdom denies me contact with Him except through others. So my partner in love is one in whom I can see the divine principle of femininity, and she can see in me the divine principle of masculinity. If I say: "I want you to love *me*, not the God in me," I become opaque, and fall; and that is the danger of the left-handed path. There is the flaming sword, and I feel anxiety; and that anxiety is what brought a lot of ideas about celibacy into religion—fear of allowing that danger. But there is no life where there is no danger.

DD: *Would you say that what is really alive in Jewish mysticism now is in the left-handed path?*

ZS: Not quite. If I say the left hand is alone, it is chaos. For instance, this delight I feel while eating on Shabbat, offering it all to God, can easily get into an eating orgy; finding God in every person in sex can lead to a sexual orgy. There have to be limits so that I don't transgress, so that it isn't corruption and vice that are energized, instead of the love of God. I sometimes use the terms silly and serious: serious is right-handed, silly is left-handed. Serious needs silly very badly, because otherwise it is all work and no play. But silly must not become the rule for more than one day. Silly always has to be the tickler of serious in order to keep serious awake; but serious has to keep a roof over silly's head. If the left hand and the right hand collaborate, as they must in everything, then the experience of the past is kept alive. You see, I really believe in tradition; I believe, however, that tradition is what a group of souls leave behind so that when they become reincarnated they don't have to learn from the beginning of the alphabet again. There is a depository of the teaching; the *magisterium*, the *depositum fidei*. The next time we come back we find it here. Now into whose hands do we entrust it? It is the parable of the talents again; we find the most conservative investors and give them the trust fund to manage. So the *depositum fidei* gets handed to the most conservative people, and that is the right-handed-path element. But when we come back, if we are wise, we realize that while we entrusted it to the right people, the money isn't there to stay in the trust fund, it is there to be used.

What souls leave behind in order to find again, that is what I think is tradition; therefore I don't think I should throw anything out of tradition—I need the whole junkyard, well catalogued and available—because what one generation can't use, another may need and can find again. The nineteenth century couldn't stand mysticism—at least, in the West; it needed to get to rationalism, it had to get rid of so much mystification and the way people were manipulated by it. And of course we can't allow mysticism to be an opiate, as Marx called it, that we give people in order that they should not think or function rightly. The nineteenth century did a good job; but they threw out a lot of baby with the bath water. It would have been wonderful if they could have said: "Now we don't need mysticism, but we still want to keep a living school of the ancient past," as for instance in eastern Europe Chassidism kept mysticism alive. Now, after the two world wards, the world is looking into the blazing H-bomb and saying: "We can't continue on this path, we have got to do something else." So this old way that was lying dormant all of a sudden blossomed. It was like spring in Manitoba where I used to live: the buds on the bare trees get thicker and then seem to burst into leaf. After World War II, we first had existentialism, then the beats, then the whole greening of America and the optimism that came with that; and now there is a very rich bed for all those mysticisms to flourish again.

DD: *So what do you think people are specially needing now?*

ZS. I think people are starving for fantasy. What Aldous Huxley called the antipodes of the mind—if I don't go there from time to time, I live an impoverished life. If I go to the fantasies of TV, they are all commercialized—

DD: *Is it fantasy we need, or myth?*

ZS: I think fantasy is the way to get into myth. If I say that thinking leads me to reason, to a system of philosophy, and sensing leads me to experience, and feeling is the response to experience, in the same way I would say that fantasy is the door into myth. You remember that fantastic parable by Kafka about the man who couldn't understand parables? We need a door to get in. For most people, the door has been slammed in their youth. Most teachers don't know how to make use of the energy of fantasy—or any of the youthful energies, for that matter. I was working with a group of high school kids who were so full of pepper they couldn't sit still. Instead of trying to make them be quiet, I said, "Let's say the Sanctus moving our arms like this: *Holy*, with the arms crossed;

Holy, with the arms lifted; *Holy*, raising them as high as possible; then turning in a half circle, with the arms out, Heaven and earth are full of Thy glory! Holy, Holy, Holy—" and for five minutes the whole place was transformed, by giving a channel to the energy that was there—not asking it to change, but to make a connection. In the same way, fantasy is the door to myth because it exercises that element that our teachers exorcized from us as youngsters.

DD: *Where would Chassidism stand today, for instance, on the subject of fantasy?*

ZS: When Chassidism first appeared, its opponents said that antinomianism was raising its ugly head: "Here is this Ba'al Shem Tov telling people to be free and happy; this leads to leaving the law and following one man. We don't want that." So Chassidism tried to avoid the Scylla of form and the Charybdis of antinomianism. It came first as a middle road between silly and serious.

DD: *But now it has become serious, hasn't it?*

ZS: And the reason for it is that the people who were supposed to take care of serious stopped taking care of it. Orthodoxy is always necessary in order to keep the right-handed element together. But orthodoxy fell apart; it didn't have any vitality any more. So the only place where vitality was left was in Chassidism, the Chassidism had to man the bastions, as it were. And while it does that, and it teaches people how to keep the forms, it has very little energy left.

The left-handed way only shows itself in opposition to the right-handed way; so if Yeshiva University and all the orthodox people would do their job, then Chassidism could do more of the left-handed things—dance in the streets, celebrate, stop people and ask them outrageous questions. But there isn't the energy. So it's not perfect. But it helps just to recognize that the growing edge is never in the center of the tree, it's always on the outside. Conservatives want to be in the center where it's safe; but the new development, the new life, the new juice is on the growing edge. Chassidism used to be on the growing edge, but now having opted for keeping the structure, or the centrist position, it's crazy people like myself who are on the circumference, on the growing edge. And it means we have to stay in touch with other such crazies in other traditions and have a new kind of devotional dialogue with them, in which we learn so much from one another. This helps some of what we have to do now, which is to bring back things that Judaism had, but has lost, like the mantra. We had a martial art, for instance—a form of belt wrestling; there are echoes of it left—but we lost it, and I think I know just when and why. We had fertility rites, many things, that were thrown out the door for one reason or another, and they come back in through the window, but in disguise.

We need to get back what we have lost. The Christians can gain a great deal, I think, from rediscovering sacred dance; some people are trying to bring it back into Christian worship. The Sufis have it, and among the Chassidim you see some dancing.

DD: *This brings up an interesting point about the interdependence of the right- and left-handed paths, in the art and ritual of all the traditions. The prescribed movements of the sacred dance, the sacred dance of the Mass, for instance, or of many other rituals, the repetition of the mantra, the chanting—when do they become empty forms? There is no blueprint for that, of course.*

ZS: Yes, there is, and no, there isn't. Here again there is a curve—worship has to have a curve. It has to go up from the prayers at the foot of the altar until I go to the Kyrie, the Gloria, the consecration and consuming of the elements. Most of the time it just stops abruptly and falls down. Obviously it is necessary to descend with prayers, with thanksgivings—

DD: *To make the full parabola, in other words.*

ZS: Right! That's the word. Now the feminine is very strong in the descent; the masculine does the initial arousing, gets to the top and then collapses. The feminine knows how to maintain and to bring it to fruition and to take it down. This is why if women are going to be priests, I would want a man to lead the first part of the Mass, and a woman the second part. Climbing the mountain is masculine; descending, and entering the cave, is feminine. The rising part of the curve is masculine and the descending is feminine. And the reason the world is in such a mess is because we haven't had feminine "priests" take us gently down and connect us again to earth in a loving way. We can be taken up the mountain and left stranded there, and if there is no right coming down, we just suddenly fall down, and there is no re-entry. I can't stress enough the importance of that. It takes me back to what we were talking about at the beginning: the purpose of creation. God is very good at doing the masculine thing (at least the way we understand that now)—Heaven loving the earth; it is the earth responding to Heaven for which man was created. One might say that in all mysticism the function of the human being is seen to be the feminine, the beloved, the responder to God, who is constantly saying to Him, "Come, build a home with me. You have taken me up the mountain, given me the great vista; now come down and build a cabin and help me raise a child."

So I think the function of man is to be woman!

I feel women teachers are such a necessity. Only one Chassidic master was a woman; and there was one Rabi'a in Sufism, but the trouble was the men couldn't leave her any space.

DD: *Must it be necessarily two different people, "man" and "woman"? Couldn't it be two different forces in the same person that bring the energy up, and down?*

ZS: Agreed. That opens another aspect: it was my father who taught me how to be a man in the world; my mother taught me how to love. What flowed between my mother and me is what allows me to meet people in love; what flowed between my father and me allows me to function in the world. What flowed between my mother and my sisters allowed them to be women in the world, and what flowed between my father and my sisters allowed them to love.

DD: *What is it really to be men and women in the world? Going back to the idea of the functioning of the human being in the continuing process of creation, what is "duty" in the sense of behavior, of action in life, of a way of living?*

ZS: I think it has to do with communication between people, and the feeling that is communicated. For instance, two people meet for the first time—like you and me. They may be worlds apart in their upbringing and education and ethnic background; but sometimes there is a door open between them and they recognize each other as fellow conspirators in the universe. And they feel something special about each other. We need fifteen or twenty words for "love"; C. S. Lewis points out the different qualities that the Greeks expressed in words like *philios, agape, eros*—

DD: *I'm told the Quechua Indians had a hundred and twenty different words for love.*

ZS: Marvelous! Wouldn't it be great if we could get such a vocabulary into print, with all its nuances and connotations? It's the same thing with *soul*. English is such a poor language; that word has so many connotations, and we need to be as precise as the Eskimos are about different kinds of snow. So the problem is how to key our communication so it should be familiar and not too familiar, so it should be friendly but not too vulnerable, because we don't know each other's virtue-vice combinations and I may touch some button inside of you that will make you turn on me. There are so many land mines hidden in the human psyche that can blow up and that we have no notion about; there are so many dangers. We need to learn to give each other signals of how we are inside, so we can let go safely when things aren't right, and we have to make room for each other's ups and downs; we have to have relations that are strong enough so that true feeling can show. Every relation calls for a kind of covenant, a sort of contract, implicit or explicit. With the majority of people we don't have the explicit contract to stay with truth, but we do have it implicitly.

And of course we need not only communication from the head but from the heart—nonverbal communication, an exchange of emotional energy, and sometimes an even higher, spiritual energy. We haven't the vocabulary to describe that in words; but I think that in the next fifteen or twenty years we are going to sharpen this kind of communication very much.

And that reminds me of a story: Someone asked Rabbi Pinchas of Koretz: "How can we pray for someone else to repent when this prayer, if granted, would curtail another person's freedom of choice? Is it not said by the rabbis that everything is in Heaven's hands, except the fear of Heaven?" Rabbi Pinchas answered: "What is God? The totality of souls. Whatever is in the whole can also be found in the part. So in any one soul, all souls are contained. If I turn, in *t'shuvah* [which means the turning, or returning, to God or to our inmost Selves] I contain in me the friend whom I wish to help, and he contains me in him. My t'shuvah makes the him-in-me better and the me-in-him better. This way it becomes so much easier for him-in-him to become better."

Parabola
Volume: 31.4
Home

OUR HOME IS GOD'S HOME:
DIRAH B'TACHTONIM

Rick Blum

There is a Hassidic song that tells a story.[1] One day God made an angel who, like every other angel, had his own particular job to do. The angel was sent to our world in order to bring back the most valuable object in all creation. He could not return without it.

First, the angel retrieved the most beautiful jewel anywhere on Earth. This was promptly rejected. Next, the angel discovered a horrifying yet moving scene. A soldier had thrown himself upon a bomb to save the lives of his comrades. The angel brought home a drop of the soldier's spilled blood. This time, the angel was very close to completing the task, but he learned that he needed to find something even more precious than the soldier's blood.

Searching again, the angel encountered a troubled man who had lost his way and made the wrong choices, and who was now rapt in anguished yearning to reconnect with God. After capturing one of the man's tears and returning, the angel learned he had succeeded—that to Heaven, this was the most precious item on Earth.

The meaning within this story speaks of more than an angel's successful mission. It also teaches us about our need for a path back to the original Source of our lives. Yet we have not noted the most startling facet of the story. Notice that Heaven directs the angel to look for something on earth, something lacking in Heaven. Note also what the angel learns is the most valuable earthly object to God, revealing a glimpse of how Heaven responds to the same spirit-matter gap that we seek to bridge. In the last line of the song, God says that such a teardrop "is the thing I cherish most." This story offers a road home that runs in two directions. At the same time that we are looking for access to Ultimate Reality, God is somehow seeking our plane of existence in return. As surprising as it may be, we have something that Heaven is looking for.

On the Literal Level

The biblical epic evokes a dynamic rhythm between two truths: God insists that we inhabit the physical realm, and the Divine wants to be close to us here. We are meant to wander through the concrete world we call Creation, and the Creator will both seek and find us wherever we go. God puts us here, watches us get lost, and then goes looking for us, over and over. The Torah's narrative speaks of little but this search by Heaven for Earth.

First, Adam decides to break the connection between divine will and human choice. God's response: "Where are you, Adam?" Yet after explaining the results of Adam and Eve's choice, God prepares and even dresses these first children for their journey. In these ways, beginning with that first question, the Divine discloses a clear and continuing message that Adam and Eve can turn off track and be hurt by their wandering, but they will never be left alone.

As matters worsen with each generation, God comes for Noah, lifts up his family, and bathes the world clean for them (a worldwide *mikveh* or baptism). After this divine bath prepares the world for future contact with Heaven, God finds Abraham, then Isaac, then Jacob. God watches over their battles, gives parental encouragement (which actually starts with Cain), lets them win arguments with Heaven (Abraham and Moses), and makes them promises that amaze them.

We learn from the Torah that, for God, this contact is profoundly cherished and even tender. This affection includes new names for some of those who most deeply return God's love—Sarah (from *Sarai*), Abraham (from *Avram*), and especially Jacob, who evidently needs two extra names: *Yisra'el* ("he who wrestles with God") and *Yishurun* ("the upright one"). Much later, in a private glimpse of His world, we find God exulting to Heaven's prosecuting attorney (the angel named "the adversary," *ha-Satan*) about one named Job who loves God no matter what.

The overall story is about being lost and found, about leaving and returning, about a dance in which God lets us swing as far away as we can stretch, before bringing us back full circle into a tight embrace. For this reason, God picks the most stubborn group of people in creation, lets them get deeply lost (Egypt), and orchestrates the rescue in a show of shows, in front of every one of them. God presents the Torah to all the people at once, promising a plan to bring them to a special home, to the place waiting for them since the very Beginning. This place is to be both their home and God's.

In picking these "stiff-necked"[2] slaves for the mission, God knew that they would never let go of the Torah and that they would never really follow it. They would eventually have to be sent away again.

After the children of Israel have made all the mistakes that the Torah predicts that they will make, God steps aside as their enemies gradually scatter them, like birds that swallow and then scatter seeds, all over the Earth. This exile fits both strains of their response to God and the Torah, both their forgetting and their remembering. Divinely inspired prophets arise to prepare for the remembering, even before the people experience the results of their forgetting. In this way, God sends the cure before the disease.

Again and again, God gives the prophets visions of His gathering the people and bringing them back home: "I will take the children of Israel from among the nations where they have gone. I will gather them from all around and bring them to their Land. ... I will save them in all the communities where they sinned, and I will purify them. They will be My people and I will be their God" (Ezekiel 37:21, 37:23).

On the Mystical Level

On the literal level of understanding, the Torah expresses one extended love song of God's wish to live closely with His children. We might expect this symbolism to disappear on the mystical (Kabbalistic) level of Torah exploration. This is the deepest of the four traditional levels of meaning (called the *pardes*), and it teaches that only God is ultimately real. In the mystical rendering of Torah, however, the world is depicted as existing because of a profound cosmic wish to dwell in the lowest realms.

The phrase for this divine journey is *dirah b'tachtonim*. It means "a dwelling place in the lowest realms," and it is a pervasive mystical message throughout the Hebrew biblical narrative. From creation to exile, it sheds a light that reveals further depths within each story, making them our stories as well. Dirah b'tachtonim is the quintessential Kabbalistic perspective on the purpose of the physical plane of existence; it can be understood as the most profound reason that the Creation was manifested at all. It begins with the Torah's innovation in describing the Creation as "good," and adds that the physical plane is in fact a better place for God than for people.

Just as the Hebrew Bible is God's story of us, the dirah b'tachtonim system is essentially God-centered. It is as if we are imagining God's meditation: the One's spiritual wish. While our urge is to journey toward higher planes of existence, God's desire is to be here with us, and the divine meditation is upon the finite.

We and our world look far different through divine vision, according to this teaching. The sublime, spiritual aspects of our human experience are, from a God's-eye view, no higher than our grossly material experience. God does not reach down to us from the top of a metaphoric ladder spanning from the lower material levels, upward through spiritual experience, and gradually ascending toward Heaven.[3] Just as infinity is fully as far from seven billion as from seven, and just as light speeds away at a constant rate no matter what relative speed you are traveling, the Infinite Essence is equidistant from every element of our world.

This truth is ultimately a touching affirmation of our lives, but at first it collides with every spiritual intuition we have. We cannot escape our sense that the unified levels, the exalted and rarefied worlds beyond gross distinctions, are higher and better. We yearn for these levels, and understandably so. Still, the desire of the One is to find a home in the world that It projects, the very world that looks so Godforsaken to us.

God's intention of dirah b'tachtonim teaches us that the world before our eyes is supposed to appear Godforsaken. To us, this is the world's limitation and our myopia. To the Divine, it is the special and exquisite power gifted to the world: the capacity to apparently and almost completely hide the Essence.[4] It is the world's unique endowment.

As a result, the further the Essential Light ventures and the more deeply Its radiance becomes hidden within the hologram of the world, all the greater does the Divine range express Itself. After all, what can we tell about the power of an intensely strong searchlight by standing next to it? Only by traveling as far as the light can shine can we measure its scope.[5] The Universal Essence extends Itself so far that we cannot even tell It is there, while It remains all that truly exists. According to the Jewish mystical outlook of dirah b'tachtonim, this furthest span from Heaven is exactly where the One wants to live.

Kabbalah teaches that this is the reason that the Torah instructs us in the physical rituals (*mitzvos*) of Jewish practice. Indeed, the oddly physical and seemingly unspiritual rituals with which the Torah overflows seem to be the most delightful to God. It is as if the more opaque the meaning of a religious act, the more it answers the Divine call.

Spiritual Homebuilding

From both the literal and mystical levels of our experience of Torah, we understand that the angel is not the only one who goes searching. The seeker's single tear is the most precious object to Heaven because it heralds fulfillment of the cosmic wish. God seeks closeness with people and wants to join us in the manifested world. This is the essential point of Creation. The Torah lets us in on the plan and asks us to agree to become partners in it. In this way, God supplies the blueprint, and we are instructed to apply it in order to complete Creation. Just as God dressed the first couple, the Torah teaches us to dress ourselves in physical mitzvos, which in turn make the entire physical plane a dirah b'tachtonim. By performing the physical commandments, we are to make a home within the Godforsaken realm for the most transcendent One.

Just as God masks the higher reality of infinity and touches us through the tangible world around us, we are to reach back through the directions in His-story, the Torah. We are not supposed to seek escape from our world in order to live in God's transcendent realm, though we innately crave it. Instead, we are to embrace even the exile and become the legs of the Torah. God intends that we carry it.

Notes:

1 It is one of the modern songs in English that are included in booklets that follow the Chabad Hassidic tradition for grace after feasts and special occasions.

2 *Am k'shai oref* in biblical Hebrew.

3 Faitel Levin, *Heaven on Earth* (New York: Kehot Publications, 2002), pp. 116-117.

4 *Ibid*, pp. 60-62.

5 *Ibid*, pp. 9-10.

Parabola
Volume: 10.1
Wholeness

THE VERTICAL ADVENTURE

Interview with Rabbi Adin Steinsaltz

Rabbi Adin Steinsaltz's work in Israel and abroad as a teacher, translator, writer, and lecturer is rooted in traditional ideas expressed through the ancient Jewish sources and the Wisdom of the Fathers. Jean Sulzberger spoke to him about wholeness in our lives.

Jean Sulzberger: *It says in the Zohar, "The Holy One, blessed be He, created man in the likeness of the All." Does this mean that the wholeness possible for man is on the scale of the universe?*

Adin Steinsaltz: It is said that God created man in His own image. The only way that can be understood is that man was created on the same scale and on the same level. The same idea is expressed when it is said that God turned to all of creation and said, "Let us create man." Let *us* create man. He turned to the whole universe and said, "Let us all participate," and each of the parts of the whole gave something of itself to create man.

JS: *But the whole universe—what does it mean? We are taught that there are worlds within worlds.*

AS: One of the stories is that Adam was created tall—that he reached from earth to heaven. And God put his hand on him and squashed him to a certain size. We do believe that a human being is a multi-leveled being, a being that is made of, so to say, several stories, one above the other. The highest one is really identical with the Godhead: the highest one. But there is a point of the self, and the point of the self is the point on a column that goes from earth to the highest heaven. I would say that self-consciousness and self-image are at a certain level of this column. Perhaps very small children are almost entirely on the physical level. Later on, perhaps a person may move slightly higher into something that is less corporeal or not entirely corporeal. The column itself can become higher and higher still, which means that the self can reach to higher and higher levels.

Now, when the self is on a particular level, a man can understand only that one level. The words and the notions he can speak about are connected solely with the images and notions of that level. Because humanity as a whole is usually on more or less the same level, one of the problems of every kind of prophet is that even when he sees, he cannot tell. There are no words to describe what he perceives. These perceptions don't have words, so they have to be translated into images which are symbolic.

JS: *Would you describe a whole man as one who can see, indeed* be, *in more than one world?*

AS: Every human being lives in more than one world. We are living in the world of emotion, the world of thought, and so on. In some ways we are always living in more than one world, almost by definition. More than that, some of us at least have a grasp, to a greater or lesser extent, of some existence that is beyond the purely mental plane of existence, and occasionally find a way to a world or worlds above us. But usually for most people, existence is just the "amphibian" state between the purely material and the mental-emotional. There are people who can achieve a state beyond this more perfectly, but it is perhaps only once in a generation that someone like this may appear. It is as though he doesn't really belong to this existence—not that he doesn't have a physical body, but his physical body is just what it should be: only a small part of his whole being. As it is, it's as though I inherited a skyscraper and I'm living only on the first story, or sometimes even below, in the basement.

JS: *Are you saying that most men have only physical bodies?*

AS: I think each of us inherited the whole building. Most people stay in the basement, some people climb to the first story, some go higher still. We know that even climbing a mountain in a quite ordinary way requires a great deal of hard work. And in relation to the climb we are speaking of, even though the potential is inborn, it needs a huge amount of training. In another kind of example, human beings seem to have the inborn ability to learn to read and write—a very abstract and complicated ability, but every human being possesses it to some degree. Still, there is a necessary period of turning this potential into practical ability, even though there is the capability inherent which makes it possible.

JS: *Can a person move from the basement to the next story through his own efforts, or does he need a guide, a teacher?*

AS: A teacher is always a great help. We would have to say that this climb is theoretically possible almost independently, because it is the individual's heritage, but practically speaking for most people it is impossible without help. Some people have living teachers, some have dead teachers, but they still have teachers. How many people learn to read and write on their own?

JS: *So most of us need a guide.*

AS: We need someone who has gone a part of the way and who can show how it is to be done and what can be done. There are people who have an inborn aptitude for this climb; for others it is necessary to work harder. Though there are guidelines which may be more or less true for everyone, each person has an individual form of growth. We are not identical—unless we would reach the highest point of our being, in which, possibly, we are entirely identical.

JS: *What is the Jewish method for moving up in the building? There are many Jews who search, but who can't find a method. So many Jews go into Zen Buddhism or Sufism because there seems to be no one within our own tradition to tell us how we can grow.*

AS: There are two reasons for this. The first is practical and historical. For many years, the number of people wishing for this was very limited. Most people, if they want adventure, want horizontal adventures. Those who had a deep desire were always very few. The many disruptions in the history of the Jews caused many of the teachers and their pupils to disappear along with many other things. So this is historical. And it is also true that there are always places where such teachers exist, but you cannot find them listed in a telephone directory.

The second reason is far deeper. The major part of Jewish tradition holds that while there are methods to achieve many great and even holy powers on many levels, the question is, what use is it? Clairvoyance, levitation, "second sight"—it was a firm belief that all these are possible on a certain way of development. The question is, should there be what is called a systematic, well-taught way of spiritual growth *per se*? What is the aim? Let's say that I grow twice or three or ten times bigger in a spiritual way. The only thing that makes this worthwhile is the worship of God and not spiritual growth. The spiritual growth may be an outcome.

JS: *Worship doesn't seem to be enough. We can worship to the end of our days and say the Psalms to the end of our days and come no closer to God.*

AS: We reach here a basic theological point. We believe that God is infinite in such a way that the human being of whatever size and whatever growth can never reach Him. The greatest, highest human soul is still separated from God by an impassable gap. There is an impassable gap between the Creator and the created. Now, this impassable gap can only be passed on one side, on God's side. He can, so to say, give a hand to the people on the other side, to pass, to cross. I can grow as tall as I want and I am still almost at the same distance away: unless He gives me a hand I will never be able—because whatever I become I am still a creature. Even the highest man stands on the brink of an impassable gap. The main question therefore becomes, how do I jump over? From that point of view, whatever I am as a person becomes only a personal query, because the real question is, how do I make this jump? And the size I have achieved is not always entirely helpful at this point. It has been said many times that you cannot have growth only in one direction. It is as certain as Newton's law of reaction. There is always some kind of danger with growth—they go together. The higher a person aspires, the stronger the forces below draw him. For every move in the direction of good, there is a natural balancing power that reacts and drives toward evil in one form or another. One of the sages of the last century put it in a very beautiful way. He said, "In a diamond, you have what is called the diamond part and the plain stone, which is the carrier of the diamond." Now, if you have a huge diamond, it is bigger as a diamond, but the stone is also much bigger. That is why there are stories in all literature about the simple, the ignorant, the innocent sometimes making this jump while higher people who had really great souls could not overcome their own problems, the problems that come, I would say, from the size of their own personalities. So the question is, what can we do to achieve the one, the only great achievement?

JS: *The jump is a process, isn't it?*

AS: It is, but in a very real sense it is irrational—it is above any type of reasoning process. Because of that we have to do it, we have to do it every day—possibly every minute. It is almost impossible for a person who did it not to achieve greatness as a kind of by-product. But some people are using their whole powers without knowing what they are doing, while others who have far more knowledge of it never manage to do it. It comes back to the separation at the beginning. You can be of the highest size, you can be made in the image of God, but you are not immune to sin.

JS: *The mystery is still how. To be whole we must begin with a kind of unity in ourselves. And if one sees that the mind is going in one direction and the body is going in another and the emotions in yet another, then how to bring them together? It's a work, isn't it?*

AS: Oh, that's a work. Here is one of the basic differences among spiritual formulas, or paths. Many of the Far East traditions, for example Zen Buddhism that you mentioned, one may call a kind of secular spiritualism, because they are so very much interested in the growth of man, in the enlightenment of man. There are very many similarities, but one of the basic differences is that it represents a kind of anthropocentric spirituality. In Judaism some of the great masters put far more stress on the basic man-God relationship than on what man is. As I have said, it has been a debate whether a systematic form and method of growth will end in something more than just the growth of the human being.

JS: *Sitting here listening to you, I feel a little more collected, as though my head and body were not so separated. With that comes more of a feeling of presence. What is that process?*

AS: These two parts are not basically enemies. We speak about them as the informed and uninformed parts, and one of the problems is, how do you inform someone that is in a way stupid? The body—and not only the body, we can call it the simple animal spirit, and the soul—have the problem of coming to a mutual understanding. The example of riding a dumb animal has been used many times. At first there may be no communication—not enmity, but lack of understanding. Later, rider and animal can become so very close that they begin to understand one another. With a good horseman, the horse does not have to be beaten—they have become, so to say, almost a unit. When the soul and the body and every part of it become a unit, then they in fact help each other. The rider will never achieve the same thing without the horse. The soul needs the body because the body has tremendous powers that reinforce it. If we take the parable of the building again, the body is the foundation, and it is very powerful because it has to support the whole structure.

JS: *What is man's part? It is God who has to bring down His hand, you said. What is our part?*

AS: First of all, one of the first conditions is to listen. He is speaking all the time. The Ba'al Shem said, "The voice inside me never stopped speaking." The voice doesn't stop. We just stopped hearing it. It isn't a phenomenon in time, but a phenomenon in eternity. It is our work to be ready to do the listening.

There are moments when a person is given a gift. Sometimes it is for a minute, sometimes it can last for a day or for months. Usually it is not a permanent change—just a gift, so to say, a loan. To use entirely different symbols: it is like giving someone a million-dollar check on the condition that it be returned after a certain time. The real question is, what use can he make of it in the meantime? Sometimes we get such a big "check" and it will have to be returned.

Sometimes there is a beginner's gift. At that stage I told one of my teachers about my experiences and he said, "Well, you have to know that these things will only last a certain time—you don't know how much time, but they will pass. The only significant thing you can do is make use of them. If you don't make use of them, they will disappear and leave you in the same position that you were before." So many times as a beginner you receive so much more than you do after you work for years, and sometimes you wish again for the days when you could achieve things so much more easily.

We don't know why or when a person is given such a gift, but again, it is only a loan, which is given for a certain period of time. On a different level, Maimonides speaks about the prophets. He says, "Humanity should be seen as a group of people being in the darkest night. From time to time there is a flash of lightning and then you get your bearings and you see everything, but it disappears after a moment. That is prophecy." That is his symbol of prophecy. On a lesser level, almost everyone gets such a gift. Sometimes it's once in a lifetime, sometimes it is far more frequent—but that is something exceptional. There is no way of ensuring that it will ever come, or come again, and sometimes it is very disappointing. One is waiting and preparing for that. ...

JS: *Is the most important thing, then, just to try to be open?*

AS: It helps up to a certain point, but whether it comes or it doesn't come—there are many Jewish ways, as one called it, of becoming a "vessel." Another called it becoming a violin that can be played upon. I have to do all the tuning of the violin and only then will it be fit to play. What can one get from an imperfectly prepared instrument? Some people say that the whole of what Judaism is about is a way of preparing body and soul for having this ability.

Some things are repeated again and again in our tradition as well as in others. One that was very much stressed is that the biggest and most terrible danger is thinking about oneself. This was considered almost a definition of evil, being self-centered. In a practical and spiritual way, the less I am motivated by my ego in every way, in every form, the more I am able to become a receptacle, a vessel, for receiving what is there. It is there. It is something in the air. I have to have an instrument that can pick it up. We have a soul—we have it *all* in us. We make too much noise. If I am always listening to myself, I cannot listen to any other thing that passes through me. That is a part of it. Part of it is the relation of the individual and others.

More than that, sometimes I may be doing something that in itself is good, but it is not a thing that *I* should do. Sometimes I am trying very hard to do something which is not necessary for me while neglecting to do something which is necessary. I am speaking about instruments. You see one person is a violin, another is a cello.

JS: *What has the perfected man attained?*

AS: I would say he has attained his whole stature. That means he is able to move on all the scales of all the worlds that correspond to his soul, to all the levels of his soul. The idea of the perfect man is that he can move on this ladder—in his lifetime, during his existence—that he can move from the physical to the highest heaven and he can understand every level with his own images, with his own ideas. He is going from one heaven to another, or from earth to heaven, and he is at home in all of them. He has a consciousness that attains, I would say, in theory, the whole universe—not just the horizontal. Perfection is not just attaining a certain level, say, the level of an angel. It is the ability to have a double, treble, five or tenfold mode of existence, of understanding. It's a multi-layered existence.

It won't do any harm to tell a story. It is told about two great men, a father and a son. They were great leaders, both of them, and the father was possibly one of the outstanding people of his time. He was passing through his son's home one day and he heard a baby crying. He looked and found the baby, and his son sitting near the cradle immersed in meditation. The father soothed the baby and then he shook his son and said to him, "My son, I didn't know you had such a little mind, because when I am in the deepest meditation I can still hear a fly moving about."

JS: *Does God need perfection from us? Is God in search of man? In a time when everything seems to be going downhill, is there at this moment, which could almost be called the "end of days," a need for conscious men? A cosmic need?*

AS: A definition of our times is complex. In one way things are becoming worse—in another, many more people are conscious about it. What's more, it seems that they used to say that each period has different souls, different sizes of souls, that behave in a different way in each period. It seems that we are living in a time in which there is a possibility for extreme changes. The extreme changes we can see from one direction to another didn't seem possible thirty or forty years ago. People moved in these directions much more slowly. So it seems that the movement—or the ability—has become accelerated.

The search for man is constant. God is searching for man—the saints and the evil-doers alike. The need *vis-a-vis* God is the same as it ever was. The need in the world is perhaps greater. There were times when it seemed that humanity was distributed in a more even way. Now there seems to be great diversity of levels and great complexity.

There is certainly a need for the teachers to be greater. In an enlightened age you don't need such a great teacher, even though it seems just the opposite. As I said, perfection is the ability to operate on many different levels. Now, we are living in a time in which there are souls scattered from every level one can imagine. They are interconnected, not only socially, because an age is not just a random mingling of people who happen to be together, who were born together by some mischance. They are interconnected. And in complicated times like these a teacher must be very great.

A teacher needs two things—perhaps three things. He should understand the subject that he wants to teach. He should know methods of teaching it. And he should understand the level and understanding of the pupil. If he is not able to do any of these things, or all of them, he is no good.

JS: *Could it be said that we must first know ourselves as we are? Would that be a first step?*

AS: I sometimes say that the first step is to acknowledge our yearning towards something. To acknowledge it. It is far below having a desire, but to acknowledge that there is something in ourselves, just to acknowledge it.

I had a friend who passed away many years ago. He wasn't troubled in a personal way, but he was troubled about his spirit. We used to meet many times for years off and on, and I once asked him what was it that made him go on, because it was obvious he was a person who was troubled for years, surely more than twenty years. He said that there was a sentence in the Book of Job that was the key sentence for his life. Job is speaking to the Lord and saying, "You are yearning for your handiwork." And my friend said, "If God is yearning for me, how can I say no?" And that was pursuing him, as I say, for twenty very troubled years, and possibly toward the end of his life that was the main point. ...

JS: *What is the mark of a real teacher?*

AS: One thing that is always a clear mark and true of every real teacher is humility. The reason is a very simple one. It is not a moral reason. It is because the greater a person is, the greater he feels his insignificance and his lack. By definition, a great teacher will have great humility. Another mark of a real teacher is the feeling of responsibility. It is essential for a teacher and is also a mark of the personality. Sometimes you can look at two teachers and you don't see the difference. Outside they may look very much alike. One of the ways to find out is when you look at their disciples, and then you see what was in the teacher. It appears in the disciples in a far more marked way and so it is a good way of assessing the kind of person the teacher is.

JS: *At the same time, what can a teacher really transmit? Can unity be transmitted? Can consciousness or will be transmitted?*

AS: Seemingly, partially it can. Partially. Sometimes you feel in the presence of someone that something is transmitted beyond whatever was said, something very definite. But the main work of a teacher is as a teacher. Quite a number of people are capable, to one degree or another, of giving somebody else a push. But the real demand on a teacher is that the pupil doesn't want only to be pushed. Sometimes a person can become just a puppet. Whatever he has is the handiwork of someone else. The person becomes a kind of implant, or transplant. You can transplant something in a person, but it really isn't his. It works, but it isn't his and he can't do anything with it.

What a teacher has to transmit, if he is really a teacher, is how I can utilize myself. They are giving a map. I have my own road to walk on and nobody can walk it for me. What I really need is for someone to show me the way. There are very few mystical descriptions in the Talmud—it is traditionally a hidden literature—but in one place Rabbi Akiva, the oldest of a certain group, says, "When you come to a certain place, don't say so and so." That is the work of a teacher. You come to a certain pathway, you have a right turn or a left turn, one way of doing things and another way. Someone can tell you the right direction and then you have to walk on. He can't walk instead of you. You walk on. Then you get to something else.

JS: *What do you think is the real question about wholeness?*

AS: I would say that the big question about it is the question of defining it. The basic question is that wholeness, completeness, may mean so many different things, and can be understood in so many partial ways. And misleading ways. Sometimes achievement is taken for it, or attainment, or talent, or even fame. These things may be good things or not but they are different from wholeness.

JS: *Doesn't the definition depend on the level on which it is being defined?*

AS: The problem is that the best definitions are the least useful. The best definition is that man is made in the image of God—that image is wholeness. That image is perfection. I'm saying that is the best definition. It is also the least useful one. It is the least useful one because there is the same danger of being misled, and perhaps in an even worse way. A definition closer to the measurable world would be a harmonious relationship between the different parts. That is not on the same level—it is a far lower level—but one can deal with it better. I think that wholeness is a kind of standard by which almost everything can be judged. The degree to which something is whole can help evaluate it—not how big it is but how far it has become harmonious and proportioned. This is true whether it is an apple, a glass, or a human being. A blemish, by this standard, would mean that there is something lacking, or something out of proportion, inharmonious. In many cases a lack is indicated by the fact that there is something which could function perfectly which is not functioning.

Here we come to one of the problems of a person who has achieved what could be called this perfection. Actually it is not a problem for them so much as for others. Such people sometimes do not want to be moved, don't want to disturb their harmony. Sometimes they don't care for others. Caring for others is the problem of every great teacher, because when he gets in contact with other people he is destroying his own balance. You see, if you make a connection with someone else then you become, at least for the time being, a unit with that person. But this new unit is not balanced, and to try to balance this new unit requires a very, very different effort on the part of the person who is by himself and on his own a balanced person. That is why so many people, including most of the prophets, did not want to be teachers—not because they were blemished, but because they did not want to destroy their balance. The story of Moses and the Burning Bush, his repeated refusal to be the Redeemer, is not just caused by humility. He is being asked to take an interest in other people, to be involved with people, some of whom are perhaps, so to say, nasty people. And you cannot work with a person or speak with a person without having contact and having, at least, his image imprinted on you. So there is a great sacrifice involved for the harmonious person to agree to be connected with others.

So as I said this wholeness requires harmony, and other people entering disturb it constantly. The deeper his connection with others, the more his balance has to become a kind of moving balance. If he succeeds, of course, he gains—he is able to incorporate all the others into a greater wholeness. So he is growing enormously. This is true of a figure such as Moses, of any true and real leader of the people: everything is magnified a hundredfold, a thousandfold. The individual becomes like a powerful lens in which forces from below are focused and transformed.

•

CHAPTER FOUR

THE STRUGGLE: HARMONY AND EQUILIBRIUM

He that is slow to anger is better than the mighty; and he that ruleth his spirit than he that taketh a city.[1]

—Proverbs 16:32

Parabola
Volume: 28.3
Chaos and Order

"As a tree torn ..."

Abraham Joshua Heschel

As a tree torn from the soil, as a river separated from its source, the human soul wanes when detached from what is greater than itself. Without the holy; the good turns chaotic; without the good, beauty becomes accidental.

Parabola
Volume: 9.1
Hierarchy

Becoming Unstable

Interview with Rabbi Adin Steinsaltz

*Whether we are aware of it or not, levels of authority every-
where govern the course of our lives. Bosses oversee our places
of work, guardians of the law enforce civil order, red lights
and green regulate the public bustle in our streets. Within
us, mysterious stops and starts curb and give rein to jostling
mitochondria and avid enzymes in the spaces of our cells.
Moral codes weigh heavily on us all; good and bad alike, we
are plagued by the hierarchical demands of our conditioned
ethical imperatives.*

*Yet confronted as we are on every hand by its impact,
the hierarchical principle has, in our time, a bad name and
tends to be denied, discounted, ignored. The fault may lie with
hierarchies of doubtful authenticity, such as those imposed by
political knavery. But even legitimate ones are uncongenial
to those living in an age bemused by the dream of equality,
freedom, and the importance of "me."*

*To be sure, those in search of spiritual understanding are
primarily concerned with the essential truth and the way to
it. Whatever their attitude toward hierarchy, they may find*

that what is required of them first off is obedience and, moreover, the only obedience worthy of the name—that which is voluntary. When rebellious nuns and monks jump over the wall, it is rarely the rigors of poverty or sexual deprivation that motivate them. Resistance to authority is far more likely to be the root of the trouble.

Be that as it may, the fact is that the interstices of our lives are laced with subtle skeins of authority; a maze of hidden hierarchies exert their inevitable impact on our comings and goings. When the opportunity came our way, we were grateful to be able to turn for light on this troublesome subject to a man widely schooled at the interface between reason and revelation.

Adin Steinsaltz, head of the Israel Institute for Talmudic Publications in Jerusalem, is a scholar, teacher, scientist, writer, social critic, and a formidable rabbi, held in the highest esteem by his colleagues. His achievements include an ongoing translation into modern Hebrew of the Babylonian Talmud, and treatises on such disparate subjects as French literature, science fiction, archeology, mysticism, Israeli politics, and zoology.

He received us kindly in Jerusalem and later consented to be interviewed in New York. We soon realized why his evening seminars in Jerusalem attract devoted students, scholars, and notables from around the world.
—William and Louise Welch

Parabola: *We live in an egalitarian moment in which it is considered that everyone is equal and everyone is free, and the idea of hierarchy is perceived as an arbitrary imposition on the freedom of man. I wonder how realistic this conception is from your point of view.*

Adin Steinsaltz: My point of view is almost the opposite. Egalitarian ideas are not supported by any evidence. The inequality of man is blatantly apparent. The only way one can find any support for the idea of equality is in a very difficult religious concept: the concept that people are born in the image of the Lord and are therefore equal. There is no other argument that I have heard that serves any purpose. All egalitarian movements are an outcome of Judeo-Christian ideas that contain within them the notion of receiving a divine soul that for everyone is more or less the same. We can speak—in a way—of the equality of souls mostly because we can't see them! But it is very hard to speak about equality in any other way. All forces everywhere, within and without, work against equality. People are so inherently different—not only different, but unequal—that it requires a constant struggle to accept the notion of some kind of equality. The only justification for the idea is what you may call a mystical one; even though people don't appear to be equal, there is something equal in them.

From this point of view, whether it is a good thing or not such a good thing, hierarchy seems to me to be a given element; inherent in creation and in nature. This is nature—everything else is an attempt to change nature.

P: *The evidence of hierarchy in the physiological organization of man is quite clear; from above downward, with semi-independent functions, each with a certain autonomy but subject to control from above. Might there be a relationship between the higher and lower in our psyche and some corresponding potential, if not actual, authority?*

AS: The physiological model has the advantage of stressing that hierarchy involves interdependence. For instance, the mind is far superior to the legs—anyone would prefer to have his leg cut off rather than to have his head cut off. On the other hand, there are functions that the legs perform which the head cannot. Recently I taught some ancient texts that spoke about inner spiritual hierarchy—for hierarchy exists not only as an outer biological and social structure, but also as an inner one. There are higher and lower forces within our world, within our souls, and within our concepts. And even there, hierarchy is interdependent. There are lower elements—clearly lower by every definition—that have a basic power which makes them not only worthwhile, but in certain situations far more important than higher ones.

There are many discussions in Jewish mystical tradition about inter-relationships between mind, or intellect, and emotion. In our view, in the hierarchy of the soul emotions are below mind, because mind gives meaning and direction to emotions. The powers of conceptualization and of thinking are called the father and mother; the emotions are called the children. It is a common way of describing them; but even so, we know that in the working of the soul there are instances when the mind cannot do anything. The intellect is powerless to achieve things. That which emotions can achieve, the mind cannot, but the emotions cannot operate without some kind of subject-object relationship. Emotions, dependent on information and direction supplied by the mind, can only work within that context. The mind works as a watcher, or censor, of things without and within.

It has often been noted that the strength of emotional and intellectual ties is very unequal. Whether we like it or not, emotionally we get attached to things and aren't able to change our attachment with the intellect.

P: *Isn't there also a hierarchy within the realms of thinking and feeling?*

AS: There is an internal hierarchy, and another hierarchy of different sets of things, one above the other. There are also complete cycles that go one into another.

P: *Where do you place the sense of values? I think different levels exist in what we value, and how we value it.*

AS: We consider the sense of values as something that comes before, or hierarchically above, conscious mind. We believe there are powers within every framework that give direction. I am speaking now not about mystical experiences but in a practical context: on one level my mind is made up about whether it wants to be for or against something. Then it creates the network and the building blocks for my basic attitude. Later, some kind of appropriate emotion arises. Because emotion is secondary, in order to develop it needs something to build upon. If I don't have any picture of whatever it is, I cannot have any emotion—love or hatred—

P: *Or reverence.*

AS: Or even reverence. I have to have a point of view; and to have a feeling of awe, of facing the unknown, on an emotional basis, one has to have a very deep intellectual background. In the Middle Ages people said that the peak of knowledge is "I don't know." The question is: if that is so, what is the difference between the person who has no knowledge whatever and the person who knows? The difference is that the person who knows, knows that he doesn't know. The person who does not know, doesn't even have knowledge of his ignorance. So the feeling of reverence is enhanced by knowing the distance. Even if I think that something is far beyond me, I need to know the gap in order to have the feeling of reverence and awe. If I don't know about the gap, the distance doesn't make any sense to me. To know that I don't know is more than just making a statement; to be emotionally involved in it, I have to have an idea of what the meaning of it is. Newton supposedly said that he felt like a small child playing with pebbles on the shore of the sea of knowledge—to feel that really and truly, you have to know as much as Newton did. Those who don't know may say it, but they don't feel it emotionally.

Emotional life is hierarchically dependent on conceptual life; conceptual life makes it possible to have emotional life. And conceptual life is hierarchically below a value system that makes things desirable or nondesirable. I have given lectures concerning what philosophers say about the nature of proof. Philosophy has no real way of defining proof, except what is said by some conservative philosophers: that the proof that something is true is that it clicks. That is the only way I know that something is true, that I have proved it: there is some kind of click. That is possibly the highest hierarchy in our conscious minds—that which says one relationship is true, and another is not. So we are, in fact, judging things, and we say: that fits and that doesn't fit. Now, we cannot explain the way something fits together, because explanation itself comes back to the same question: does it click? If it does, the explanation makes sense. The nature of proof is something that, within the soul, is above anything in the conscious mind—even above the power of pure reason. Above pure reason stands something—we don't know what it is—but it convinces us that something *is*.

P: *Is the vision of hierarchy essential, then, for the movement upwards of the sense of values, and the spiritual search?*

AS: There is something that has to be achieved. If there is no hierarchy, nothing can be achieved by moving from one point to another. When there is a difference, movement makes sense; when there is no difference movement does not make sense. If one goes into it further, one gets into very complex concepts of movement and what movement means; we would be speaking about the theory of relativity. In the abstract, when there is no interrelation, movement or size doesn't make any sense. Without a scale, there is no movement; to advance or retreat depends on having a direction—a beginning and an end.

P: *One has the sense that along with the force of emotion, and the polarity of like and dislike, there can be at times an intelligence of feeling that has its own quality. You place the mind above emotion, but where do you place this intelligence of the emotions?*

AS: People say that the heart has its own reason. We believe that every emotion is made, roughly speaking, of three parts, as mind is made up of the same three parts. There is the intelligence of the emotion; the emotions of the emotion; and the mechanics of emotion, getting it expressed. So the intelligence, or mind of the emotion, does exist. We believe that the intellectual powers are also made like this. There is intellectual thought and emotional thought, because intellect has in it an emotional part. That is one reason why the process of thinking sometimes becomes enjoyable per se; intelligence is not pure, it also has a part that is emotion. The reason of the emotion works in a different way, on a different level; that is the inner hierarchy. Emotion has its own way of conceptualizing, not intellectually but by creating images.

P: *Is there a concept in Judaism that this model within the individual is a reflection of an order which exists on another level? Do the same elements exist on a cosmic scale?*

AS: Given the creation by God of a complete universe, it is a basic assumption that everything is interconnected. One can see something like that by looking at drops of water; one sees reflections, smaller ones and bigger ones, like in a house of mirrors; the same thing, the same nature, reflected in different ways. It follows that if I would know perfectly, completely, entirely, one part, then I would know the whole.

It is a beautiful thing: When God says, "Let us make man," He is calling the whole universe—"Let *us* make man." And each contributes something: the foxes and the lions, the monkeys and the angels all give something! So we are the result of everything that is. The idea is that we contain (and this point is considered essential) the mind-body point of connection; the same hierarchy that exists in the body exists in the mind.

One of the ways to explain the basic concept of our religion is to say that because we are men, we have to correct. We have free will, and we have the ability to repair. Because we have free will, we are also the only ones who have the ability to distort. One of our problems is that of choice. There is an attempt to become better; it is like making corrections for a lens. The lens became for some reason not right, so it distorts whatever is seen through it. We believe the main duty, the chief work of man, is to make corrections until it is possible to transmit the right picture.

P: *The question in my mind, before you said that, is that there is an order evident in our bodies and in all nature; everything is perfect—except me. If I am a reflection of this perfect order, why am I not perfect?*

AS: Free will is an element of disorder. It is also the only element of advancement.

Any kind of movement is a way of destroying a system of order. Walking, for example, is *becoming unstable.* Running is becoming even more unstable. Flying in a plane creates a different kind of instability; the plane becomes less and less stable until it takes off, and then it restabilizes and gains equilibrium. Movement destroys equilibrium all the time; the power to move is also the power to destroy order. The imperfection is inherent, because I am the only creature that has independent volition, and the only creature in the universe that can distort. These distortions are part of our common human work for coming to a higher point, because other creatures, seemingly, cannot move of their own volition, and we can. And being able to move means that we can move in different directions. We don't have the same biological point of view as other creatures; we are free of instinct—not entirely, but to a very great degree. That is our power, and that is our downfall.

P: *You almost say* choice, *don't you?*

AS: Yes, I am always saying *choice*. Animals and plants don't have that element of choice. It used to be a habit of mine, when I felt angry or discontented, to go to the zoo and watch the animals; animals have a certain type of perfection that we don't. In a way, it's the same thing that makes babies beautiful. Sometimes you wonder why so many babies are born wise and beautiful, and why when they become adults, they lose both those qualities! It is because babies are innocent; they reflect the power of relation and choice. They reflect something which we call the great order of things. The bigger they become, the more they are able to move. There are some people who, as they grow older, clearly become wiser—not just more knowledgeable; there is a great difference between the two—and also more beautiful. Their choice, their achievement of consciousness, was a growing from one set of relationships to another, a bigger one, a better one, which is what all this is about. On the other hand, there are some people who make the choice of distorting, and they become less wise and less beautiful, everything less. So as I say, this difficulty of mankind, being the one creature that is not in order, is my strength and my weakness.

P: *You are speaking of levels of order, aren't you? Because doesn't a human being then choose to love according to another, higher order?*

AS: That is what I am saying. We are in movement. In every set of circumstances, every level of hierarchy, there is stability of some kind. Movement is a disturbing element, and also rather dangerous. Between one step of a ladder and another, there is a void; the void is necessary because it makes the difference between the levels. But if I want to move from the first rung to the second or the third, I have to take the risk of passing through this void, of abolishing my foothold in one place in order to get to another, and in between I may fall down. It often happens. So our process of growing, from the physical to the spiritual, is getting from one set of ways of behavior, and so on, to a different one, which we hope is a higher one. It is not necessarily so, but it is a movement into a different order in which things, after some time, again become more or less stabilized. In any process of inner growth or evolution, there is the same problem of getting from one point to another. Being born is in a way ceasing to exist in one set, one type of order, and getting into a different type of order in which almost all the rules are changed. As a fetus, I don't breathe, and my life system is entirely different. Being born is the shock of transfer to a set of circumstances in which almost everything is done in a different way, in which there is an order of a different kind. Dying is doing the same thing—again, in a different way, perhaps coming to a point where I discard certain things about my being. The shock there is clearly that of transferring from one set of circumstances to another. Our notions of people going to hell has to do with this transfer. I might be magnificently suited to survive in this world, but now I have to go into another world with other rules, whether I want to or not. And the things that equipped me to be, for instance, a financial success in this world will send me to hell in a different world! If a person doesn't grow through adaptation to a certain order and then moves into another one, he is unable to deal with it. It is like the tadpole and the frog. We see this all the time: men who were wonderful as boys in school are not necessarily wonderful as adults out of school. Because a change creates a necessity for a different order.

P: *The transformation of a tadpole to a frog, or from one set of conditions in life to another in death, is something that happens automatically; but isn't there another possibility of transformation for human beings, an intentional one?*

AS: Oh, that is what it *should* be! That is what I meant about a person going to heaven or hell; the process of learning, of education, determines which way one takes. It is a process of knowing the direction consciously and following it consciously to a different state, so that one is not thrown into the workings, so to say, but is preparing consciously to go into them. I would call any type of school or learning preparation for entering into a different order—a conscious preparation. The tadpole doesn't learn to become a frog; but for man, as we know, it is very hard work. What I said about emotional hell refers to when a person is kicked into a different set without being prepared. Imagine: all your desires, images, ways of thinking are tied to a very particular set of values and notions. If you are put into a place where none of this applies, then you don't need devils to torment you, you will be as miserable as anybody can imagine, because of your inability to deal with something you are not equipped for.

As a human being, I have some ability to change consciously to a different order, but actually, we set our hearts on a certain place and don't want to get any higher. There is an old Russian story about a simple soldier who rescued the Czar from some danger. The Czar told him he could ask for whatever he wanted, and the soldier said, "Please, change my commanding officer!" Instead of moving upward in the hierarchy, I just want to shift into a more comfortable position on the same level.

P: *What is the difference between mechanical and conscious equilibrium?*

AS: Conscious equilibrium is not a stationary stability, but rather a constant readjustment. If I consciously want to remain in equilibrium, in quiet, in peace, it means I have to work very hard, to adjust all the time. In a mechanical equilibrium, forces are more or less in balance, they can go on in the same way until something changes. In a conscious equilibrium, I have to work very hard to stay in the same place. What Alice said is a very good definition of conscious equilibrium: to run very fast in order to stay in the same place.

Some people seem to have such equanimity that they do not mind anything, but this may come from two very different ways of being; one, in which the person does not care about anything, and the other, in which he cares very much, but is able to make constant adjustments in order not to get angry or sad or overjoyed. This sort of conscious equilibrium is very, very hard work. You have to work all the time. It's like what a pilot does in a plane. You can't fall asleep.

If someone makes me angry or does something I don't like, then I may say something or think about something that is just the opposite. But I don't only want to learn, as every adult person learns, not to *show* a reaction—I wish to learn how not to be overwhelmed by the reaction. If I just escape the situation, nothing really happens. When events occur that I don't like and I'm not prepared for—there is the test.

I would say that hierarchy is an infinite number of orders of laws, one above the other. Each order has within it an inner order; and with this interdependence, all in all, the whole hierarchical situation is a complete set in which different parts are working. So there is a context in which we are all equal, in which existence is equal in this eternal interdependence.

P: *What you have said raises the question, What is equality? Are you saying that authority is determined by the degree of consciousness?*

AS. I am a part of something. Authority is the rule of the higher over the lower. I think that, as you say, possibly hierarchy is defined by greater consciousness. Julian Huxley seems an unlikely source to quote, but in speaking about evolution he says that only in this sense of growing consciousness can we make sense of evolution as a progressive line. Advance is not in terms of "fitness"; if evolution is simply a matter of the survival of the fittest, it would have stopped with the cockroach. But there is a different striving, for more consciousness; and in this way we may say we have something above the cockroach.

So power or authority is connected with the level of consciousness, in every level, in every degree. It determines what is bigger, what is smaller; the bigger is bigger because it can encompass the smaller. In every hierarchy the one that knows where to put the others is the one who is in charge. The highest in the hierarchy is the one who can put all the parts in some kind of complete order. Otherwise, whatever the official, apparent order may be, it is a false hierarchy. In a real hierarchy, the one who is most conscious about what is happening is the higher. Other people may perhaps be more powerful, but they are not higher.

One of the things that makes life so complicated is that there is not one type of hierarchy, but many. And because there are conflicting hierarchies, we get confused. There is the hierarchy of the good, the hierarchy of the wise, the hierarchy of the powerful. Each is different. I would say that all designs somehow end up at the infinite, at a convergent point; but in our world they are not convergent. The problem of existence is that different hierarchies are not aligned, not compatible with each other. It has been said before that in this world we have the clever and the good—and they are usually not the same people! A world in which they would become more and more identical would be a better world.

So our problem is not lack of hierarchy, but too many hierarchies. Our problem is to make order among them, to arrange the different hierarchies in a hierarchical formation. We have different types of ladders, and when they are not arranged among themselves, they don't lead anywhere. We have the feeling that we have lots of ability and can climb higher. What we need is a way of attaching the separate ladders into one which becomes far bigger. But every group has its own ladder and doesn't want to share it, and because of this we come to the point where no one in his separate way can go any higher. So we divide and come to a sort of compromise that says: because we don't agree on which is better, let us assume that nothing is better. Because we don't agree on who should be on top, nobody should be there.

P: *What authority will we all accept?*

AS: We all accept that there is a certain ladder; what we dispute about is which one. The ladders seem incompatible; they don't meet. We are dealing in different areas. The differences between us—for instance, between the believing man and the knowledgeable man—often take precedence over something that is more urgent: which ladder is the more important one.

P: *Is it finally a matter of agreement or decision? Or is there one which simply is more important? It seems there would have to be, if there is real hierarchy.*

AS: I would say there definitely is one; that we don't agree about it doesn't mean anything. All of us agree that what is most positive should be at the head. The question is not so much about hierarchy as about what hierarchy to adopt. Almost every religion tries to give some way of measuring things, some kind of scale. We need a way of bringing different things to some kind of common scale, some common value into which they can all be translated. That is what we are in search of.

Parabola
Volume: 20.2
Stranger

A Glimpse of Eternity

Martin Buber

To the man the world is twofold, in accordance with his twofold attitude. He perceives what exists round about him—simply things, and beings as things; and what happens round about him—simply events, and actions as events; things consisting of qualities, events of moments; things entered in the graph of place, events in that of time; things and events bounded by other things and events, measured by them, comparable with them: he perceives an ordered and detached world. It is to some extent a reliable world, having density and duration. Its organization can be surveyed and brought out again and again; gone over with closed eyes, and verified with open eyes. It is always there, next to your skin, if you look on it that way, cowering in your soul, if you prefer it so. It is your object, remains it as long as you wish, and remains a total stranger, within you and without. You perceive it, take it to yourself as the "truth," and it lets itself be taken; but it does not give itself to you. Only concerning it may you make yourself "understood" with others; it is ready, though attached to everyone in a different way, to be an object common to you all. But you cannot meet others in it. You cannot hold on to life without it, its reliability sustains you; but should you die in it, your grave would be in nothingness.

Or on the other hand, man meets what exists and becomes as what is over against him, always simply a *single* being and each thing simply as being. What exists is opened to him in happenings, and what happens affects him as what is. Nothing is present for him except this one being, but it implicates the whole world. Measure and comparison have disappeared; it lies with yourself how much of the immeasurable becomes reality for you. These meetings are not organized to make the world, but each is a sign of world-order. They are not linked up with one another, but each is a sign of the world-order. They are not linked up with one another, but each assures you of your solidarity with the world. The world which appears to you in this way is unreliable, for it takes on a continually new appearance; you cannot hold it to its word. It has no density, for everything in it penetrates everything else; no duration, for it comes even when it is not summoned, and vanishes even when it is tightly held. It cannot be surveyed, and if you wish to make it capable of survey you lose it. It comes, and comes to bring *you* out; if it does not reach you, meet you, then it vanishes; but it comes back in another form. It is not outside you, it stirs in the depth of you; if you say "Soul of my soul" you have not said too much. But guard against wishing to remove it into your soul—for then you annihilate it. It is your present; only while you have it do you have the present. You can make it into an object for yourself, to experience and to use; you must continually do this—and as you do it you have no more present. Between you and it there is mutual giving: you say *Thou* to it and give yourself to it, it says *Thou* to you and gives itself to you. You cannot make yourself understood with others concerning it, you are alone with it. But it teaches you to meet others, and to hold your ground when you meet them. Through the graciousness of its comings and the solemn sadness of its goings it leads you away to the *Thou* in which the parallel lines of relations meet. It does not help to sustain you in life, it only helps you to glimpse eternity.

Reprinted from Martin Buber, *I and Thou* (New York: Charles Scribner's Sons, 1970), pp. 31-33. Reprinted by permission of the Agent for the Estate of Martin Buber.

Parabola
Volume: 29.3
The Seeker

Harmonizing the Passions

Geoffrey Dennis

In the West it is often assumed that our choices are stark: between virtue and vice, between those qualities that align with the good and those that carry the taint of evil. But can the denial of any part of ourselves lead us to wholeness?

The first and greatest of the Jewish *kalam*, the dialectic theologians, was Saadia ibn Yusuf al Fayyumi (882–942 CE). A seeker after virtue, he sought to express traditional Jewish wisdom through the language of Greek philosophy. That Saadia was himself a virtuous man there can be no doubt. His contemporaries raised him to the pinnacle of religious authority and called him *Gaon*, a term that conveys both intellectual and moral excellence.

Yet for all his spiritual authority and towering wisdom, Saadia was a man driven by his passions. He was also thoroughly modern in those desires; he was ambitious, contentious, and proud. Born the son of a laborer in Egypt, he proved a polymath genius: translator, poet, astronomer, mathematician, philosopher, and communal leader. Those gifts and his own ambition brought him to a position of prominence in the *kehillah* of Babylon. The greatest Jewish community of his time, where he was invited to become chancellor of its ancient academy—an honor never before offered to a non-Iraqi.

But even after he achieved that high office, his life was one of ongoing struggle. He had to grapple with the religious persecutions and conflicts of his time. He also had to contend with the jealousy of rival scholars and teachers. But he especially had to contend with the rising hegemony of Greek philosophy, whose attractiveness and influence threatened to uproot the traditional teachings of his community. Yet out of all these experiences he came to discern a path for those seeking virtue that was completely grounded in the human condition, a path both psychologically deep and profoundly humanistic.

Saadia rejected the monistic tendencies of Greek ethics; instead he took selected elements of philosophic thought and blended them with the experiential wisdom of Solomon and the traditional dialectic teachings of the Talmudic Sages. From ancient traditions he crafted a remarkably modern approach to being a decent person.

Saadia expounds his teaching on human conduct in his magnum opus, *Sefer Emunah v'Daat* (*The Book of Beliefs and Opinions*). In Chapter 10 he begins his meditation in a distinctly philosophic mode: humans, he states, are composite beings. We possess a "multiple nature." This, he notes, accords with the way of all nature, as well as the way of God; for though the Divine is one, all God's works are manifold. From this it is reasonable to conclude human conduct cannot be based upon a single trait. He then illustrates his philosophic point in a most Solomonic fashion, with a parable: An architect making a well-built house is foolish to limit himself to a single material; a house built entirely of stone, or teakwood, or reeds, would not be as attractive and well made as one constructed from all these products. If a structure as simple as a house will lack quality if it is made from only a single ingredient, how much more will this be true of a person?

For Saadia then, the key to a virtuous life is "balance," giving each inclination in life its due measure. Notice here, however, that Saadia is already taking us away from Western thought, for he does not speak of balancing those qualities commonly thought of as "virtues." Instead he speaks of harmonizing *actual human motivations*. Specifically he identifies thirteen human "passions" that, brought into proper balance, will serve as the material for constructing a good life. The list of these useful passions is startling: self-denial, hunger, sexual drive, love, avarice, progeny, achievement, longevity, power, revenge, knowledge, devotion, and ease. Many, if not most, of these impulses would not make it onto any conventional list of desirable motives. Yet each in its proper measure, Saadia insists, has something to contribute to making an ethical person.

In his interpretation of these desires, Saadia treats each trait dialectically. None is good in and of itself; each is potentially a virtue or a vice; the key is combining them in proper proportion to each other. Saadia exhorts the seeker with a quote from the proverbs of Solomon: "Balance the course you take" (Prov. 4:26). Thus, the desire for sexual pleasure is not a vice; rather, vice results from allowing intercourse to become one's single-minded concern.

Even a passion that seems an out-and-out vice, like the desire for revenge, has a role in a quest for virtue. God implanted this impulse within us "in order that God's justice might be carried out ... and the welfare of mankind might be served." What is more, pursuing a resolution to wrongs has a psychological benefit, for it "relieves the sorrow in which it is wrapped." Thus the wise seeker after virtue will not pursue revenge for one's own sake, but neither will he simply tolerate injustice as a Stoic might.

By the same token Saadia finds a seemingly obvious virtue, like self-denial, to be a vice if one treats it as *summa bonum*, as the ultimate good. He addresses this as he does each passion, by first presenting the arguments in favor of asceticism: the transitory experience of pleasure, the illusionary nature of satisfaction, and the value of removing oneself from all the cruelties that accompany a worldly existence. But to reject utterly the essentials of life—sustenance, clothing, and shelter—leads one perilously close to rejecting the value of life itself. Worse, constant self-denial inures one to the suffering of others. We are not conceived solely for suffering, and to make it a supreme good is to deny one's (and possibly someone else's) essential humanity. Instead, abstinence is commendable as a discipline against excess and transgression, but no more than that.

The perceptive reader will realize that though Saadia uses the language of Western philosophy, his thinking is really more thoroughly grounded in Hebrew wisdom traditions. His entire treatment of human conduct is actually a powerful meditation on traditional Jewish dialectics on human nature. For the Talmudic Sages taught that God has created each person with two impulses, the *Yetzer ha-Tov* and the *Yetzer ha-Ra*. Though these translate literally as "good" and "evil" impulses, the Sages use these expressions more in the sense of altruistic and selfish desires. Neither, the Rabbis taught, is adequate in itself for human life. Thus in a rabbinic commentary on Genesis we read:

> *Rabbi Samuel bar Nachman said: The words "behold it is good"*
> *refer to the impulse to good, and the words, "behold it is very good"*
> *(Gen. 1:31) refer to the impulse to evil. But how can the evil impulse*
> *be called "very good?" Because ... were it not for the evil impulse, a*
> *man would not build a house, take a wife, beget children, or engage*
> *in commerce (Genesis Rabbah 9:7).*

This perspective is further illustrated in a marvelous rabbinic myth: The ancient Sages once actually captured the personified Yetzer ha-Ra. Just as they were about to slay it, they realized that if they did, procreation and creativity would cease in the world. So instead they merely blinded the Yetzer in order to weaken its power, but then let it go (Yoma 69b).

So while the virtuous impulses are good, the self-serving impulses are, in their own way, better, for it is such robust human motivations—lust, ambition, and greed—that compel a person to build up the world and to fulfill the human potential to be co-creators with God. The key to a good life is less a matter of embracing virtue and rejecting vice than it is to harmonize all aspects of human nature in God's service.

Saadia summarizes his approach by writing "Since ... the harmonious blending of the sensations is generally beneficial to man, how much more must this apply in the balancing of tendencies of his character ... to each of the objects of human striving ... a person should devote himself at its appropriate time." At the conclusion of his ethics, Saadia quotes the wisest of Israel's kings: "There is nothing better for a man than that he should eat and drink, and make his soul enjoy what is good from his labor; this also I saw is from the hand of God" (Eccl. 2:24).

Saadia ibn Yusuf ha-Gaon was a two-fold seeker. As a spiritual thinker, he saw that the individual is driven by multiple impulses, so he sought to find a way for the individual to reach for virtue *by means of these impulses*. As a spiritual leader, he saw his people confronted with a new, faith-challenging worldview, so he searched for a way that they might remain faithful, *using the ideals of that same worldview*. His solutions reveal the true depth of his wisdom, and they are especially valuable, for they show us a balanced way to virtue. Saadia teaches how to make spiritual tools out of the very obstacles that confront us on our journey.

Parabola
Volume: 21.3
Peace

To Strive Toward Spirit

Rabbi Adin Steinsaltz

Peace of mind has come to be regarded in our time as one of life's highest ideals. Clergymen, leaders of cults, psychologists, advertisers—all seem to agree that this is the thing most to be desired. And of course all of them are in some measure prepared to provide it. Rest and relaxation are no longer the exclusive province of resorts and sanitariums. Peace of mind is regarded not merely as something pleasant and desirable but as a spiritual ideal and significant life goal, the final achievement to which various schools of thought and meditation aspire.

The reasons for this longing for tranquility are not hard to find. Modern life, particularly in its characteristic urban form, is beset by political and economic upheaval, insecurity and fear. It is an unquiet life. Global tensions impinge not only on the body politic and its functionaries but on each individual citizen. People in general, even those most concerned with peace of mind—be it for themselves or as a "commodity" to be sold to others—have very high *material* expectations, which in turn necessitate ceaseless striving.

The shattering of accepted values and the distrust of established frameworks create confusion and changed, sometimes contradictory, expectations. All this makes modern man tense, pressured, discontented. Hardly anyone escapes this stress or the measure of difficulty it adds to life. Home, family, friends, and good works all gradually disappear or are drastically altered in form, and to the extent that they survive at all they tend themselves to become sources of tension and competition. Thus, beyond all the internal and external turbulence, what man seeks is tranquility, relaxation, and peace, at least with himself. The almost physical need for quiet and surcease quickly received legitimation and even reinforcement from psychology, philosophy, and religion. Tension and stress of all kinds have come to be seen not only as discomforting and harmful but as morally invalid. Peace and quiet have become the great motive forces of all striving, including the spiritual.

Of course, the quest for peace in all its forms is quite ancient, as old as mankind itself. So, too, is the elevation of peace as a supreme value. Nevertheless, there is still room to question the notion of peace of mind and its place in the hierarchy of human needs. What, first of all, does it really mean? One important definition is provided by the Jewish sages in the context of a lengthy discussion of the many virtues of peace: "The Holy One, blessed be He, found no vessel but peace which could contain all blessing." This beautiful passage, which makes peace the very basis of all good things, goes on to make a telling distinction: peace is a vessel that can contain blessing, but it can also contain nothing at all, can be an *empty* vessel. Here is a truth with wide applicability, be it in the international or the interpersonal realm, or in the life of the individual soul. Peace with no content, meaningless tranquillity, rest without sanctity—all are empty vessels. At best, the emptiness is soon filled with positive content. In all too many cases, however, the empty vessel becomes a repository for whatever comes along. In the absence of anything else, rubbish and abomination can fill the void. It is the same with empty peace of mind: the tension and pressure seem to be gone, but nothing positive comes to take their place. A vacuum results, an existence devoid of effort or thought, which is in no sense better than what preceded it. A life of vain struggle can be relieved of pressure and anxiety and yet remain as vacuous and meaningless as before. Furthermore, while stress is likely (particularly when unremitting) to be unpleasant, it has the potential of achieving meaningful, valuable change. An equilibrium from which stress has been eliminated can be a terminal state, a condition from which all further development is likewise excluded—in short, the peace of death.

The notion of peace of mind as a supreme value, as a standard by which to judge all other aspects of life, is worse than inadequate. It carries with it the real danger of apotheosizing emptiness and negation—negation of good as well as evil, release from achievement as well as stress. The Torah's identification of life with good and death with evil (Deuteronomy 30:15) is cast in different, less exalted and more down-to-earth imagery in the Book of Ecclesiastes: "Better off the living dog than the dead lion" (9:4). And the reason given has to do with the potential for change, however bitterly expressed: "For the living know that they shall die, while the dead know nothing at all" (9:5). In other words, as long as there is activity, as long as there is struggle—however lowly, however reduced to the level of the "dog's" struggle for bare existence—it is better than the empty tranquillity of death, the peace which contains nothing and points nowhere beyond itself.

The underlying issue here has to do with the positioning of a scale of values. As soon as there is some kind of ordering leading to a final goal—be it material, spiritual in a broad sense (knowledge, truth, love), or specifically religious (divine enlightenment, etc.)—one must judge each situation and each action, not according to its "comfortableness" but according to whether or not it is likely to bring one nearer to that goal. In our case, peace of mind may come as pleasant relief to one sorely pressed by the exigencies of life; but as long as he aspires to more in life than escape, such peace cannot be for him an end in itself. Inner tranquility and turmoil, relaxation and tension, must be judged in light of the ultimate goal. And there are goals that cannot be attained except through struggle waged within the soul.

The path of inner conflict is neither easy nor pleasant. Every struggle, first of all, carries the risk of an undesirable outcome. Every attempt to reach a higher level of existence, to break out and ascend, entails not only the possibility of failure to rise but also the possibility of falling even lower than the point where one began. Then too, no spiritual ladder can be ascended without constant effort, tension, and anguish. In many ways, this struggle is between different and often opposing values. But in a much broader sense, it is an ongoing struggle between the given, present reality and that which has not yet come into existence but waits to be created. The inertia of what already exists is always the great enemy and can never be fully overcome. The never-ending conflict between the existent and not-yet-existent is at the root of man's whole inner struggle.

In fact, it is in the nature of inward, as opposed to outward, political or economic struggle, that it knows no termination, no clear-cut end point at which victory or defeat can be pronounced. There may be brief pauses for rest or changes of pace along the way, alternations between stretches of acute, violent exertion and stretches of slower, more measured progress, but there is no real conclusion. Not only are the goals of spiritual struggle loftier and more difficult to attain than other kinds of goals, they are enlarged by the very process of achieving them, by the inward growth of the struggler himself. Thus, when quiet overtakes the spiritual struggle, it is in itself a sign of backsliding and descent. There can be no greater danger to one laboring to reach a higher spiritual and moral plane than the feeling that he has achieved it. Such feelings of self-satisfaction generally indicate a blurring of the vision of the goal itself.

In every serious discussion of spiritual matters there arises from time to time the question of whether man is capable of reaching any goal whatsoever except through such protracted inner conflict. This is not just a theoretical question. In fact, everyone whose life is oriented toward goals beyond his present reality, goals that are not simply the direct and natural outcome of his present way of life, is already involved in such a conflict. Is there no alternative? For most of us, the answer is no. There does not appear to be any magical way, without deception, to resolve, conclude, and thus dispense with the inner struggle.

True, there are in this world people with extraordinary gifts who are able to bring the opposed forces in their own souls into genuine harmony that these forces energize rather than undermine. But such abilities result not from following any particular teaching or path but from rare inborn attributes. The latter are not unlike other sorts of native endowments—natural beauty, for example, which radiates from every movement and gesture and needs no artificial enhancement; or genius in a particular discipline, which is reflected in nearly total mastery. People with such endowments do not need to make a certain effort, but it is mainly to avoid spoiling what they already possess. There are, likewise, rare cases of people especially gifted in the moral realm, and here too, the quality is not one that can be achieved by any sort of exertion. Of course, many who are not particularly gifted are responsible for significant and even decisive achievements in this realm, but never without effort or by taking an easy way. The extraordinarily talented are like rare works of nature—orchids or birds-of-paradise—whose character is something to marvel at and enjoy but not imitate. Nor do such people usually reach the same heights or depths as others in their grasp of truth. For there are certain precious insights that cannot be acquired except through tribulation, things born of struggle and effort that can never be harmonized, and it is the pursuit of these that makes for the highest levels of aspiration. It is, in any case, the unavoidable lot of most men to choose, not between turmoil and tranquil perfection, but rather between a harsh struggle to find themselves and a degeneration that in the last analysis offers no peace of mind either. Instead of waiting for a miraculous rescue, let a man take the other path, the only meaningful one, and prepare himself to do battle within.

Part of the preparation lies in this very recognition, that without inward strife there can be no life, that what a man endures is no mere "punishment" being exacted of him as an individual but the way of all men. And in a wider perspective, man's inner struggle is part of the larger process of life itself. On one level, the struggle within the human soul is likely to be between good and evil, while on another level it is between the natural (animal, biological) and supernatural (divine) elements in the human makeup. Taking yet a broader view—and one that does not contradict but complements the picture already presented—it is a struggle in cosmic terms between chaos and Creation, or, in physical terms, between entropy and life. In a sense, all physical existence represents the struggle of mute form to preserve itself, its weight, its volume, its component elements; and the same is especially true of life forms whose very being is a perpetual process not only of maintenance but of metabolic transformation, not only of self-preservation but of growth. This ceaseless tension between being and nothingness is no mere epiphenomenon or superstructure but part of existence itself, at all levels and in all manifestations. It is thus impossible for man to escape this tension or negate it entirely. It can be ignored or not recognized, but there is no release from it.

Indeed, man's question should not be how to escape the perpetual struggle but rather what form to give it, at what level to wage it. The tension of existence is to be found even in a molecule of inarticulate matter; in man, as in all living creatures, there are the tensions of biological growth and change. He can live his life and carry on his struggle entirely on that plane. If he does, that, too, will be the plane on which his spiritual life is lived, for even at its basest, human life cannot be lived without consciousness. At whatever level man struggles, there will his consciousness be involved. What differentiated the saint from the lowly creature of instinct, cunning, and cruelty is not the life-tension within him but the level at which his conscious being joins the struggle he must wage for survival. The choice between good and evil is preceded by an even more fundamental choice: whether to give spiritual or moral expression to the contradiction inherent in one's humanness or to try to ignore that contradiction. Difficulty and tension, bitterness and pain, are to be found as much in the ash heap as in the heavens. Each human being must decide where to take his stand and fight his battle.

Reprinted from Adin Steinsaltz, *The Strife of the Spirit* (Northvale, NJ: Jason Aronson, Inc., 1988). Reprinted by permission of the publisher.

Parabola
Volume: 25.1
Threshold

RUNNING BETWEEN THE SUNS

Mordechai Beck

In the beginning was night; in the beginning, too, was day. But what came between them? A sudden leap, a cosmic on/off switch? No, what came between was dusk, to soften the transition with a swath of time that was neither day nor night but a unique mixture of the two. The ancient Hebrews had a name for it—*erev*, "evening," from the triple-consonant root *ayin*, *resh*, *vet*, offering associations of something less than pure, a commingling of the elements, a world out of focus.

Hundreds of years later, the sages of the Babylonian Talmud (redacted circa the fifth century) invented another, even stranger term—*beyn hashmashot*, meaning literally "between the suns," somewhat similar to the word "twilight" in Medieval and Old English, which also means between two lights. Though the term is used widely in Talmudic literature, nowhere is it actually explained. Only much later, in the late nineteenth to early twentieth century, does the great scholar Dr. Marcus Jastrow cite an obscure text in the rabbinical commentary to "The Song of Songs." There, says the learned Dr. Jastrow, the term is used to refer back to the very beginning of creation where the phrase signifies the changing of the guard, as it were, between "the two great luminaries"—the sun, which rules or serves the day, and the moon, which serves the night. Here the term hashmashot is used to signify the verb *leshamesh*, "to serve."

Yet even with this piece of detective work to our credit, we are only touching the surface. For much ink is spilled over the phrase in Talmudic literature, since it is precisely in this obscure, midway place that so many laws and rules have to be clarified, just where nature itself is unclear. At what time, for example, does the Sabbath day or the slew of Biblical festivals commence—a crucial item since the ancient Hebrews, basing themselves on the opening lines of the Book of Genesis, ushered in their days in the evening and thus, too, the rabbis of the Talmud, from about the third century at least, fixed their calendars. At this soft edge of the day began all the strictures but also all the delights identified with these sacred times. It was crucial not to miss even one second.

Primitive humans, perhaps, had an understandable fear of night and darkness. For them twilight was filled with foreboding, dark magic; it presaged doom. Twilight was the diurnal passage into fearful night. The rabbis retained something of this in their approach. In the only openly philosophic work of the sages, *Pirke Avoth* (which can be understood as *Chapters of the Fathers*, or the *Book of General Principles*), they refer to another ancient legend that also harks back to the days of creation.

> On the eve of the first Sabbath day, at twilight, ten things were created—the mouth of the earth which swallows Korach, Miriam's well, Balaam's ass, Noah's rainbow, the manna, Moses' rod, the stone-splitting shamir, *the writing on the tablets of stone of the Deca-logue; some say, too, the destroying spirits, the burial place of Moses, Abraham's ram; others say the primal tongs that forged the tongs of creation.* (Pirke Avoth 5:8)

Perhaps these various items, which were later on to have such a significance for the Children of Israel, signify God's providential care for His children, overriding the rational processes of the creation. If these things properly belong to the realm of the irrational, God's last-minute introduction of them into His creation would suggest that magic, too, had a place in His universe, as long as it was within the boundaries of the Divine and did not fall into the realm of the forces of the Other Side. Yet even these delicious speculations do not give us, the baffled readers, a reason for these particular items to be created at this specific time of the day or week.

One clue, admittedly indirect, appears in the story of the famous teacher of the first century, Rabbi Shimon bar Yohai (*Tractate Shabbat* 33b). Rabbi Shimon is forced to flee his home, with his son Elazar, for insulting the Roman overlords, whom he accused of perverting the holy land with their apparently advanced civilization. For thirteen years, father and son hide in a cave where they study the deepest secrets of the sacred Torah. According to some it was here that the mystical tradition was formulated, eventually emerging as the *Book of Splendor* (*Sefer haZohar*). After twelve years, Elijah the prophet appears to the pair announcing that the Caesar who had originally put a price on their heads had died and that his decree was therefore annulled.

Emerging from the cave, Rabbi Shimon is appalled at the apparent waste of time in which the people are indulging themselves. So enraged is he that when he observes men plowing and sowing the soil instead of studying holy texts, they are burned to death. A heavenly voice emerges and orders father and son back to the cave. "This is why you left the cave—to destroy my world?" asks the voice. They are given another twelve months in the cave, equivalent to the length of time the wicked spend in Gehenna, and at the end of this period are again ordered back into the workaday world. This time Rabbi Shimon and Elazar are reconciled with their contrary situation. "What we study," says the chastened father to his son, "is sufficient for the entire world."

As though to prove their change of heart they meet an old man carrying two branches of myrtle. It is the twilight hour before the Sabbath day and the man is "running between the suns," i.e., on his way to greet the Sabbath before nightfall. When they ask him why he is carrying his two bundles, the old man replies that they are to fill his house with a pleasant fragrance during the Sabbath day. If that is so, they ask him, would not one bundle suffice? One, says the man, is for the Biblical verse commanding us to "remember the Sabbath day" (Exodus 20:8) the other is for the command to "keep the Sabbath day" (Deuteronomy 5:12).

The answer pleases the fiery rabbi and his son. The custom of bringing fragrance into the house was not required by the many and intricate laws of the Sabbath day. It was an addition that this anonymous old man had supplied out of his deep love of the tradition, even without spending thirteen years away from the world in utter deprivation, studying God's word. This spontaneous act fused the spiritual and material universes, something that Rabbi Shimon with all his study and meditation seemed incapable of doing. This simple expression of overflowing gratitude revealed to Rabbi Shimon that it was possible to be in the world simultaneously on both spiritual and material levels: that it was possible to live in the world of contrasts and extremes without sacrificing one's integrity. This is why the time of their encounter is so significant.

This old man, of whom we know no details, is "running between the suns"—between the secular week and the Sabbath day, between the natural and supernatural world, between this world of rocks and stones and trees and the supernal word of the spirit. Twilight is no longer the frightening zone of conflict. The rabbis of the Babylonian Talmud in which this incident is recorded were perhaps conscious of what their Babylonian neighbors had made of night and day—how for the Zoroastrians, for example, night and day reflected the irreconcilable nature of good and evil, the two gods representing these contrary domains, and the dualism that was built into the cosmos. Rabbi Shimon's old man shows that these dualities can be transcended. The world does not have to be either/or, the threshold can be faced and crossed, we can all "run between the suns" without fear of being burned. Instead of fright and foreboding, twilight can be filled with a fragrant redolence of higher worlds. Ultimately, there is one source that unites heaven and earth, a majestic presence that can be glimpsed at the interstices of day and night, and that can be wooed with a bunch of myrtle, the fragrance of Venus.

Parabola
Volume: 21.4
Play and Work

THE RUNG OF SERVICE

Martin Buber

The Nature of Service

This is the service man must perform all of his days: to shape matter into form, to refine the flesh, and to let the light penetrate the darkness, until the darkness itself shines and there is no longer any division between the two. As it is written: "And there was evening and there was morning, one day."

One should not make a great to-do about serving God. Does the hand boast when it carries out what the heart wills?

Imitation of the Fathers

Question: In the Book of Elijah we read: "Everyone of Israel is duty-bound to say: 'When will my works approach the works of my fathers, Abraham, Isaac and Jacob?'"

How are we to understand this? How could we ever venture to think that we could do what our fathers did?

Answer: Just as our fathers invented new ways of serving, each a new service according to his own character: one, the service of love; another, of stern justice; a third, of beauty; so each one of us in his own way should devise something new in the light of the teaching and of service, and do what has not yet been done.

The Gate

It is written: "Open to me the gates of righteousness."

Man is serving in the right way as long as he feels that he is still on the outside and begs God to open the gate to true service for him.

Only a Beginning

A man ought never to say that he is perfect in his fear of God; he should always say that now he is only about to begin to serve God. For did not Moses, after forty years of wandering, say to God: "Thou hast begun to show Thy servant Thy greatness"? And that is why it is written: "As a beginning God created the heaven and the earth." He created all in Heaven and all on earth as a beginning of the fear of God, as a beginning of the knowledge of him.

New Every Morning

Unless we believe that God renews the work of creation every day, our prayers and doing the commandments grow old and accustomed and tedious. As it is written in the psalm: "Cast me not off in the time of old age"—that is to say, do not let my world grow old.

And in Lamentations it is written: "They are new every morning: great is Thy faithfulness." The fact that the world is new to us every morning—that is your great faithfulness!

The Manifest and the Secret

The two things that Israel stated on Horeb: "We will do and obey," represent what is manifest in the teachings and the commandments, what can and should be done, as well as the mystery which surrounds the teachings and the commandments, the mystery which is not revealed within them, which we become conscious of only when we pray. And this we grow aware of in prayer only when our prayers cling to the boundless. The two exist in every world; everyone has both, each according to his rung.

And he who rises to a higher rung converts his obeying into doing, and then is given a new "we obey," and so on from rung to rung. The same holds for the worlds. What in this, our world, is a "we obey," is a "we do" for the world of heavenly spheres, and the heavens have a higher "we obey," and so on from world to world.

Valid Sacrifice

It is written: "And Abel, he also brought." The "he" is what he brought: he brought himself. Only when a man brings himself, too, is his sacrifice valid.

To Die and to Live

It is written in the psalm: "I shall not die, but live." In order really to live, man must first give himself to death. But when he has done so, he discovers that he is not to die, that he is to live.

Fulfillment

This is the secret of the unity of God: no matter where I take hold of a shred of it, I hold the whole of it. And since the teachings and all the commandments are radiations of his being, he who lovingly does one commandment utterly and to the core, and in this one commandment takes hold of a shred of the unity of God, holds the whole of it in his hand, and has fulfilled all.

The Way

It is impossible to tell men what way they should take. For one way to serve God is by the teachings, another by prayer, another way by fasting, and still another by eating. Everyone should carefully observe which way his heart draws him, and then choose that way with all his strength.

Infinity

Infinity shall be contained in every deed of man, in his speaking and seeing, listening and walking, standing still and lying down.

Adam's Sin

Question: What was Adam's real sin?

Answer: Adam's real sin was that he worried about the morrow. The serpent set out to reason with him: "There is no service you can perform, for you cannot distinguish between good and evil and are unable to make a choice. Eat of this fruit and you will be able to distinguish; you will choose the good and receive your reward." That he gave ear to this —that is where Adam was at fault. He worried that he would not be able to serve, yet at that very hour he had his service: to obey God and to resist the serpent.

The Ten Principles

Said the Great Maggid to Rabbi Zusya, his disciple: "I cannot teach you the ten principles of service. But a little child and a thief can show you what they are.

"From the child you can learn three things:

He is merry for no particular reason;
Never for a moment is he idle;
When he needs something, he demands it vigorously.

The thief can instruct you in seven things:

He does his service by night;
If he does not finish what he has set out to do in one night,
he devotes the next night to it;
He and those who work with him love one another;
He risks his life for slight gains;
What he takes has so little value for him that he gives it up for
a very small coin;
He endures blows and hardship, and it matters nothing to him;
He likes his trade and would not exchange it for any other.

Participation

This was Rabbi Mikhal's comment on the words of Hillel, "If I am not for myself, who will be for me? And if I am for myself, what am I?":

"'If I am not for myself,' that is, if I do not work for myself alone, but continually participate in the congregation, 'who will be for me?' In that case, whatever 'who,' that is, whatever any member of the congregation does in my place, counts just as though I had done it myself. But if I am 'for myself'—if I do not participate with others, if I do not join with them—'what am I?' Then everything in the way of good works which I have wrought alone is less than nothing in the eyes of God, who is the source of all good."

From *Ten Rungs: Hasidic Sayings*, collected and edited by Martin Buber (Secaucus, NJ: Citadel Press, 1995), pp. 49–56. Copyright © 1947, 1995 Estate of Martin Buber. Reprinted by permission.

Parabola
Volume: 5.3
Obstacles

THE GREAT TRANSITION

Rabbi Jonathan Omer-Man

Somewhere in the life-voyage of certain religious people there is a great transition, which can also become a major crisis of significance. The traveler enters this great transition as a man or a woman of God, as a man or woman of truth, and emerges as a Lover of God, as a Seeker of Truth. Each tradition employs its own imagery to describe this transition, and it is known variously as the initiation, the end of apprenticeship, death and rebirth, the sojourn in the wilderness, the passage through the gate, etc. When a traveler passes through the great transition, the significance of the voyage is totally transformed. From the perspective of one who has passed through it, the first leg, the first part of one's life, is perceived as a period of preparation in which the traveler learns the skills of his trade—the basic geography of the cosmos, the rudiments of navigation and map-reading, and the recognition and avoidance of dangers. The great transition is both a summons and a revelation. The traveler opens his sealed sailing instructions, and, for the first time, his true destination becomes clear. He also discovers that although the knowledge he had gleaned and the competences he had acquired previously are of great value—he could not have reached his present station without them—the total picture they give is, ultimately, an illusion, from which he must move into a deeper reality. This great transition is also the point at which many travelers are broken. The new route is so strange when compared with the old that the two appear to be incompatible, or even mutually exclusive. It is a sad but commonplace fact that the life of a religious person, especially in our times, is often no preparation for the tasks facing a Seeker of Truth.

I perceive precisely such a crisis, a breaking point in the religious lives of many of my Jewish friends today. They have come so far as Jews, have learned the traditional wisdom of the Jewish religion, and have accepted, with some degree or other of commitment, its praxis, its skills. And then, suddenly, comes the summons, comes the revelation. The response is frequently one of shock, of despair. No matter how clear the recognition that the call is of truth, and to truth, they feel that they have not been prepared to make the crossing, that nothing that they have learned as Jews has equipped them for the life of a Seeker of Truth. The great transition is seen as impossible. At this point, many shrug off the summons, and justify themselves by saying that the new route is not part of the Jewish way; some attempt to continue as if nothing had taken place, and tend to live rather impoverished, automatic, religious lives. Others, and their number seems to be growing, accept the summons, but feel that they cannot pursue it within Judaism, that they cannot reach completion as Jews; these are the Jewish dropouts, the recruits to other, especially Eastern, religions.

Personally, I believe that this crisis can be navigated, and that it is possible to make the passage and to emerge as a religious Jew. The difficulties are formidable, especially for those outside the orthodox, fundamentalist camp. Those who wish to undertake it must be willing to seek out and to find the Jewish wisdom that deals with the path to enlightenment, forewarned that the access to it is obstructed; the texts are obscure, and teachers are few. Such travelers must be prepared to question and to challenge much of what they have previously learned of Judaism, even, on occasion, to the point of smashing apparently sacrosanct structures in order to extract a few holy stones. Nevertheless, I believe that it can be done, and that the effort will be richly rewarded. What follows is an offering of insights, derived from my own work and that of my friends, into the nature of some of the obstacles we have encountered. There are, of course, no answers, but the very understanding of a difficulty is often a step towards confronting it.

The first obstacle is one that derives from a confusion of means and ends. Is one a Jew primarily in order to serve God, or is one a Jew for a variety of valid, though ultimately extrinsic reasons, among which religion, at least ontologically, is secondary? Now, it is clear that membership of any religious community is determined to a large extent by psychological and sociological factors, but in the case of the Jews, with the burden of three thousand years of troubled history and a community structure that was fashioned at least partially by external pressures, these are particularly heavy. Thus, for example, even a person who finds little satisfaction in Judaism is likely to feel bound to it by a sense of guilt. How can one abandon a path that one's forefathers fought so ferociously to defend, on many occasions at risk to their lives? How can one opt out of a nation that was threatened so barbarically with extinction in the most recent past? How can one desert a community under siege?

Parallel to, or flowing from, this continued association out of a sense of guilt, another, more positive and certainly more acceptable mechanism develops: the growth and reinforcement of personal identity by means of membership in a group. The Jew learns to love and to be proud of the values of his group, its path and its praxis; and he receives warm rewards for this loyalty. On the most basic level he acquires a strong identity and a support group upon which he can call in time of crisis. On a higher level, he discovers the rich spiritual resources that are his heritage, a well-tried way to worship God, a world view that attributes deep significance to the cycles of life, and a theology that promises—despite the vagaries of history—divine protection and ultimate vindication. Now, there is nothing reprehensible in such mechanisms. They are both commendable and essential for a group that has every right to desire to continue to exist. Nevertheless, for the Jewish traveler who approaches the great transition, they can constitute a serious obstacle. He learns that in order to proceed with his work—which is to understand God's will and to align his whole being with it—he must strip ego from self, must rid himself of all habits of thought that inhibit the freedom of his soul. He has to learn to purify his praxis, so that it will serve the one goal. The Jewish identity we have described makes this task very difficult, for it has welded together the functions of the soul and the process of survival.

So far we have dealt with problems whose provenance is sociological, the effects of a recruitment to a religious community for reasons that are not primarily associated with the worship of God. Let us now turn to another group of obstacles, those that derive from an apparent incompatibility between what the traveler has learned in the first part of his voyage—that is, the Judaism he has received—and what he perceives as the path beyond the great transition—to become a Seeker of Truth. These difficulties are of a mixed etiology, but can broadly be attributed to the sad state of contemporary Judaism. I have no intention here of embarking upon a critique of Jewish theology, and shall limit my diagnosis to a single sentence: Judaism appears to be suffering from a lack of knowledge of the old and from an inability to confront the new.

The first obstacle in this group is one that all but the most extraordinarily fortunate seekers are certain to encounter: the almost universally accepted, but quite false, hypothesis that Judaism does not acknowledge the "inner path of quest" as a legitimate route to God. Had I not been so sternly warned by my academic teachers to reject out of hand all "conspiracy" theories, I would be greatly tempted to adopt such an explanation. Ask a hundred rabbis, and you find that ninety-nine will say that it is not the Jewish way. "Enlightenment is not a goal in Judaism." Survey the numerous scholarly works on Jewish mysticism, and with one or two remarkable but little known exceptions, you will find no reference to it. Even accounts of small closed groups that were clearly established as holy communities are generally written in a way that emphasizes other, secondary characteristics, such as the messianic aspirations of the members. Scan the textbooks, the manuals, the encyclopedias for material on meditation, and you are likely to conclude that it was never part of Jewish praxis. Nevertheless, there is a vast body of Jewish wisdom on the inner path, dispersed in books on the Kabbalah, and especially in the later Hasidic works. True, it is not presented in monographic discourses (Hasidic books are notoriously nonsystematic), and there are few explicit manuals of instruction, but it is possible to glean a mass of important teachings from these sources. Some Hasidic writers, for example, deal extensively with the processes of cognition, the migration of attention through the various levels of consciousness, and specifically with the problem of the painful descent from the holistic mode, the ecstatic perception of an all-pervading oneness, to the individuated mode, the perception of particularized reality. Many other topics of a related nature, comprising together what could be called the basics of the mystic's craft, can be located in a good Jewish library.

This obstacle, this systematic denial of access to information, is in fact a new manifestation of an ancient and perennial struggle, that between priest and prophet, dogmatician and mystic, the community and the ecstatic. When perceived as such, it is relatively easy to confront: it is not that no path exists, but that there are powerful social forces that wish to prevent one from following it.

The problems that derive from the inadequacies of modern Jewish theology, however, are far more difficult to resolve. The traveler needs theology; it is an essential navigational aid, and he cannot proceed without it. The task of theology is to provide a reliable map, a concept of the universe in which every detail is significant and the life of the individual is meaningful. Furthermore, theology must describe the features of the universe in such a way that the mystery that enshrouds them is untouched. Divinity resides in mystery. The major failing of theology today is that it has restricted its own applicability to a few relatively safe areas of existence. Most of the universe is no longer mysterious, or at least not so in religious terms.

Traditionally, Jewish theology relates to and portrays four interrelated areas of existence, which may be envisaged as four concentric circles. The innermost is the human soul; the second circle is the individual's immediate environment, which starts with his body and reaches out to the entire Jewish people; the third is the cosmos, everything that God created; and the outermost circle is the Creation, the mythical key to an understanding of the personality of God and the nature of his relationship with the world.

Most of the work of Jewish theologians and thinkers in recent years has been directed towards the second circle, most specifically towards the contemporary problems of the Jewish people. Thus serious attempts have been made to grapple with the agonizing problem of the Holocaust, and, on the brighter side, the significance of the establishment of the State of Israel. Now, although an understanding of what it means to be the Chosen People is extremely important in such traumatic and dramatic times, its value is limited when the universe as a whole is unfathomable from the perspective of religion.

For centuries theology (both Jewish and non-Jewish) fought against the encroachments of science into what it considered to be its private territory. Frequently, however, it seems to have done so for the wrong reasons. By focusing the issue on the conflict between religious dogma and scientific fact, the theologians failed to perceive the deeper significance of the scientific world view. When, in recent years, they were willing to accommodate, to concede that, for example, there was no inherent contradiction between dogma and the discoveries of Galileo and Darwin, and that the book of Genesis was in many ways an allegory and not a textbook of history, it was too late. The scientific cosmology had won the day, and its significance is not that the earth is not the center of the universe, or that man evolved from amoebas by way of worms and apes. The cosmological teaching of modern science is that man is utterly insignificant: in terms of the infinite reaches of time and space, human history is but an ephemeral, local event of minute proportions; not only is man not the final stage of Creation, he is not even necessarily the highest form of life, just the most recent development on this particular planet. The effect of this onslaught of science upon religion has been devastating. Instead of confronting an exciting new world, theology has restricted its concerns to safe familiarities, and even these seem at times to be demystified.

For the traveler who becomes a Seeker of Truth, such a theology is of no more value than a broken toy. He must relate to the mysteries of astrophysics, and must face with awe his own minute proportions in relation to the cosmos. He must ponder once again the question posed so powerfully in the Bible, by Ezekiel, by Job and the Psalmist: In such a terrifying world, is there any significance to my life? The Jewish seeker cannot determine his coordinates exclusively within the narrow bounds of Jewish history and peoplehood; he must plot his course also by the most distant galaxies.

Paradoxically, this is not a particularly difficult task, though it does seem formidable. Whereas much modern theology appears to be paralyzed in the face of the new cosmology, that embodied in the old Jewish mystical tradition, the Kabbalah, appears to be alive and pertinent. These strange theosophical works depict a universe of infinite size and complexity in which, on the one hand, man is insignificantly small, and yet, on the other, he is the observer and the actor who stands at the center.

It is obviously an inane pursuit to attempt to find equivalences between the details of the Kabbalistic picture of the universe and, for example, the Big Bang (though, needless to say, it has been attempted), but the modes of cognition, and even the theory of knowledge, seem to coexist in peace. What I wish to say here is that the Kabbalah offers a map of the cosmos that is not incompatible with our new knowledge, and can match it in excitement. A friend of mine once remarked that were the great mystics of the Middle Ages alive today, they would surely employ science fiction as a vehicle for their works. In my opinion, the writings of Isaac Luria, a major Kabbalist who lived in the sixteenth century, were just such science fiction.

So far I have reviewed a few common obstacles of a more general nature. Before concluding with a short discussion of what is most frequently considered to be the most serious difficulty of the Jewish seeker, the lack of teachers, I shall list three or four more problems, each a cluster of closely related questions, and shall devote no more than a few words to each.

Is the Jewish praxis really the way? Is compliance with a complex set of commandments an aid or an obstacle to the path? Do not the details obscure the essential work? Is it possible to be confident that, in performing a particular minor ritual, one is making manifest the will of God? My response to these questions is to repeat what has been given to me: It is the way if one chooses it as the way.

Does not the great emphasis placed on study in the Jewish tradition introduce an element of achievement orientation, of personal involvement with success, precisely in the area in which one must be free of the constrictions of ego? The answer to this is that there is such a danger, but that the great teachers, especially of the Hasidic movement, were aware of it, and fought against it on both the personal and social levels.

Does not Jewish self-consciousness, drawing on centuries of apologetics, engender a rather over-serious, humorless way of looking at the world? Can the Jew giggle in his prayers? Can he perceive the laughter in the universe? Can he hear the Almighty chuckling? This one is difficult. The perception of the humorous is certainly a requirement of many seekers, but many others have done without.

The final item I shall mention in this survey is the lack of teachers. Whereas the western world appears to be inundated with great (and less great) gurus and spiritual guides, there are very few who can lead the seeker on the Jewish path. Once there were many. A Jew living in Eastern Europe in the eighteenth century, in the heyday of the Hasidic revival, could probably choose between a dozen or more great *rebbes*, and he would be able to select the one whose path and regimen seemed to suit him best. What then must the modern Jewish traveler do, as he approaches the great transition and desperately needs the direction of a spiritual mentor? There appears to be but a single answer: He must realize that he is not alone, and that there are many others in the same predicament. Seekers of Truth who have no spiritual teachers must come together and teach each other.

•

CHAPTER FIVE

PRAYER AND MEDITATION: TALKING TO GOD

The purpose of all prayer is to uplift the words,
to return them to their source above.
The world was created
by the downward flow of letters:
The task of man is to form those letters into words
and take them back to God.
If you come to know this dual process,
your prayer may be joined
to the constant flow of Creation—
word to word, voice to voice,
breath to breath, thought to thought.[1]

—Liqqutim Yeqarim

Return

Exodus 3:1-5

Now Moses kept the flock of Jethro his father in law, the priest of Midian: and he led the flock to the backside of the desert, and came to the mountain of God, even to Horeb.

And the angel of the Lord appeared unto him in a flame of fire out of the midst of a bush: and he looked, and, behold, the bush burned with fire, and the bush was not consumed.

And Moses said, I will now turn aside, and see this great sight, why the bush is not burnt.

And when the Lord saw that he turned aside to see, God called unto him out of the midst of the bush, and said, Moses, Moses. And he said, Here am I.

And he said, Draw not nigh hither: put off thy shoes from off thy feet, for the place whereon thou standest is holy ground.

Hasidic prayer

A person may come to sense two kinds of movement
   taking place within him as he prays.
At times he feels the left hand of God
   pushing him away;
   at other times God's right hand draws him near.
But even as he is pushed away,
   he still should know
   that this is only for the sake of his return.

Even as he feels
   the might
   of God's left hand upon him,
   he should see
   that it is God Himself who touches him.
This too he should accept in love,
   and, trembling, kiss the hand that pushes him—
   for in that very moment,
   the right hand awaits his coming near.

Psalm 137

By the rivers of Babylon, there we sat down,
yea, we wept, when we remembered Zion.
We hanged our harps upon the willows
in the midst thereof.
For there they that carried us away captive
required of us a song; and they that wasted us
required of us mirth, saying,
Sing us one of the songs of Zion.
How shall we sing the Lord's song in a strange land?
If I forget thee, O Jerusalem, let my right hand forget her cunning.
If I do not remember thee, let my tongue cleave
to the roof of my mouth; if I prefer not Jerusalem
above my chief joy.
Remember, O Lord, the children of Edom in the day of Jerusalem;
who said, Rase it, rase it, even to the foundation thereof.
O daughter of Babylon, who art to be destroyed;
happy shall he be, that rewardeth thee as thou has served us.
Happy shall he be, that taketh and dasheth thy little
ones against the stones.

Isaiah 55:10-11

For as the rain cometh down, and the snow from heaven, and returneth
not thither, but watereth the earth, and maketh it bring forth and bud,
that it may give seed to the sower, and bread to the eater: So shall my
word be that goeth forth out of my mouth; it shall not return unto me

void, but it shall accomplish that which I please, and it shall prosper in the thing whereto I sent it.

Mendel of Kotzk

He who is about to pray should learn from a common laborer, who sometimes takes a whole day to prepare for a job. A wood-cutter, who spends most of the day sharpening the saw and only the last hour cutting the wood, has earned his day's wage.

Parabola
Volume: 26.4
The Heart

Building a Sanctuary

Geoffrey Dennis

At the heart of Israelite religion, the discipline of silence reigned supreme. While neighboring Semitic cults offered sacrifices to their gods accompanied by prayer and incantation, the Priests of the cult of the one God performed their oblations unaccompanied by speech. While the outer courts of the Temple echoed with the Levites intoning their psalmodies and while the people spoke, sang, and danced their devotion, the inner precincts were, in the words of Biblical scholar Yehezkel Kaufmann, "a sanctuary of silence." The absence of speech served the priesthood in many ways. Aside from dramatically distinguishing Israelite *avodah* (sacrificial service), it also created an atmosphere of awe before the Divine Presence as the offerings were made. Priests were more mindful of their tasks and concentration marked all their actions. Quiet made the Temple a suitable dwelling place for God amidst the people. Silence was the very catalyst by which the mechanical and punctilious acts of animal and grain sacrifice were transformed into *avodat ha-lev*—sacrifice of the heart (Deut. 11:13).

In the Zohar, the pre-eminent book of Kabbalah, we find this enigmatic statement: "Silence is the means of building the sanctuary above and the sanctuary below" (2a). To make sense of this we first must know that the Temple in Jerusalem was more than just a geographical center for the Jewish people; it was also a spiritual template. Its form was a physical representation of two supernal realities. The rabbis believed that the Temple was modeled on the form of the celestial domain, as well as on the contours of the human soul. The universe and the individual, therefore, are reflections of each other and dwelling places for the divine.[1] While the Temple in Jerusalem existed, it served as a conduit between the twin sanctuaries of the human soul and the World Soul.

By the time the Zohar was written, however, the earthly temple service had ceased to exist. The "sanctuary below" to which the Zohar refers, therefore, is the temple of the human soul. Prayer, the service of the heart, continues there, and with it the need for silence. But just as the heart, which makes life possible, beats largely without our awareness, so too the soul's need for silence goes unnoticed. While prayer continues to be a vital concern for religious Jews, silence as a spiritual practice is virtually forgotten. Yet one is hardly possible without the other. Cultivating quiet is essential if we wish the offerings of our lips to open for us the perspective of the heart. It is the key to drawing together the twin sanctuaries of heaven and earth—it is the essence of prayer.

To understand the significance of silence we must begin at the Beginning. Creation begins with words. In Genesis God creates through speaking. Based on Isaiah 43:7, the Kabbalists teach that divine speech brought into existence otherness, a chain of four universes: the World of Emanation and the dimension of pure spirit, the World of Creation and the dimension of intellect, the World of Formation and the dimension of emotions, and the World of Action and the dimension of the material.

To be in any phase of this chain of being is to experience duality, a sense of our being separate from our surroundings. So even though Judaism teaches the unity of all things, as humans we see the world around us as multiplicity. The Jewish mystic understands that the human perspective innately distinguishes self from other, for the very act of creation imposes this perspective on us. For example, we are conscious of a distinction between our thoughts and ourselves. And what is true in the dimension of thought is true at all levels of creation. In our thinking, feeling, and actions, therefore, we find pervasive duality. "One who descends from the Root of roots to the form of forms must walk in multiplicity."[2]

Human beings, as the last act of creation and foremost in the World of Action, find themselves in an ironic condition. Seemingly the culmination of God's creation, we also seem the farthest removed from the root. Judaism describes this as the condition of *galut*, exile. Like duality, it is an existential reality arising from the very act of creation itself. And even though we sense that an aspect of God, the *Shekhinah*, the Divine Presence, remains with us, a rabbinic myth teaches that Shekhinah Herself is in a kind of exile. This is crucial in accounting for modern feelings of alienation. Excepting those saints blessed with the innate spiritual talent to draw worlds together, we feel trapped in the lower worlds and God is distant from us. More radical still, we even experience the one God as bifurcated, fragmented into transcendent and immanent domains. Jewish mysticism does not deny this feeling of remoteness or the experience of multiplicity; it frequently speaks in such terms. God is described as "above," "transcendent," or "distant."

At the same time, the teachers of Kabbalah emphasize that our experience is ultimately subjective. It is foremost a matter of perspective. For, while we feel ourselves at the periphery, God experiences everything as at the center. From the divine perspective all is caught in unity, all worlds, whether "above" or "below," are still One. Duality and exile, then, are the human starting points; unity, return to the center, our desire. Return through the Four Worlds to the Root of roots is possible. Or more precisely, we can unify Intellect, Emotion, and Action and so return to the realm of Spirit.

Spoken prayer is the vehicle of that return to the center and silence is the power that transports us. We receive a hint of this when the prophet Ezekiel reveals the *Maasei Merkavah* (the "workings of the Divine Chariot"). In describing his vision of the "chariot," he reports, "A storm wind came out of the north, a huge fire surrounded by radiance, and at the center of it, in the center of the fire, a gleam as of *chashmal*" (Ezek. 1:4). In expounding on the mysteries of this vision, the Talmud includes an oral tradition on the word *chashmal*. The word, it is taught, should actually be read as two abbreviated words, *chashah* (to be silent) and *milah* (speech) (Chagigah 13b). Thus "silent speech" is both the heart of Divinity and the essence of God's self-revelation. From our perspective, of course, "silent speech" is self-contradictory. But if we desire to be at that center then we must grapple with this paradox: spoken prayer, the royal pathway to God, demands silence.

There are two dimensions to prayer: speech and silence. Of the two, speech is necessary, but silence takes precedence. This is in some ways self-evident. Without silence there is no speech. Without the pauses before, between, and after each sound, communication through words would be impossible. Returning metaphorically to "building the sanctuary," words are building blocks, but silence is the foundation. There is an innate inequality between experience and expression, because experience does not require words—and often defies adequate expression. While speech is a necessary act, silence engages the higher domains of thought and emotion. In the Talmud, Simeon ben Gamaliel declares: "In all my days growing up among the Sages, I have not found anything better for oneself than silence" (B. T. Avot 1:17). The Zohar offers an even more earthy evaluation: "Speech is worth a penny, silence is worth two" (2a).

Silence is the authentic medium of prayer, the rich matrix in which true communion becomes possible. And being a medium, silence has a positive existence. For the one who truly understands prayer, silence also conveys a message; it too speaks. And therein lies another modern challenge. Modernity teaches us to experience silence, not as a presence, but as a void, a lacuna in our consciousness that needs to be filled. The modern person seems only to know of "uncomfortable silences" and "awkward silences." We prefer to fill our environment with sound—any sound. We equate silence with loneliness rather than with aloneness with God. It is because of this reality, along with our sense of God's remoteness, that we today have become so alienated from authentic prayer—for we have come to abhor silence. If it is the pauses in speech that make expression possible, then prayer particularly suffers for the lack of contrast. The consequence has been to cause our words of prayer to disappear against a background of constant speech. In a world blanketed with sound, our supplications are just so much verbiage bled of their potency and their potential. Prayer simply blends into everything else being said. For prayer to be powerful, it must be reunited with its antipode, the discipline to be quiet.

The discipline of quieting ourselves is also twofold: quieting the tongue and quieting the heart. Quieting of the tongue is the type of discipline most of us imagine as the way of silence. And, in fact, restraining oneself from constant speaking is a discipline prized and admired by Jewish spiritual practitioners. Just as silence has both a value and a presence, so too it has power—"The cry one holds back is the most powerful of all."[3] Observing a fast from words has greater transformative power than a fast from food,[4] for to restrain our tongue, especially from gossip, tale-bearing, or frivolous speech, is to offer up a blessing, itself a form of "silent speaking." Such silence of the tongue prepares the soul for prayer. It also opens a way for empathy. In silence one can now hear the pain of others, the pain of the world. Silence is a hammer that breaks our heart of stone and then replaces it with a heart of flesh—a heart that understands what flesh is, a heart that may be pierced by the suffering of others, and that is open to Divinity.

This in turn prepares us for the discipline of quieting the heart. In the Hebrew imagination, the heart is the seat of consciousness; therefore this is the practice of inner quiet that soothes the soul and calms the mind. Quieting the heart is the process of cultivating intentionality, the ability to concentrate wholeheartedly on a single object or task, a critical element of prayer. In the tradition of Jewish meditation, quieting the heart is achieved through the discipline of *hitbodedut*, or "self-seclusion." To the practitioners of Jewish meditation it refers to quieting the mind and reining in the distracted self,[5] even if one finds oneself in a crowd or amidst much commotion. The practitioner of quieting the heart seeks only to reduce the cacophonous voice of the *self*, so as to open an avenue through which the transcendent dimension of God can commune with the immanent dimension of God (that is, the soul) and unite the two. Such was the discipline exercised by Elijah the prophet, who though surrounded by thunderous tumult upon Mount Horeb, quieted his heart to the point where he could hear the "sound of sheer silence" (1 Kings 19:12)—the voice of divine unity. Those who practice silence truly can hear a "silent sound."

So how does Judaism teach one to integrate silent meditation into a moment of worship? In Mishna Tractate Berachot 5:1 we are told that "the early pietists would sit silently for an hour and then pray in order to concentrate their minds on their Source in heaven."[6] The Talmud (Berachot 31b) adds that these spiritual masters continued this sitting meditation for an hour after prayer. The prayer itself they would recite very slowly in an undertone. Thus these Talmudic pietists expressed their prayer embedded in silence.

All of which brings us once again to the problem of duality and the paradox of "silent spoken" prayer. That paradox is resolved by bringing the two elements together in such a way that we may fully experience God. When we begin our prayer with silence, we begin with an act of supreme adoration, for "Silence is praise to You" (Ps. 65:2). To conclude with silence is to invite divine disclosure: "My soul waits silently for God" (Ps. 62:2). Together they bring us before God like the ancient priesthood. By binding our prayer to concentration born of silence, we may enter the Divine precincts.

And it is through silence that God in turn "speaks" to us. The Talmudic interpretation of the word chashmal concludes by stating, "When they are silent, the Holy One speaks." Which is to say, only in quiet does the unmediated, unbound nature of Divinity become accessible to one who prays. The twentieth-century Hasidic Master, Kolanymus Kalman Shapira, also know as the Piasetzner Rebbe, writes extensively on the metaphysical role of prayer in mystically experiencing the Divine:

> "And so one must isolate himself from the world prior to spoken prayer, separating from the noise of the world with the intent that he now draw near to speak with the Eternal. Once he has isolated himself from the world and its uproar, then—if one could say such a thing—the "garments" that separate Divinity from him (for he has masked that Divinity with his ego: his thoughts, his will, his actions) pass away. Then the Divinity within them reveals itself."[7]

Through the simplicity of quiet and stillness, we expose our soul to the upper worlds so that it might achieve fusion with God. Silence makes this union possible because it preceded the Worlds of multiplicity. The created universe is made of words. Before God's words/worlds, there was the silence that speaks only of utter unity. To transcend the world, therefore, we need silence. The Piasetzner Rebbe explains that prayer without attending silence only penetrates the three "lower worlds" of Action, Formation, and Creation. Our prayers can ascend to the highest world of Emanation only when we bind our prayers to simple silence.[8]

Through bridging and binding these worlds, we reverse the flow of multiplicity and achieve the unification of divine aspects, and fusion with God. Silence transforms one from a seeker of the Divine into a vessel of the Divine:

Thus we can transcend [the limitation of] speech by means of an hour's silence … in truth, every person has in one's self a portion of Divinity … if only we could stop for an hour, then that Divinity, stripped of its concealing garments, would become apparent to him.[9]

The silence of adoration allows us to draw close to the Beloved, while the silence of response shows that our love is requited and the Divinity below and the Divinity above merge in primordial embrace.

Just as performing avodah in silence allowed the priests to serve in the Jerusalem sanctuary, through the silence of adoration our prayers enter the transcendent Sanctuary of God's dwelling. There we make the avodat ha-lev, offerings of our heart, offerings of our wholeness.

Notes:

1 That the Temple building is a representation of both the celestial and the human parallels the Greek notion of Macrocosm and Microcosm. This myth of the Temple as cosmic model is common in Judaism. It appears in non-esoteric works, such as the *Avot de Rabbi Natan* (Ch. 31), but is most elaborately expounded in mystical works, such as the Kabbalistic commentary on the Torah by Bachya ben Asher (*Midrash Rabbeinu Bachya* on Exodus 25:19).

2 Azriel of Gerona (thirteenth-century Kabbalist), *Sod Ha-Tefillah*, 216, as translated in Dan Matt, *The Essential Kabbalah* (Edison, NJ: Castle Books, 1997), p. 76.

3 The Kotzker Rebbe (Menachem Mendel of Kotzk, nineteenth-century Hasidic master), as quoted in David Wolpe, *In Speech and in Silence* (New York: Penguin Books, 1992), p. 186.

4 The Vilna Gaon (Elijah ben Solomon Zalman, eighteenth-century Ethicalist), *Iggeret HaGra*.

5 Chayyim Vital (sixteenth-century Kabbalist), *Shaarei Kedushah*, part 4, as quoted in Aryeh Kaplan's *Meditation and Kabbalah* (New York: Weiser, 1989), p. 342.

6 Referring to the "Tefillah," the spoken prayer a Jew is to recite three times daily.

7 *Derekh Ha-Melekh*, Merkaz Chasidei Piesetznah, p. 2. The translation is the author's. This writer owes a great debt to my teacher Dr. Elliot Ginsberg for introducing me to the works of the Piasetzner Rebbe.

8 *Ibid*, p. 3.

9 *Ibid*, p. 5.

Parabola
Volume: 12.4
The Sense of Humor

THE THREEFOLD LAUGH

Martin Buber

On a Friday evening, when the Ba'al-Shem sat with some
of his disciples at table and had just spoken the blessing
over the wine, it happened all at once that his face shone
with a joyful light as from within, and he began to laugh
and laughed much and in a hearty manner. The disciples
glanced at one another and looked around the room, but
there was nothing there that could have been the cause of
his laughter. After a short while the Ba'al-Shem laughed
a second time in the same manner, with the unexpected
gaiety and brightness of a child. Then a short while
elapsed, and his laugh rang out for a third time.

The disciples sat silent around the table. In their eyes
this occurrence was a rare and incomprehensible thing.
For they knew the master well and knew that he did not
lightly surrender himself to such an impulse. So they sus-
pected a significant ground for this joyousness and would
gladly have known it, yet none found the courage to
approach the Ba'al-Shem about it. Therefore, they turned
their eyes to Rabbi Wolf who was in their midst, that he
should inquire of the master the cause of his laughter. For
it was the custom that at the end of the Sabbath Rabbi
Wolf should go to the Ba'al-Shem when he rested in his
room in order to learn from him what might have taken
place in the course of the Sabbath.

Thus it happened this time too, and this disciple questioned him about the meaning of his laughter of the day before.

"Well now," said the Ba'al-Shem, "you would like to know from whence joy flowed into me. Come with me and you shall hear." Then he bid the servant harness the horses in order to take a drive in the open country, as was the custom after the expiration of the Sabbath. He climbed into the coach with his disciples, and they did not return home after a few hours as usual, but rather drove silently through the darkness the whole night. In the morning they reached a village. The Ba'al-Shem had the carriage stop at the house of the leader of the community. Soon his arrival was known to all the Jews. Everyone came and surrounded the house in order to do him honor. But he commanded the leader to send for Shabti, the bookbinder.

The leader replied, a little dissatisfied, "Master, what do you want with this man, who lives in our community without being especially noticed by anyone? He is an honest Jew, but never have I heard him praised for the sake of even the slightest learning. What good can he be to you?"

"Nevertheless," said the master, "it is my wish that you call him for me." He was sent for, and he came—a modest, grey-haired old man. The Ba'al-Shem regarded him and said, "your wife too should come," and she also was soon present.

"Now," said the Ba'al-Shem, "you shall tell me what you did on the night of the last Sabbath. But say the simple truth, have no shame and hide nothing from us."

"Sir," Shabti answered, I shall conceal nothing from you, and if I have sinned, then you behold me ready to accept penance at your hands as if it came from God Himself.

"All the days that heaven has given me, I have been able to live by my work; indeed, in good seasons I was able to lay aside a little savings for myself. But from the beginning it was my custom that my wife should go out at noon of the fifth day of the week to buy with great care all the necessities for the Sabbath—our wants in flour, meat, fish, and candles. After the tenth hour of the day before the Sabbath, I left my work and went to the prayer house to remain there until after the evening prayer. I have done this since my youth.

"But now, since I am beginning to age, my wheel of fortune has turned; my possessions have flown out of my hands, and my strength for work has been lamed. Now I live a life of care, and often I do not succeed in providing for all the needs of the Sabbath by the fifth day. My consolation is that whatever else may come, one thing I do not need to give up; ending my week's work on the tenth hour of the day before the Sabbath, entering the prayer house, and remaining there until evening speaking the holy psalms and the festive songs.

"On the tenth hour of the day before this Sabbath, I did not have a farthing in my hands to supply the wants of the holiday, and my poor wife did not have a pinch of flour in the bin. Yet I have never in all the days of my life required assistance of other men, and I wanted to get through this day too without alms. So I decided to fast during this Sabbath. But I feared that seeing no light burning on the table would weigh on my wife's heart all too heavily and that she might accept a candle and some Sabbath bread or a little fish if a well-meaning neighbor offered it to her. Therefore, I demanded of her that she not take help from any man, even though he pressed her to do so. For understand, Master, that the Jews among whom we live are of a kind disposition and would find it difficult to accept our Sabbath table's standing empty. My wife promised to do as I asked. Before I went to the prayer house I said to her, 'Today I shall tarry until the day declines. For if I should go home with the others from the prayer house and they should see no light in my house, they would ask me the cause, and I would not know how to answer them. But when I come then, my wife, we shall receive with love what heaven will allot us.' Thus I spoke to my old spouse to comfort her.

"She, however, remained and cleaned the house in every nook and cranny. Since the hearth was cold and she had no food to prepare, she had a lot of time on her hands which she did not know how to spend otherwise, so she opened an old chest and took out the yellowed clothing of our youth in order to brush it and neatly put it in again. There she found, under all the old, worn-out clothes, a sleeve that we had missed once years ago and that since then had never been found. On the piece of garment there were some buttons in the form of little flowers, made out of gold and silver wire, a charming ornament such as one is likely to find on old clothes. These my wife cut off and took to the goldsmith and he gave her so much money that she was able to purchase the food that was needed for the Sabbath and also two good, strong candles and, in addition, even what we needed for the next day.

"In the evening when all the people had gone, I walked slowly through the streets to our house and saw already from a distance a light burning. The candlelight appeared festive and cozy. But I thought, 'My old wife has acted in the manner of women and could not refrain from accepting something.' I entered and found the table fully set and ready with Sabbath bread and fish, and I also found there wine over which to say the blessing. But I restrained myself from getting angry since I did not want to break the Sabbath. So I held myself back, spoke the blessing and ate of the fish. After that I said to my wife—but I spoke in a soft voice, for her poor, troubled soul moved me to pity—'It turned out then that your heart was not in a condition to accept hardship.' But she did not let me speak to the end, rather said in a bright voice, 'My husband, do you still remember the old material with the gold and silver buttons that we have been missing for years? When I cleaned out the great chest today, I found it. I gave the buttons to the goldsmith, and with the money I provided for the Sabbath.'

"Master, when I heard that my eyes filled with tears, so great was my joy. I threw myself down and thanked the Lord that he had remembered my Sabbath. I looked at my wife and saw her good face beam back my joy. Then I became warm, and I forgot the many wretched days. I seized hold of my wife and danced with her around the room. After that I ate the Sabbath supper, and my mood became ever lighter and more thankful; then I danced in joy and laughed a second time, and when I had consumed dessert, I did the same for the third time. You see, Master, so great was my happiness that this blessing had come to me from God alone and not from men. My joy was too great for me to be able to hide my feelings. It was in my mind to do reverence to God, thereby, but if, Rabbi, it was an unworthy piece of foolishness that I danced thus with my wife, then give me a merciful penance, and I shall not fail to perform it."

Here Shabti the bookbinder ceased speaking. The Ba'al-Shem said to his disciples, "Know that all the hosts of heaven rejoiced with him and turned round with him in dance. And I, who saw all this, was moved to laughter the three times." Then he turned toward the two of them and said, "A child of your old age will be born to you who are childless. Call him Israel after my name."

Thus it happened. This boy became the Maggid of Kosnitz, the great man of prayer.

Reprinted by permission of Schocken Books Inc. from *The Legend of the Ba'al-Shem* by Martin Buber, translated by Maurice Friedman. Copyright © 1955 by Harper & Row. First Schocken edition 1969.

Parabola
Volume: 24.2
Prayer and
Meditation

THE INNER BOOK OF PSALMS

*The Book of Psalms is a sacred book, read sometimes as scripture
and sung sometimes as hymns. Psalms of lament, of petition and
penitence, of praise and thanksgiving are its mantle for an inner
movement, a vertical exchange, up and down the scale of being.*

*The Psalmist is searching, searching for his place in the order
of the universe, and searching for the way to reach union with
God. He is summoned to return to himself: "Commune with
your own heart upon your bed, and be still." (Psalm 4:4) Self-
knowledge and understanding, conveyed in single sentences and
short passages, are the rungs of a ladder ascending and descending through sleep and awakening to the realm of the Word.*

—Jean Sulzberger

*When I consider thy heavens, the work of thy fingers, the moon
and the stars, which thou hast ordained;
What is man, that thou art mindful of him? and the son of
man, that thou visitest him?*   8:3–4

*The Lord looked down from heaven upon the children of men, to
see if there were any that did understand and seek God.*   14:2

I shall be satisfied, when I awake, with thy likeness.   17:15

He brought me forth also into a large place.   18:19

The heavens declare the glory of God; and the firmament sheweth his handy-work. Day unto day uttereth speech, and night unto night sheweth knowledge. There is no speech nor language, where their voice is not heard. Their line is gone out through all the earth, and their words to the end of the world. In them hath he set a tabernacle for the sun, which is as a bridegroom coming out of his chamber, and rejoiceth as a strong man to run a race. His going forth is from the end of the heaven, and his circuit unto the ends of it: and there is nothing hid from the heat thereof.   19:1–6

The steps of a good man are ordered by the Lord.   37:23

He asked life of thee.   21:4

Show me thy ways, O Lord; teach me thy paths. Lead me in thy truth, and teach me.   25:4–5

I sought the Lord, and he heard me.   34:4

In thy light shall we see light.   36:9

Lord make me to know mine end, and the measure of my days.   39:4

I am a stranger with thee, and a sojourner.   39:12

Mine ears hast thou opened.   40:6

Deep calleth unto deep.   42:7

Send out thy light and thy truth: let them lead me.   43:3

Be still, and know that I am God.   46:10

The meditation of my heart shall be of understanding.   49:3

He bringeth out those which are bound with chains.   68:6

Violence covereth them as a garment.   73:6

Both the chariot and horse are cast into a dead sleep.   76:6
My spirit made diligent search.   77:6

I will open my mouth in a parable: I will utter dark sayings of old: which we have heard and known, and our fathers have told us.   78:2–3

He brought streams also out of the rock.   78:16

I am shut up, and I cannot come forth.   88:8

Lord, thou hast been our dwelling place in all generations.
    Before the mountains were brought forth, or ever thou hadst formed the earth and the world, even from everlasting to everlasting, thou art God.
    Thou turnest man to destruction; and sayest, Return, ye children of men.
    For a thousand years in thy sight are but as yesterday when it is past, and as a watch in the night.
    Thou carriest them away as with a flood; they are as a sleep: in the morning they are like grass which groweth up.
    In the morning it flourisheth, and groweth up; in the evening it is cut down, and withereth.   90:1–6

Teach us to number our days, that we may apply our hearts unto wisdom.   90:12

He that dwelleth in the secret place of the most High shall abide under the shadow of the Almighty.   91:1

The Lord knoweth the thoughts of man, that they are vanity.   94:11

Blessed is the man whom thou chasteneth.   94:12

Today if ye will hear his voice.   95:7

My days are like a shadow that declineth.   102:11

As for man, his days are as grass: as a flower in the field, so he flourisheth. For the wind passeth over it, and it is gone; and the place thereof shall know it no more. 103:15–16

Awake, psaltery and harp: I myself will awake. 108:2
I called upon the Lord in distress: the Lord answered me, and set me in a large place. 118:5

The stone which the builders refused is become the head stone of the corner. 118:22

Open thou mine eyes. 119:18

It is time for thee, Lord, to work. 119:126

The entrance of thy words giveth light; it giveth understanding. 119:130

Lord have mercy. 123:3

How shall we sing the Lord's song in a strange land? 137:4

O Lord, thou hast searched me, and known me.
Thou knowest my downsitting and mine uprising, thou understandest my thought afar off.
Thou compassest my path and my lying down, and art acquainted with all my ways.
For there is not a word in my tongue, but, lo, O Lord, thou knowest it altogether. Thou hast beset me behind and before, and laid thine hand upon me.
Such knowledge is too wonderful for me; it is high, I cannot attain unto it.
Whither shall I go from thy spirit? or whither shall I flee from thy presence? If I ascend up into heaven, thou art there: if I make my bed in hell, behold, thou art there. If I take the wings of the morning, and dwell in the uttermost parts of the sea; Even there shall thy hand lead me, and thy right hand shall hold me.
If I say, Surely the darkness shall cover me; even the night shall be light about me. Yea, the darkness hideth not from thee; but the night shineth as the day: the darkness and the light are both alike to thee. 139:1–12

The Lord looseth the prisoners: the Lord openeth the eyes of the blind.   146:7–8

Sing unto the Lord a new song.   149:1

Let them praise his name in the dance.   149:3

Parabola
Volume: 2.2
Creation

Psalm 19

David Rosenberg

The universe unfolds
the vision within:
creation

stars and galaxies
the words and lines
inspired with a hand

day comes to us
with color and shape
and night listens

and what is heard
breaks through deep silence
of infinite space

the rays come to us
like words
come to everyone

human on earth
we are the subjects
of light

a community
as it hears
the right words

creating time
the space of the sky
the face of the nearest star

that beats like a heart
in the tent where it sleeps
near the earth every night

then rises above the horizon
growing in our awareness
of the embrace

of inspiration
we feel as we turn
toward the warmth

starting at the edge of the sky
to come over us
like a secret love we wait for

love we can't hide
our deepest self-image
from

nobody holds back that fire
or closes the door
of time

words My Lord writes shine
opening me
to witness myself

conscious and unconscious
complex mind
warmed in an inner lightness

that moves me
to the simple beat
of time

testimony
of one author
speaking through history's pages

commanding my attention
bathed in light
around me

clean perfect notes
hearts play
make us conscious

we become the audience
amazed we can feel
justice come over us

our minds become real
unfold
the universe within

silence becomes real
we hear
clear words

become the phrasing of senses
lines of thought
stanzas of feeling

more lovely than gold
all the gold in the world
melting to nothing in light

sweet flowing honey
the right words
in my mouth

warming your subject
as he listens
breaking through his reflection

his image in the mirror
what mind can understand the failure
waiting in itself

silent self-image
created in the dark alone
to hold

power over others!
but justice comes over us
like a feeling for words that are right

absolutely
a mirror is pushed away
like a necessary door

we're free to look at everything
every shape and color
light as words

opening the mind
from nightmares of social failure
desperate routines

we're inspired above
the surface parade
of men dressed up in power

we see the clear possibility
of life growing
to witness itself

let these words
of my mouth
be sound

the creations
of my heart
be light

so I can see myself
free of desperate symbols
mind-woven coverings

speechless fears
images hidden within
we are the subjects of light

opening to join you
vision itself
my constant creator.

•

CHAPTER SIX

REPENTANCE

Why do we say the prayer beginning, "Forgive us,"
during the Evening Prayer at the close of Yom Kippur:
lo, Yom Kippur has already made atonement for all sins?
This may be compared to a parable about a king who
was passing through a field. A countryman saw him and kicked him.
The king's men wanted to kill the man. But the king said:
"Let him be, for he does not know who I am. If he knew me,
he would not have done what he did; put him in a school and let him get
understanding and manners." They put the man in a school,
and he became a man of understanding. When he saw the respect
the king was held in, and remembered what he had done to the king,
he grew faint with shame and began to cry,
"Forgive me!" For all the time he had been a coarse man
he had not known how great his sin was, and it had not been
clear to him in what way he had sinned.[1]

—S. Y. Agnon

Parabola
Volume: 10.1
Wholeness

Portrait of Moses

Haggadah

The whole world was shaken and enthralled by the miracle of the Exodus. The name of Moses was on everyone's lips. Tidings of the great miracle reached also the wise king of Arabistan. The king summoned to him his best painter and bade him go to Moses, to paint his portrait and bring it back to him. When the painter returned the king gathered together all his sages, wise in the science of physiognomics, and asked them to define by the portrait the character of Moses, his qualities, inclinations, habits and the source of his miraculous power.

"King," answered the sages, "this is the portrait of a man cruel, haughty, greedy of gain, possessed by desire for power and by all the vices which exist in the world."

These words roused the king's indignation.

"How can it be possible," he exclaimed, "that a man whose marvelous deeds ring through the whole world should be of such a kind?"

A dispute began between the painter and the sages. The painter affirmed that the portrait of Moses had been painted by him quite accurately, while the sages maintained that Moses' character had been unerringly determined by them according to the portrait.

The wise king of Arabistan decided to verify which of the disputing parties was right, and he himself set off for the camp of Israel.

At the first glance the king became convinced that the face of Moses had been faultlessly portrayed by the painter. On entering the tent of the man of God he knelt down, bowed to the ground and told Moses of the dispute between the artist and the sages.

"At first, until I saw thy face," said the king, "I thought it must be that the artist had painted thy image badly, for my sages are men very much experienced in the science of physiognomics. Now I am convinced that they are quite worthless men and that their wisdom is vain and worthless."

"No," answered Moses, "it is not so; both the painter and the physiognomists are men highly skilled, and both parties are right. Be it known to thee that all the vices of which the sages spoke have indeed been assigned to me by nature and perhaps to an even higher degree than was found by them from my portrait. But I struggled with my vices by long and intense efforts of the will and gradually overcame and suppressed them in myself until all opposed to them became my second nature. And in this lies my greatest pride."

From P. D. Ouspensky, *A New Model of the Universe* (Alfred A. Knopf, 1934).

Parabola
Volume: 8.1
Guilt

Repentance

Rabbi Adin Steinsaltz

Repentance is one of the ultimate spiritual realities at the core of Jewish faith. Its significance goes far beyond the narrow meaning of contrition or regret for sin, and it embraces a number of concepts considered to be fundamental to the very existence of the world.

Certain sages go so far as to include repentance among the entities created before the world itself. The implication of this remarkable statement is that repentance is a universal, primordial phenomenon; in such a context it has two meanings. One is that it is embedded in the root structure of the world; the other, that before man was created, he was given the possibility of changing the course of his life. In this latter sense repentance is the highest expression of man's capacity to choose freely—it is a manifestation of the divine in man. Man can extricate himself from the binding web of his life, from the chain of causality that otherwise compels him to follow a path of no return.

Repentance also comprises the notion that man has a measure of control over his existence in all dimensions, including time. Time flows in one direction; it is impossible to undo or even to alter an action after it has occurred and become an "event," an objective fact. However, even though the past is "fixed," repentance admits of an ascendancy over it, of the possibility of changing its significance in the context of the present and future. This is why repentance has been represented as something created before the world itself. In a world of the inexorable flow of time, in which all objects and events are interconnected in a relationship of cause and effect, repentance is the exception: it is the potential for something else.

The Hebrew word for repentance, *Teshuvah*, has three different though related meanings. First, it denotes "return," a going back to God or to the Jewish faith. Second, it can mean "turning about" or "turning to," adopting another orientation or direction in life. Third, Teshuvah signifies "response."

The root meaning is return to God, or to Judaism, in the inclusive sense of embracing in faith, thought, and deed. On the simplest, most literal level the possibility of return can only exist for someone who was once "there," such as an adult who retains childhood memories or other recollections of Jewish life. But is it not possible for someone to return who was never "there," who has no memories of a Jewish way of life, for whom Judaism is not a personal but a historical or biological heritage, or no more than an epithet that gives him a certain meaningless identity? The answer is unequivocally in the affirmative, for—on the more profound level—repentance as return reaches beyond such personal configurations. It is indeed a return to Judaism, but not to the external framework, not to the religious norms that man seeks to understand or to integrate into, with their clear-cut formulae, directives, actions, rituals; it is a return to one's own paradigm, to the prototype of the Jewish person. Intellectually, this paradigm may be perceived as a historical reality to which one is personally related, but beyond this is the memory of the essential archetype that is a part of the soul structure of the individual Jew. In spite of the vast range of ways in which a Jew can alienate himself from his past and express himself in foreign cultural forms, he nevertheless retains a metaphysically, almost genetically, imprinted image of his Jewishness. To use a metaphor from the world of botany: a change of climate, soil, or other physical conditions can induce marked alterations in the form and the functioning of a plant, and even the adoption of characteristics of other species and genera, but the unique paradigm or prototype persists.

Reattachment to one's prototype may be expressed in many ways, not only in accepting a faith or credo or in fulfilling certain traditional obligations. As he liberates himself from alien influences, the penitent can only gradually straighten himself out; he has to overcome the forms engraved by time and place before he can reach his own image. He must break free of the chains, the limitations, and the restrictions imposed by environment and education. If pursued aimlessly, with no clear goal, this primal search does not transcend the urge to be free; without a vector, it can be spiritually exhausting and may never lead to a genuine discovery of the true self. In this respect, not in vain has the Torah been perceived as a system of knowledge and insights that guide the individual Jew to reach his own pattern of selfhood. The mutual relationship between the individual Jew and Judaism, between the man and his God, depends on the fact that Judaism is not only the Law, the prescribed religious practice, but is a life framework that embraces his entire existence; furthermore, it is ultimately the only framework in which, in his aloneness and in his search, he will be able to find himself. Whereas potentially a man can adapt himself, there exists, whether he acknowledges it or not, a path that is his own, which relates to him, to his family, to his home.

Repentance is a complex process. Sometimes a man's entire life is no more than an ongoing act of repentance on several levels. It has been said that a man's path of spiritual development, whether he has sinned or not, is in a certain sense a path of repentance. It is an endeavor to break away from the past and reach a higher level. However, not withstanding the complexity and the deeply felt difficulties involved, there is a clear simplicity in the elemental point that is the point of the turning.

Remoteness from God is, of course, not a matter of physical distance, but a spiritual problem of relationship. The person who is not going along the right path is not farther away from God but is, rather, a man whose soul is oriented toward and relating with other objects. The starting point of repentance is precisely the fulcrum point upon which a person turns himself about, away from the pursuit of what he craves, and confronts his desire to approach God; this is the moment of conversion, the crucial moment of repentance.

It should be noted that generally this does not occur at a moment of great self-awareness. Though a person may be acutely conscious of the moment of repentance, the knowledge can come later. It is in fact rare for repentance to take the form of a sudden, dramatic conversion, and it generally takes the form of a series of small turnings.

Irrespective of the degree of awareness, several spiritual factors come together in the process of conversion. Severance is an essential factor. The repentant cuts himself off from his past, as though saying: "Everything in my life up to this point is now alien to me; chronologically or historically it may be part of me—but I no longer accept it as such." With a new goal in life, a person assumes a new identity. Aims and aspirations are such major expressions of the personality that renouncing them amounts to a severance of the old self. The moment of turning thus involves not only a change of attitude, but also a metamorphosis. When the process is fully realized, it includes a departure from, a rejection of, and a regret for the past, and an acceptance, a promise of change in the future. The sharper the turning, the more deeply conscious it is, the more prominent will these aspects be—a shaking free of the past, a transfiguration of self, and an eager thrust forward into a new identity.

Repentance also includes the expectance of a response, of a confirmation from God that this is indeed the way, that this is the direction. Nevertheless, the essence of repentance is bound up more with turning than with response. When response is direct and immediate, the process of repentance cannot continue, because it has in a way arrived at its goal; whereas one of its essential components is an increase of tension, the tension of the ongoing experience and of yearning. As long as the act of repentance lasts, the seeking for response continues, and the soul still strives to receive from elsewhere the answer, the pardon.

Response is not always given; and even when it is, it is not the same for every man. Repentance is a gradual process; final response is awarded not to specific isolated acts but to the whole; the various components, the desire to act, the performing of the deed based on anticipation, the yearning, disappointment, and hope, are rewarded, if at all, by partial answers. In other words, a response to turning is given to a man as "something on account," the rest to be paid out later. A person generally hears the longed-for answer not when he puts the question, not when he is struggling, but when he pauses on a summit and looks back on his life.

Jewish thought pays little attention to inner tranquility and peace of mind. The feeling of "behold, I've arrived" could well undermine the capacity to continue, suggesting as it does that the Infinite can be reached in a finite number of steps. In fact, the very concepts of the Divine as infinite implies an activity that is endless, of which one must never grow weary. At every rung of his ascent, the penitent, like any person who follows the way of God, perceives mainly the remoteness. Only in looking back can one obtain some idea of the distance already covered, of the degree of progress. Repentance does not bring a sense of serenity or of completion but stimulates a reaching out in further effort. Indeed, the power and the potential of repentance lie in increased incentive and enhanced capacity to follow the path even farther. The response is often no more than an assurance that one is in fact capable of repenting, and its efficacy lies in the growing awareness, with time, that one is indeed progressing on the right path. In this manner the conditions are created in which repentance is no longer an isolated act but has become a permanent possibility, a constant process of going toward. It is a going that is both the rejection of what was once axiomatic and an acceptance of new goals.

The paths of the penitent and of the man who has merely lost his direction differ only in terms of the aim, not in going itself. The Jewish approach to life considers the man who has stopped going—he who has a feeling of completion, of peace, of a great light from above that has brought him to rest—to be someone who has lost his way. Only he whom the light continues to beckon, for whom the light is as distant as ever, only he can be considered to have received some sort of response. The path a man has taken is revealed to him only in retrospect, in a contemplation of the past that grants confidence in what lies ahead. This awareness is in fact the reward, and it is conditional on the continuation of the return.

The essence of repentance has frequently been found in the poetic lines of the Song of Songs, "The King has brought me to his chambers (1:4)." This verse has been interpreted as meaning that he whose search has reached a certain level feels that he is in the palace of the King. He goes from room to room, from hall to hall, seeking Him out. However, the King's palace is an endless series of worlds, and as a man proceeds in his search from room to room, he holds only the end of the string. It is, nevertheless, a continuous going, a going after God, a going to God, day after day, year after year.

Repentance is not just a psychological phenomenon, a storm within a human teacup, but is a process that can effect real change in the world, in all the worlds. Every human action elicits certain inevitable results that extend beyond their immediate context, passing from one level of existence to another, from one aspect of reality to another. The act of repentance is, in the first place, a severance of the chain, of cause and effect in which one transgression follows inevitably upon another. Beyond this, it is an attempt to nullify and even to alter the past. This can be achieved only when man, subjectively, shatters the order of his own existence. The thrust of repentance is to break through the ordinary limits of the self. Obviously, this cannot take place within the routine of life, but it can be an ongoing activity throughout life. Repentance is thus something that persists; it is an ever-renewed extrication from causality and limitation.

When man senses the wrongness, evil and emptiness in his life, it is not enough that he yearn for God to try to change his way of life. Repentance is more than aspiration and yearning, for it also involves the sense of despair—and, paradoxically, the sin that precedes it—that gives man the possibility of overleaping his past. The desperation of the endeavor to separate himself from the past, to reach heights that the innocent and ordinary man is not even aware of, gives the penitent the power to break the inexorability of his fate, sometimes in a way that involves a total destruction of his past, his goals, and almost all of his personality.

Nevertheless, this level of repentance is only a beginning, for all the penitent's past actions continue to operate: the sins he committed and the injuries he inflicted exist as such in time. Even though the present has been altered, earlier actions and their consequences continue to generate a chain of cause and effect. The significance of the past can be changed only at the higher level of repentance called *Tikkun*.

The first stage in the process of Tikkun is one of equilibration. For every wrong deed in his past, the penitent is required to perform certain acts that surpass what is demanded of an "ordinary" individual, to complement and balance the picture of his life. He must build and create anew and change the order of good and evil in such a way that not only his current life activity acquires new form and direction, but the totality of his life receives a consistently positive value.

The highest level of repentance, however, lies beyond the correction of sinful deeds and the creation of independent, new patterns that counterweigh past sins and injuries; it is reached when the change and the correction penetrate the very essence of the sins once committed and, as the sages say, create the condition in which a man's transgressions become his merits. This level of Tikkun is reached when a person draws from his failings not only the ability to do good but the power to fall again and again and, notwithstanding, to transform more extensive and important segments of life. It is using the knowledge of the sin of the past and transforming it into such an extraordinary thirst for good that it becomes a divine force. The more a man was sunk in evil, the more anxious he becomes for good. This level of being, in which failings no longer exert a negative influence on the penitent, in which they no longer reduce his stature or sap his strength, but serve to raise him, to stimulate his progress—this is the condition of genuine Tikkun.

Thus the complete correction of past evil cannot be brought about merely by acknowledgment of wrong and contrition; indeed, this acknowledgment often leads, in practice, to a loss of incentive, a state of passivity, of depression; furthermore, the very preoccupation with memories of an evil impulse may well revive that impulse's hold on a person. In genuine Tikkun, everything that was once invested in the forces of evil is elevated to receive another meaning within a new way of life; deeds once performed with a negative intention are transformed into a completely new category of activity. To be sure, forces of evil that had parasitically attached themselves to a person are not easily compelled to act in the direction of the good. Spiritual possibilities of which a man who has not sinned can never even gain an awareness have to emerge and become a driving force.

The penitent thus does more than return to his proper place. He performs an act of amendment of cosmic significance; he restores the sparks of holiness which had been captured by the powers of evil. The sparks that he had dragged down and attached to himself are now raised up with him, and a host of forces of evil return and are transformed to forces of good. This is the significance of the statement in the Talmud that in the place where a completely repentant person stands, even the most saintly cannot enter; because the penitent has at his disposal not only the forces of good in his soul and in the world, but also those of evil, which he transforms into essences of holiness.

This essay is reprinted from *The Thirteen Petalled Rose* by Adin Steinsaltz (Basic Books, 1980).

Parabola
Volume: 8.1
Guilt

THE WISDOM OF JEWISH MYSTICS

Rabbi Nachman

Rabbi Nachman's teaching includes: "Through depression and sadness a man can forget who he really is. Therefore it is necessary to be continually in a state of joy, no matter what low level a person may be at ... A man needs to have faith in himself believing that he is beloved in the eyes of God ... Feeling unimportant and distant from God is not humility ... And in speaking of how a person becomes capable of repentance, he said: "The main thing is truthfulness, for everything depends on truth, and one must follow the truth according to the level one is on. As the rabbis teach: 'The seal of God is truth.'" Whenever he fell from the spiritual level he had attained, he did not grow depressed because of this. He merely said that he would begin anew as if he had not yet begun to enter the service of God, and that only now was he beginning for the first time. Sometimes he would have to begin again several times in one day, because even in the course of one day he might fall several times from the intensity of his service of God.

From Unterman, ed., *The Wisdom of the Jewish Mystics* (Sheldon Press, 1976).

Parabola
Volume: 12.3
Forgiveness

NEILAH IN GEHENNA

Isaac Loeb Peretz

The town square ... an ordinary day, neither a market day nor a day of the fair, a day of drowsy small activity. ... Suddenly there is heard, coming from just outside the town, approaching nearer and nearer, a wild impetuous clatter, a splutter and splashing of mud, a racket of furious wheels! In-ter-est-ing, think the merchants, wonder who it is? At their booths, at their storefronts, they peer out, curious.

As the galloping horse, the thundering wagon, turn into and careen through the square, they are recognized! The townsfolk recoil, revulsion and fear and anger upon their faces. The informer of the neighboring town is at it again! Posthaste to the capital! God alone knows on whom he is going to do a job now.

Suddenly a stillness falls upon the marketplace. Reluctantly, with loathing, the townsfolk look around. The wagon has come to a halt. The horse is lazily nuzzling in the mire of the wheel ruts. And the informer, fallen from his seat, lies stretched out on the ground!

Well, even an informer has a soul; they can't just let him lie there, so the townsfolk rush forward to the body, motionless in the mud. Dead—like every other corpse! Finished! The members of the Burial Society make ready to do the last rites for the deceased.

Horse and wagon are sold to pay for the funeral expenses; the informer is duly interred: and those little imps of dispatch, who crop up just there where you won't see them, snatch up his soul and bear it off to the watchers of the gates of Gehenna.

There, at the gates, the informer is detained while the fiend of reception, he who keeps hell's register of admission and discharge, wearily puts the questionnaire to him and as wearily, with his leaking pen, enters the answers: Who, When, How.

The informer—in hell he feels cut down to size—respectfully answers: Born in such and such a place; became a son-in-law in such and such a place; was supported by father-in-law for such and such a number of years; abandoned wife and children; pursued, in such and such places, his chosen profession, until, his time having come, as he was passing with horse and wagon through the marketplace of Ladam—

At the mention of this name the fiend of reception, in the middle of a yawn, pricks up his ears. "How do you say it? Laha—"

"Ladam!"[1]

The fiend goes red in the face, little lights of puzzlement twinkle in his eyes, and he turns to his assistants. "Ever hear of such a town?"

The assistant imps shrug their shoulders. Their tongues stuck between their teeth, they shake their heads. "Never heard of it!"

"*Is* there such a town?"

Now in the records of Gehenna every community has its own file, and these files are all alphabetically arranged, and every letter has its own filing cabinet. So a careful search is made through L—Lublin, Lemberg, Leipzig, they're all there—but no Ladam!

"Still it's there," the informer persists, "a town in Poland."

"Contemporary or historical?'

"Founded twenty years ago. The baron built it up. It boasts, in fact, two fairs a year. Has a synagogue, a house of study, a bathhouse. Also two gentile taverns."

Again the registrar addresses himself to his assistants. "Any of you remember—did we ever get anybody here from Ladam?"

"Never!"

Impatiently they turn to the informer. "Don't they ever die in this Ladam of yours?"

"And why shouldn't they?" he answers Jewish-wise, by returning a question. "Close, congested hovels that stifle you. A bathhouse where you can't catch your breath. The whole town—a morass!"

The informer is now in his element.

"Never die!" he continues. "Why, they have a completely laid out cemetery! It's true that the Burial Society will flay you for the costs of burial before they bring you to eternal rest, but still they do have a cemetery. And not so long ago they had an epidemic too."

The interrogation at an end, due judgment is rendered concerning the informer, and concerning the town of Ladam due investigation is instituted. A town twenty years old, a town with an epidemic in its history—and not one soul landed in Gehenna! This was a matter one couldn't let drop.

The imps of inquiry are sent forth diligently to search the thing out.

They return.

True!

And they report as follows: That in the realm of Poland there is indeed a town called Ladam; that it is still extant; that it boasts its tally of good deeds and admits to a quantum (greater) of misdeeds; that its economy presents the usual occupations and the usual struggle; and that the spirit of evil representing hell's interest in the said place, he too is not unemployed.

Why, then, have there never been any candidates for Gehenna from Ladam?

Because Ladam has a cantor! There lies the explanation! And what a cantor! Himself he's nothing! But his voice! A voice for singing, so sweet, so poignant-sweet, that when it weeps it penetrates right into hearts of iron, through and through; it melts them to wax! He has but to ascend the prayer stand, this cantor, and lift his voice in prayer, and behold, the entire congregation of Ladam is made of one mass of repentance, wholehearted repentance, all its officers and members reduced, as if one person, to single-hearted contrition! With what result? With the result that Up There Ladam's sins are nullified, voided, made of no effect! With the result that for Ladam the gates of paradise—because of this cantor—are forthwith flung apart! When somebody comes before those gates and says he's from Ladam—no further questions asked!

It was easy to see that, with such a cantor in the vicinity, Gehenna would have to operate in Ladam at a loss. Accordingly the matter was taken over by That Certain Party himself! Head of hell, he would deal with the cantor personally.

So he orders that there be brought to him alive from the regions mundane a crowing Calcutta rooster, with a comb of fiery red.

Done.

The Calcutta cock, frightened and bewildered in its new roost, lies motionless on the satanic altar, while he—may his name be blotted out!—circles around and around it, squats down before it, never taking his eye off it, his evil eye upon that bright red crest; winds around it, encircles it, until, the spell having worked, the red crest blanches and pales and grows white as chalk. But suddenly, in the midst of this sorcery, an ominous rumbling is heard from Up There. The Holy One, blessed be He, waxes wrathful! So he—may his name be blotted out!—in alarm desists, but not before he spits out a farewell curse:

"Cockcrow, begone! Begone his singing voice! Until the hour of his death!"

Against whom he really launched this curse, you, of course, have already surmised, and indeed even before the blood returned to the crest of the comb of the Calcutta rooster, the cantor of Ladam was minus his voice. Smitten in the throat. Couldn't bring out a note.

The source and origin of this affliction was known, but known, naturally, only to truly holy Jews, and even of these perhaps not to all. But what could one do? One couldn't, of course, explain it; the cantor just wouldn't understand. It was one of those things. Now, had the cantor himself been a man of good deeds, worth, and piety, one might perhaps have interceded for him, hammered at the gates of heaven, clamored against injustice, but when the cantor was, as all knew, a man of insignificant merit, a trifle in the scales, a nothing, why, then …

So the cantor himself went knocking at the door of the great rabbis, soliciting their help, imploring their intervention before the heavenly throne.

To no avail. It couldn't be done.

At last, winning his way into the court of the *tzaddik* of Apt, he clings to the tzaddik, won't be sundered from him, weeps, begs, and, unless and until he is helped, won't budge a step from the court. It is a most pitiable thing to see. Not being able to suffer the poor cantor's plight any longer, the tzaddik of Apt reluctantly decides to tell the cantor the irrevocable, but not without mixing in it some measure of consolation. "Know, cantor," he says, "that your hoarseness will persist until your death, but know also that when, at the hour of your death, you come to say the Prayer of Repentance, you will say it with a voice so clear, you will sing it with a voice so musical, that it will resound through all the corridors of heaven!"

"And until then?"

"Lost!"

The cantor still refuses to depart. "But, rabbi, why? Rabbi, what for?"

He persists so long that at last the tzaddik tells him the whole story—informer, rooster, and curse.

"If that's the case," the cantor cries out in all his hoarseness, "if that's the case, I—will—have—my—revenge!" And he dashes out.

"Revenge? How and from whom?" the tzaddik calls after him.

But the cantor is gone.

This was on a Tuesday, some say Wednesday; and that Thursday, in the evening, when the fishermen of Apt, out on the river to catch their fish for the Sabbath, drew up their nets, they drew forth the drowned body of the cantor of Ladam!

A suicide! From the little bridge over the river! For the saying of the Prayer of Repentance his singing voice had indeed come back to him, even as the tzaddik of Apt had promised, the learned tzaddik interpreting the words of That Certain Party and stressing them, "*until* the hour of his death"—but not *the* hour of his death.

Yet despite this assurance the cantor—and this was his revenge, as you will soon see—purposely, in that last hour, both on the bridge and in the water, refrained from saying the Prayer of Repentance!

No sooner is the cantor buried, according to the rite of suicides, than the imps are at his soul and to Gehenna he is brought. At the gate the questions are put to him, but he refuses to answer. He is prodded with a pitchfork, stimulated with glowing coals—still he keeps silent, won't answer.

"Take him as is!"

For these questionings in hell are but a matter of form; hell's own agents have all these years lain in wait for the unsuspecting cantor; hell knows in advance the answer to Who, When, What for. The cantor is led to his proper place. A caldron seethes and boils before him.

But here, here the cantor at last permits himself the privilege of his voice. Clear and ringing he sings it forth: "*Yit-ga-da-al* ..."

The *Kaddish* of *Neilah*!

He intones it, he sings it, and singing his voice grows bolder, stronger ... melts away ... revives ... is rapturous ... glorious as in the world aforetime ... no, better ... sweeter ... in the heart, deeper ... from the depths ... clamorous ... resurgent. ...

Hushed are all the boiling caldrons from which up to now there had issued a continual sound of weeping and wailing; hushed, until, after a while, from these same caldrons, an answering hum is heard. The caldron lids are lifted, heads peer out, burned lips murmur accompaniment.

The fiends of calefaction stationed at the caldrons, refuse, of course, to make the responses. Bewildered, abashed, they stand there as if lost, one with his faggots for the fire, another with his steaming ladle, a third with his glowing rake. Faces twisted ... mouths agape ...tongues lolling ... eyes bulging from the sockets. ... Some fall into epileptic fits and roll, convulsed and thrashing, on the ground.

But the cantor continues with his *Neilah*.

The cantor continues, and the fires under the caldrons diminish and fade and go out. The dead begin to crawl forth from their caldrons.

The cantor sings on, and the congregation of hell in undertone accompanies him, prays with him; and passage by passage, as the prayer is rendered, hurt bodies are healed, become whole, torn flesh unites, skin is renewed, the condemned dead grow pure.

Yes, when the cantor comes to the verse where he cries out, "Who quickeneth the dead," and hell's poor souls respond, "Amen, amen," it is as if a resurrection, there and then, is taking place!

For such a clamor arises at this Amen that the heavens above are opened, and the repentance of the wicked reaches to the heaven of heavens, to the seventh heaven, and comes before The Throne itself! And, it being a moment of grace and favor, the sinners, now saints, suddenly grow wings! One after the other out of Gehenna they fly ... to the very gates of paradise.

Thereafter there remained in Gehenna only the fiends, rolling in their convulsions, and the cantor, stock still at his stand. He did not leave. True, here in hell he had brought, as he had brought on earth, his congregation to repentance, but he himself had not known a true repentance. That unsaid Prayer of Repentance … that matter of suicide. …

In the course of time Gehenna was filled again, and although additional suburbs were built, it still remains crowded.

Notes:

1 The original Hebrew has *LHDM*, which are the initial letters of the phrase "*lo hayu devarim me-olam*," meaning "these things never were," "a pure fiction."

Parabola
Volume: 16.3
Craft

Yom Kippur Prayer

Like the clay in the hand of the potter
Who thickens or thins it at his will,
So are we in Thy hand, gracious God,
Forgive our sin, Thy covenant fulfill.

Like a stone in the hand of the mason
Who preserves or breaks it at his will,
So we are in Thy hand, Lord of life,
Forgive our sin, Thy covenant fulfill.

Like iron in the hand of the craftsman
Who forges or cools it at his will,
We are in Thy hand, our Keeper,
Forgive our sin, Thy covenant fulfill.

Like the wheel in the hand of the seaman
Who directs or holds it at his will
So are we in Thy hand, loving God,
Forgive our sin, Thy covenant fulfill.

Like the glass in the hand of the blower
Who dissolves or shapes it at his will,
So are we in Thy hand, God of grace,
Forgive our sin, Thy covenant fulfill.

Like the cloth in the hand of the tailor
Who smoothens or drapes it at his will,

So are we in Thy hand, righteous God,
Forgive our sin, Thy covenant fulfill.

Like silver in the hand of the smelter
Who refines or blends it at his will,
So are we in Thy hand, our Healer,
Forgive our sin, Thy covenant fulfill.

Authorship unknown, translated by Ben Zion Bosker, *The High Holyday Prayer Book: Rosh Hashanah and Yom Kippur* (New York: Hebrew Publishing Co., 1959), p. 285.

•

CHAPTER SEVEN

REPAIRING THE WORLD

And out of the ground the Lord God formed every
beast of the field, and every fowl of the air;
and brought them unto Adam to see
what he would call them:
and whatsoever Adam called every living creature,
that was the name thereof.
And Adam gave names to all cattle,
and to the fowl of the air, and to every beast of the field.[1]

—Genesis 2:19-20

The Works of Creation

Selected Passages

Psalms 90:17

And let the beauty of the Lord our God be upon us: and establish thou the work of our hands upon us; yea, the work of our hands establish thou it.

Job 12:7-10

But ask now the beasts, and they shall teach thee; and the fowls of the air, and they shall tell thee:

Or speak to the earth, and it shall teach thee: and the fishes of the sea shall declare unto thee.

Who knoweth not in all these that the hand of the LORD hath wrought this?

In whose hand is the soul of every living thing, and the breath of all mankind.

Isaiah 2:4

And they shall beat their swords into plowshares, and their spears into pruning hooks: nation shall not lift up sword against nation, neither shall they learn war any more.

Isaiah 11:6

The wolf also shall dwell with the lamb, and the leopard shall lie down with the kid; and the calf and the young lion and the fatling together; and a little child shall lead them.

Abraham Heschel

The road to the sacred leads through the secular.[1]

Note:

1 Abraham Heschel, *I Asked for Wonder*, ed. Samuel H. Dresner (New York: Crossroad Publishing Co., 1983).

Parabola
Volume: 21.1
Prophets and
Prophecy

What Manner of Man Is the Prophet?

Abraham J. Heschel

What manner of man is the prophet? A student of philosophy who turns from the discourses of the great metaphysicians to the orations of the prophets may feel as if he were going from the realm of the sublime to an area of trivialities. Instead of dealing with the timeless issues of being and becoming, of matter and form, of definitions and demonstrations, he is thrown into orations about widows and orphans, about the corruption of judges and affairs of the market place. Instead of showing us a way through the elegant mansions of the mind, the prophets take us to the slums. The world is a proud place, full of beauty, but the prophets are scandalized, and rave as if the whole world were a slum. They make much ado about paltry things, lavishing excessive language upon trifling subjects. What if somewhere in ancient Palestine poor people have not been treated properly by the rich? ... Why such immoderate excitement? Why such intense indignation?

The things that horrified the prophets are even now daily occurrences all over the world. There is no society to which Amos' words would not apply:

> *Hear this, you who trample upon the needy,*
> *And bring the poor of the land to an end,*

Saying: When will the new moon be over
That we may sell grain?
And the Sabbath
That we may offer wheat for sale
That we may make the ephah small and the shekel great,
And deal deceitfully with false balances,
That we may buy the poor for silver
And the needy for a pair of sandals,
And sell the refuse of the wheat?
                                        —Amos 8:4-6

Indeed, the sort of crimes and even the amount of delinquency that fill the prophets of Israel with dismay do not go beyond that which we regard as normal, as typical ingredients of social dynamics. To us a single act of injustice—cheating in business, exploitation of the poor—is slight; to the prophets, a disaster. To us injustice is injurious to the welfare of the people; to the prophets it is a deathblow to existence: to us, an episode; to them, a catastrophe, a threat to the world. ...

The niggardliness of our moral comprehension, the incapacity to sense the depth of misery caused by our own failures, is a fact which no subterfuge can elude. Our eyes are witness to the callousness and cruelty of man, but our hearts try to obliterate the memories, to calm the nerves, and to silence our conscience.

The prophet is a man who feels fiercely. God has thrust a burden upon his soul, and he is bowed and stunned at man's fierce greed. Frightful is the agony of man; no human voice can convey its full terror. Prophecy is the voice that God has lent to the silent agony, a voice to the plundered poor, to the profaned riches of the world. It is a form of living, a crossing point of God and man. God is raging in the prophet's words ...

To a person endowed with prophetic sight, everyone else appears blind; to a person whose ear perceives God's voice, everyone else appears deaf. No one is just; no knowing is strong enough, no trust complete enough. The prophet hates the approximate, he shuns the middle of the road. Man must live on the summit to avoid the abyss. There is nothing to hold to except God. Carried away by the challenge, the demand to straighten out man's ways, the prophet is strange, one-sided, an unbearable extremist.

Others may suffer from the terror of cosmic aloneness; the prophet is overwhelmed by the grandeur of divine presence. He is incapable of isolating the world. There is an interaction between man and God which to disregard is an act of insolence. Isolation is a fairy tale.

Where an idea is the father of faith, faith must conform to the idea of the given system. In the Bible the realness of God came first, and the task was how to live in a way compatible with His presence. Man's coexistence with God determines the course of history.

The prophet disdains those for whom God's presence is comfort and security; to him it is a challenge, an incessant demand. God is compassion, not compromise; justice, though not inclemency. The prophet's predictions can always be proven wrong by a change in man's conduct, but never the certainty that God is full of compassion.

The prophet's word is a scream in the night. While the world is at ease and asleep, the prophet feels the blast from heaven ...

The prophet is a watchman, a servant, a messenger of God, "an assayer and tester" of the people's ways (Jeremiah 6:27) ... The prophet's eye is directed to the contemporary scene; the society and its conduct are the main theme of his speeches. Yet his ear is inclined to God. He is a person struck by the glory and presence of God, overpowered by the hand of God. Yet his true greatness is his ability to hold God and man in a single thought.

It is common to characterize the prophet as a messenger of God, thus to differentiate him from the tellers of fortune, givers of oracles, seers and ecstatics. Such a characterization expresses only one aspect of his consciousness. The prophet claims to be far more than a messenger. He is a person who stands in the presence of God, who stands "in the council of the Lord" (Jeremiah 23:18), who is a participant, as it were, in the council of God, not a bearer of dispatches whose function is limited to being sent on errands. He is a counselor as well as a messenger. ... As a witness the prophet is more than a messenger. As a messenger, his task is to deliver the word; as a witness, he must bear testimony that the word is divine.

The words the prophet utters are not offered as souvenirs. His speech to the people is not a reminiscence, a report, hearsay. The prophet not only conveys; he reveals. He almost does unto others what God does unto him. In speaking the prophet reveals God. This is the marvel of a prophet's work: in his words *the invisible God becomes audible*. He does not prove or argue. The thought he has to convey is more than language can contain. Divine power bursts in the words. The authority of the prophet is in the Presence his words reveal.

From Abraham J. Heschel, *The Prophets: An Introduction*, Vol. I (NY: HarperCollins, 1962). Reprinted by permission of the publisher.

Parabola
Volume: 23.1
Millenium

THE AGE OF TIKKUN

Rabbi Eliezer Shore

There is a word that is repeated throughout history. It is spoken in times of peace, when society builds hopefully for the future; it captures the best of our dreams and aspirations. Judaism speaks of it often, for it is at the heart of all her laws and customs, and finds expression in nearly every aspect of the religious life. It is the goal of both the legalist and the mystic, of both leaders and the simple man seeking quietude. The word is *tikkun*.

Tikkun has several connotations: correction, restoration, reform. Most often, it is used in the phrase *tikkun haolam*, usually translated as "repairing the world." It conveys a sense of putting things right, of promoting harmony, peace, and integration among the various elements of creation. Tikkun is understood to be the goal of all the Torah's commandments: "The *mitzvot* were only given to purify the world," says the Midrash.[1] It manifests itself on all levels of society, whether one works in the wide area of the public good or merely tries to refine one's own life: both contribute to the same goal of tikkun haolam. Ultimately, tikkun means imbuing the creation with such a profound sense of life and spirit that the entire world becomes a vessel for revelation. In that sense, tikkun also means "healing," for it means returning to the world its soul.

This was humanity's role from the very beginning. It was for this reason that God declared: "Let us make

humankind in Our image, after Our likeness: and let them have dominion over the fish of the sea, and over the birds of the air, and over the
cattle, and over all the earth. ..." (Genesis 1:26). This dominion is not a
form of control or manipulation; rather it is a type of stewardship, leading all the parts to a greater whole. The word "dominion" in this verse,
vayerdu, is related to the word "to go down" just as a greater person must
descend to see to the needs of a lower one, for tikkun is always concerned
with raising up that which is fallen.

According to the Kabbalah, when God first formed the universe, He
left it incomplete, one step away from Divinity. Adam was supposed to
close the circle and finish the tikkun. But when he sinned in the Garden, rather than uplifting the world, he plunged it further into darkness,
making the process of repair that much harder. There is a Kabbalistic
teaching that says that as a direct result of Adam's sin, the Children of
Israel, many centuries later, would be forced to descend into Egypt to
experience bondage and deliverance; for there is a direct relationship
between the act of tikkun and the movement from slavery to freedom.

It has been noted that the Torah, as a book of law, never speaks in terms
of rights; all its laws are phrased in the language of responsibilities—to
one's family, one's community, or to God. Though the law is preemi-
nently concerned with the welfare of the poor and the underprivileged, it
nonetheless speaks only of our obligations. However, there is at least one
area in which the law does allude to human rights: in the treatment of
slaves and indentured servants. Even in ancient times, when slavery was
common, the Torah protected their welfare. Of the rights of a slave, the
verse states, "It shall be good for him with you" (Deuteronomy 15:16).
According to the Talmud, this means that a slave must be fed and clothed
well, he must not be overworked, nor embarrassed or belittled in any way,
and if his master abuses him physically, he is allowed to go free.[2]

The Torah is making a subtle point: that the difference between rights
and responsibilities is the difference between slavery and freedom. For a
free man is not defined by the rights he deserves, but by the responsibilities that he bears. Freedom is not an end unto itself, to be the focus of
legislation; it is a means to something greater, to bring the world to perfection. Only a person under the subjugation of another needs rights, but

since the Torah views man as intrinsically free, it makes him responsible for others and for the entire world.

In the mystical teachings of Hasidism, the concepts of slavery and freedom are understood on a deeper level—as states of consciousness. "We were slaves to Pharaoh in Egypt, and the Lord our God took us out from there," begins the Passover Hagadah. The essence of slavery is not physical subjugation or restricted movement, but a limited state of consciousness in which the mind cannot recognize the truth of God in the present moment but sees only a facade of illusions and fantasies projected by the ego and the lower inclinations. Slavery means living in a world of dreams, whereas true freedom means relating to the world as it exists before one now, as an emanation from God, with all its potential for becoming a vessel for holiness. The First Commandment states, "I am the Lord Your God who took you out of Egypt ..." (Exodus 20:2). That is, the deliverance from bondage is precisely that which leads us to a perception of the "Lord our God." One who attains this state of consciousness is free, even when he is physically restrained, for he is at every moment attached to the Divine. In contrast, even a person with autonomy of movement is enslaved so long as he cannot liberate himself from the influence of his fantasies and lower self.

Thus, the act of tikkun is not merely an act of repairing the world but of repairing the consciousness, until we can see clearly what needs to be done in this world. It means freeing ourselves from personal interests and biases in order to serve the needs of the present moment. For it is in *this* moment, with all its problems and deficiencies, that God reveals himself to us. Freedom means giving to others even when the deed is unfulfilling, or putting aside one's own interests for the sake of a greater good. In a word, it means the willingness to sacrifice for the highest vision of goodness and truth. This is the process of both individual and universal redemption. Hasidism teaches that when all the illusions of the world have finally been exhausted, history will have reached its end, the world will reach its tikkun.

Seen in this light, the concepts of slavery and freedom apply to our generation as well. Never in history have these two opposites been stronger: the unbridled reign of the imagination fostered by our media culture versus the need for the most sober, realistic world view in the face of our great power for destruction; our potential to bring the world to perfection versus our total ability to annihilate it. We have finally fulfilled the verse, "You have made [man] a little less than the angels. ... You have given him dominion over the works of Your hands; You have put all things under his feet: all sheep and oxen, the beasts of the field; the birds of the sky, and the fish of the sea" (Psalms 8:6–9). We must remember, with everything that we do, that this means stewardship over the earth, with the goal of bringing it to perfection. Thus, even while we examine other traditions for alternative paradigms of society—Native American, Aborigine, earth religions—we must realize that humankind, having mastered so much of this planet, will never return to those models. And since we will never relinquish our control, we have no choice but to learn to use it properly.

The question now is how to become free, how to take responsibility for all our actions. For we can no longer afford to be slaves to our illusions, ignoring the repercussions of our acts. God created Adam and placed him in the Garden "to serve it and to protect it" (Genesis 2:15). The Kabbalah teaches that Adam was supposed to repair the world on the very first day of his creation. Yet he failed to take responsibility for the earth, insisting instead on his right to eat from every tree in the Garden. But even though he fell, the job of tikkun remains the same, only now it has to be performed by countless individuals over thousands of years, for the soul of Adam was divided and spread out over time.

That means that every human being, on whatever level of society, has something to fix, something to heal, some way in which to use the gift of his or her life for a higher purpose, correctly, responsibly. The Midrash says that while Adam still lay silent on the ground, God showed him all the generations that would emerge from him. Some were derived from his head, some from his heart, some from his feet.[3] Each person has his or her place and role; together they constitute the body of Adam. Likewise, when the Torah speaks of responsibilities, it is not just addressing those in power. The underprivileged also have obligations, and according to Jewish law, even the beggar on the street must give charity to those worse off than him.[4] By doing this, he too contributes to the repair of the world, within his own limited sphere of influence.

Now we stand on the threshold of the new millennium. So many ages have already passed over us, from the Classical Age to the Age of Technology, from the Romantic period to the post-modern age. Each one has left its mark upon the world; some have done it harm. What age will we now be facing?

We must enter the Age of Tikkun, of Healing—for the damage we have done to ourselves and the world over the past centuries, and because the earth still waits to fulfill its purpose. We exist in this world in order to fix and uplift, and we have a responsibility to all of creation. The Midrash says that when God created Adam, He took him around the Garden of Eden and showed him all the trees. "Do you see My handiwork, how beautiful and choice they are? Be careful not to ruin and destroy My world, for if you do, there is no one to repair it after you."[5] This command still applies to us. We must not despair in the face of the challenge, but only see our great potential for healing. May God help us finally fulfill what we are meant to do on this earth.

Notes:

1   Midrash Rabbah, Genesis 44:1.

2   Talmud Kiddushin 20a. See Exodus 21:26-27.

3   Midrash Rabbah, Exodus 40:3.

4   Code of Jewish Law, Yoreh Deah 248:1.

5   Midrash Rabbah, Ecclesiastes 7:13.

Parabola
Volume: 28.3
Chaos and Order

Souls of Fire

Abraham Isaac Kook

The conventional pattern of living, based on propriety, on the requisites of good character and conformity to law—this corresponds to the way of the world of order. Every rebellion against this, whether inspired by levity or by the stirring of a higher spirit, reflects the world of chaos. But there is a vast difference in the particular expressions of the world of chaos, whether they incline to the right or the left [positive or negative in motivation]. The great idealists seek an order so noble, so firm and pure, beyond what may be found in the world of reality, and thus they destroy what has been fashioned in conformity to the norms of the world. The best among them also know how to rebuild the world that has thus been destroyed, but those of lesser stature, who have been touched only slightly by the inclination to idealism—they are only destroyers, and they are rooted in the realm of chaos, on its lowest level.

The souls inspired by the realm of chaos are greater than the souls whose affinity is with the established order. They are very great; they seek too much from existence, what is beyond their own faculties to assimilate. They seek a very great light. They cannot bear what is limited, whatever is confined within a prescribed measure. They descended from their divine abode in accordance with the nature of existence to generate new life; they soared on high like a flame and were thrust down. Their endless striving knows no bounds; they robe themselves in various forms, aspiring constantly to what is beyond the measure of the possible. They aspire and they fall, realizing that they are confined in rules, in limiting conditions that forbid expansion toward the unlimited horizons, and they fall in sorrow, in despair, in anger, and anger leads to—wickedness, defiance, destruction, and every other evil. Their unrest does not cease—they are represented by the impudent in our generation, wicked men who are dedicated to high principles, those who transgress conventional norms defiantly rather than because of some lust. Their souls are of very high stature; they are illumined by the light that shines from the realm of chaos. They chose destruction and they are engaged in destroying, the world is undermined by them, and they with it. But the essence of their aspiration is a dimension of holiness, that which in souls content with measured progress would yield the vigor of life.

The souls inspired by a destructive zeal reveal themselves especially at the end of days, before the great cataclysm that precedes the emergence of a new and more wondrous level of existence, when the old boundaries expand, just prior to the birth of a norm above the existing norms. In times of redemption insolence is on the increase. A fierce storm rages, more breaches appear, acts of insolence mount continually because they can find no satisfaction in the beneficence offered by the limited light. It does not satisfy all their yearnings, nor does it unravel for them the mystery of existence. They rebel against everything, including also the dimension of the good that could lead them to a great peace and help them rise to great heights. They rebel and they are indignant, they break and they discard; they seek their nourishment in alien pastures, embracing alien ideals and desecrating everything hallowed, but without finding peace.

These passionate souls reveal their strength so that no fence can hold them back; and the weaklings of the established order, who are guided by balance and propriety, are too terrified to tolerate them. Their mood is expressed in Isaiah (33:14): "Who among us can dwell with the devouring fire? Who among us can dwell with those who destroy the world?" But in truth there is no need to be terrified. Only sinners, those weak in spirit and hypocrites, are frightened and seized by terror. Truly heroic spirits know that this force is one of the phenomena needed for the perfection of the world, for strengthening the power of the nation, of man, and of the world. Initially this force represents the realm of the chaotic, but in the end it will be taken from the wicked and turned over to the hands of the righteous who will show the truth about perfection and construction, in a great resoluteness, inspired by clear perception and a steady and undimmed sense of the practical.

These storms will bring fructifying rain, these dark clouds will pave the way for great light, as the prophet envisioned it: "And the eyes of the blind shall see out of obscurity and out of darkness" (Isaiah 29:18).

Excerpts from Abraham Isaac Kook, *The Lights of Penitence, The Moral Principles, Lights of Holiness, Essays, Letters, and Poems,* translation and introduction by Ben Zion Bokser, from *The Classics of Western Spirituality.* Copyright © 1978 by Ben Zion Bokser, Paulist Press, Inc., New York/Mahwah, NJ.

Parabola
Volume: 28.1
Compassion

Sweetening the Judgments: The Kabbalah of Compassion

Estelle Frankel

Reb David of Lelov and a group of *hasidim* were on their way to Lublin to spend the Sabbath with their rebbe, the Seer of Lublin. After encountering obstacles on the way, they arrived just as the sun was about to set Friday afternoon. Fearing they would be late for Sabbath prayers, the group of hasidim hastily abandoned their horse and carriage and ran off to the synagogue to be with the rebbe—everyone, that is, except Reb David. When the Seer realized that Reb David was missing, he sent the others to look for him. After searching far and wide they found him in the livery with the horses. When they asked him what he was doing there he responded that all the others had run off without thinking to feed and water the horses and so he had stayed behind to do just that.

Reb David was a hasid in the truest sense of the word, a lover of the divine; his love for God was expressed through his deep compassion for all living things. Observing the *mitzvah* of *tza'ar ba'alei chaim*, the commandment to prevent the suffering of animals, was much more important to him than seeking spiritual upliftment in the synagogue. Reb David understood that it is in the expression of compassion—the love and care we extend to all living things—that we find the divine.

Jewish mysticism teaches that we come close to God by *resembling* God, in the sense of being compassionate. It is through compassion that we fulfill the mitzvah (Biblical injunction) to walk in God's ways:

> *"Walking in all His ways" (Deut. 11:22). What are the ways of the Holy One? "A God compassionate and gracious, slow to anger, abounding in kindness and faithfulness, extending kindness to the thousandth generation, forgiving iniquity, transgression and sin ..."* *(Ex. 34:6). This means that just as God is gracious and compassionate, you too must be gracious and compassionate. ... Just as God gives freely to all, you too must give freely to all. Just as God is loving, you too must be loving.[1]*

In his ethical-mystical treatise, *The Palm Tree of Deborah*, sixteenth-century Rabbi Moshe Cordovero expands on the mystical dimensions of compassion. He suggests that when we act with compassion we have the power actually to open up the flow of divine compassion in the universe, reversing the usual "as above, so below," to "as below, so above." God needs our compassion in order to fully manifest divine compassion.

> *Just as you conduct yourself below, so are you worthy of opening the corresponding sublime quality above. Exactly as you behave, so it emanates from above. You cause that quality to shine in the world.[2]*

According to Cordovero, compassion involves desiring the well-being of all fellow creatures.

> *Let your compassion extend to all creatures, neither despising nor destroying any of them. For Wisdom spreads over all created things: mineral, vegetable, animal, and human. Each was created in Wisdom. Do not uproot anything that grows, unless it is necessary. ...[3]*

And through compassion we fulfill the commandment to love our neighbor as ourselves:

> *Do good to whomever needs your goodness. ... You should desire the well-being of your fellow creature, eyeing his good fortune*

benevolently. Let his honor be as precious to you as your own, for you and your fellow are one and the same. That is why we are commanded: "Love your neighbor as yourself."[4]

Interestingly, the Hebrew word for compassion, *rachamim*, comes from the same three-letter root as the word *rechem*, womb, suggesting that compassion makes us womb-like, nurturing of life. With compassion we enable all things to grow into their most beautiful and complete form, and with compassion we learn the wisdom of the womb—the ability to be flexible, to know when to expand and when to contract, when to extend and give of ourselves and when to hold back and restrain from giving.

In the Kabbalah's scheme of divine unfolding through the *sefirot*, or tree of life, rachamim is identified with the divine attribute known as *tiferet*, beauty. The perfect balance point between *chesed* (loving kindness) and *gevurah* (the limit-setting energy of discernment), rachamim is situated at the heart center on the tree of life, for to embody compassion is to have heart.

In order to become a conduit for the flow of divine compassion, many Jewish mystics made compassionate awareness the central focus of their spiritual healing practice. Among the Hasidic masters, Reb Levi Yitzhak of Berditchov stands out as one who truly perfected this practice. Levi Yitzhak was a legendary master of the "good eye," one who could bestow blessing by seeing and nurturing the good in others. A classic tale of the Berditchover Rebbe describes a conversation he had with a certain Jew whom he encountered eating in public on Tisha B'av, a ritual fast day commemorating the destruction of the Holy Temple in Jerusalem. Levi Yitzchak said to the man, "Surely you have forgotten that it is Tisha B'av?" "No," replied the man brazenly, "I know it is." "Then surely you do not realize that we are commanded to fast on Tisha B'av?" "No, I know we are supposed to fast," said the man. Once again giving the man the benefit of the doubt, Lev Yitzchak said to him: "Perhaps you are sick and the fast would endanger your health." "No, Rabbi," answered the man. "I am quite healthy, thank you. May there be many in Israel as well as I am." At that moment Levi Yitzchak looked up to heaven and said: "Master of the Universe, look down from heaven and see who is like your people Israel, a holy nation. A Jew would rather declare himself a sinner than permit a false word to escape his lips!"[5]

This practice of selectively focusing on the good that exists in each person was further developed by Rebbe Nachman of Breslov, the great-grandson of the Ba'al Shem Tov. He suggested that we must always "tip the scales of judgment towards the side of compassion" and give people the benefit of the doubt.[6]

> *And you should know that one must judge every person in such a way as to tip the scale of judgment to merit; even someone who is evil. One must search and find some small aspect of goodness in him and judge him favorably* (lekaf zechut). *Through this you tip his scale towards the good and enable him to repent and spiritually heal. This is what is meant in the passage (Ps. 37:10), "In just a bit there will be no evil one and when you glance at the place where the evil one* (rasha) *stood, he will no longer be there." This passage teaches one to tip the scale of judgment in the direction of merit. ... Even if you see he is evil you must search to find some goodness—some area where he is not evil. ... And one must also find this in oneself. ...*[7]

The Hebrew expression Rebbe Nachman uses to signify the tipping of the scales towards the side of merit (*zechut*) suggests pureness (*zach*). To tip the scales towards *zechut* is to intentionally focus on that which is most pure in each person—to see their highest and holiest potential, their essential divine being.

Rebbe Nachman's teaching is actually a powerful spiritual healing technique, for by seeing the goodness and pureness in others, even when they are unable to see it in themselves, we open up the space for them to become who they are truly meant to be. Our compassion has the power to heal and lift them up. The same is true for ourselves. When we practice self-compassion and focus on the good in ourselves, we are more able to help ourselves overcome our personal difficulties and limitations.

Unfortunately, though, many of us spend a great deal more time sitting in harsh judgment than practicing compassion. We ruminate over our own imperfections and are all too ready to criticize our friends, family, and associates whenever they fall short of our expectations. And though our intentions may be good, when we judge and find fault with ourselves and others, we often end up adding to the problems we think we are trying to remedy.

It is not always so easy to retrain ourselves to be compassionate when we have grown up in excessively critical or judgmental families, yet with mindfulness and practice we can learn to catch ourselves when we get stuck in our "judging" minds and we can lovingly redirect ourselves to focus on the good. Each day of our lives we are given many opportunities to view things either from the perspective of judgment (*din*) or compassion (rachamim). And when we view reality from the perspective of din, our vision may be objectively correct from an absolute perspective, but we are often missing the point of it all, which is that all of life needs healing and fixing and we are part of the process. When we see life through the lens of rachamim, with eyes filled with love and compassion, we become healers and have the ability to shape reality in a positive way.

In Jewish folklore, we find that many of the great sages and prophets also had to work on themselves to overcome judgmental and critical tendencies before they could fully come into their spiritual powers. Reb Zusia of Hanipol, for instance, who was famous for his ability to spiritually heal even the most wicked of individuals, didn't start out that way. As the following tale suggests, he gained these powers only after realizing how destructive his judgments could be.

One day Reb Zusia happened to walk into the house of study of his teacher, the Maggid of Mezerich, when he saw a man trying to convince the Maggid to join in a business venture with him. Being gifted with clairvoyant powers, Zusia saw that this man had a long history of getting involved in dishonest dealings and business scams. Without hesitating, Reb Zusia blurted out his perception to the Maggid, causing the man to leave in total embarrassment. Reb Zusia immediately regretted what he had done. He realized that by criticizing the man and pointing out his faults he had shamed him, and in doing so had failed to open the gates of healing and repentance for him.

Now the Maggid, wise teacher that he was, understood how Zusia's psychic powers were getting in the way of his work as a soul-healer, and so he blessed him that from that day on he would be able to see only the *good* in others. And, indeed, from that day on, Reb Zusia became blind to the evil in others. Even if someone sinned right in front of his eyes, he only saw the good in that person and in his actions, and anything bad he saw in others, he experienced as though it was his own wrong-doing.[8]

In the rabbinic imagination, it is not just *we* who must struggle to overcome our own judgmental tendencies; even God is portrayed as struggling to allow divine compassion to overcome divine judgment:

> *What does God pray? R. Zutra b. Tobi said in the name of Rav: May it be My will that My mercy should suppress My anger, and that My attribute of mercy should dominate all My other attributes, so that I may conduct Myself with My children with mercy, and that I should deal with them, not according to the strict letter of the law (but do for them more than they have rightfully earned).*[9]

Perhaps it's a bit of a projection on our part to imagine that God struggles with his own attributes as we do. But according to Jewish legend, God's struggle to overcome the attribute of judgment (*midat ha'din*) goes all the way back to the story of creation, where the unfolding of creation is described as a dynamic dance between the divine qualities of judgment and compassion, din and rachamim.

"In the beginning Elohim created the heavens and the earth" (Gen. 1:1). Creation is initiated by Elohim, the name associated with din, divine judgment and limits. Indeed, as the Kabbalah teaches, creation began with the Ein Sof (Infinite, Limitless One) withdrawing its light in order to make room for a finite, boundaried world to exist. Though creation is initiated by Elohim, when we look further into the text of Genesis, we find that another name—YHVH—is added. This name, known as the holy name of Being (*shem havayah*), represents that aspect of the divine that is beyond time and space. A composite of the Hebrew words for "was" (*hayah*), "is" (*hoveh*), and "will be" (*yihiyeh*), YHVH represents God's infinite, loving nature.

"This is the story of the creation of heaven and earth on the day that YHVH-Elohim created earth and heaven" (Gen. 2:4). Commenting on the name change, the midrash suggests:

At first God thought to create the world through the quality of din (truth/judgment), but realizing that the world could not endure at this level, God added on the quality of rachamim (compassion).[10]

This midrash can be a bit confusing if taken too literally. It's not that God had a change of mind or heart, but rather that the process of creation involved a blend or marriage of the energies of YHVH and Elohim—rachamim and din, compassion and judgment (love and limits). These two names for the divine actually coexist and balance one another as complementary, yin-yang aspects of reality that are interdependent and inseparable.

If we look at the dynamic relationship between Elohim and YHVH from the perspective of modern-day physics, we might say that while Elohim continually creates form and structure, YHVH is characterized by the absolute freedom and chaos of subatomic particles, which seemingly obey no steadfast rules. While Elohim operates according to the linear, deterministic forces of nature, YHVH exists at a level of reality where causality no longer operates, where emptiness predominates and particles of matter are transformed into energy or pure consciousness. When we open ourselves to YHVH, then we can transcend the laws and limits (judgments) of nature.

At any given moment we have the power to shift the figure-ground relationship between these two aspects of the divine. In Kabbalistic parlance, we have the ability to "sweeten the judgments." By opening our hearts to the infinite love and compassion of YHVH (infinite beingness), Elohim steps aside, as it were, making room for unpredictable and miraculous things to occur; for the limits embedded in creation by Elohim exist only as a gateway through which the boundless love and compassion of the creator can be revealed. The responsibility for opening that gate rests on us.

This is essentially what Jewish spiritual healing is all about—moving all creation from a state of separation to interconnectedness, from multiplicity to unity, and from finite to infinite. Sweetening the judgments—*hamtakat ha'dinim*—is something in which all of us can participate, in our own special way. We just have to allow our hearts to break open so that we can see the divine in all things and experience our essential unity with all being.

Notes:

1   *Sifre* Deut. 49.

2   Rabbi Moshe Cordovero, *Tomer Devorah*, translated by D. Matt in *The Essential Kabbalah* (San Francisco: Harper San Francisco, 1995), pp. 83–88.

3   *Ibid.*

4   *Ibid.*

5   S. Dresner, *The World of a Hasidic Master: Levi Yitzhak of Berditche* (New York: Shapolsky Publishers, Inc., 1986), p. 64.

6   The basis of this teaching is a saying from the Mishnah (*Pirkay Avot* 1:6): "One should judge every person meritoriously."

7   *Likutay Maharan* #282. Translation by the author.

8   Martin Buber, *Tales of the Hasidim: Early Masters* (New York: Schocken Books, 1947), p. 237.

9   *Berachot* 7a, translated by A. Y. Finkel in *Ein Yaacov: The Ethical and Inspirational Teachings of the Talmud* (New Jersey: Jason Aronson, Inc., 1999), p. 12.

10 *Bereishit Raba* 12:15. Translation by the author.

Adapted from the author's book *Sacred Therapy: Jewish Spiritual Teachings on Emotional Healing and Inner Wholeness*, Shambhala Publications © 2003.

•

CHAPTER EIGHT

HASIDIC AND RABBINIC TALES, PARABLES AND SAYINGS

*When the great Rabbi Israel Ba'al Shem-Tov saw
misfortune threatening the Jews it was his custom to go
into a certain part of the forest to meditate.
There he would light a fire, say a special prayer,
and the miracle would be accomplished and the misfortune averted.
Later, when his disciple, the celebrated Maggid of Mezritch,
had occasion, for the same reason, to intercede with heaven,
he would go to the same place in the forest and say:
"Master of the Universe, listen! I do not know how to light the fire,
but I am still able to say the prayer," and again the miracle
would be accomplished. Still later, Rabbi Moshe-Leib of Sasov,
in order to save his people once more, would go into the forest and say:
"I do not know how to light the fire, I do not know the prayer,
but I know the place and this must be sufficient." It was
sufficient and the miracle was accomplished. Then it fell to
Rabbi Israel of Rizhyn to overcome misfortune. Sitting in
his armchair, his head in his hands, he spoke to God:
"I am unable to light the fire and I do not know the prayer;
I cannot even find the place in the forest. All I can do is tell
the story, and this must be sufficient." And it was sufficient.
God made man because he loves stories.*[1]

—Elie Wiesel

Words from the Wise

Selected Passages

Yiddish proverb

When the thief is needed, he's taken off the gallows.

Learning

This is very important to consider when serving God. Most people are distressed by past events, especially during prayer. When a person recites his prayers, his thoughts are constantly disturbed by memories of the past. He may think about his business or household affairs, worrying whether he did something wrong or neglected something important. While attempting to serve God through prayer or study, he might become troubled by his many sins and shortcomings.

The best advice for this is simply to forget. As soon as an event is over with, forget it completely and never think about it again. Understand this well, for it is a very important concept. Because you can forget, you can relearn a lesson or review, and it is like learning anew.

A good illustration is provided by men hired to fill leaky barrels. The more they pour into the barrels, the more leaks out.

The fools complain, "Why are we working in vain? What good is it to fill the barrels if it leaks out?"

But the wise ones reply. "What difference does it make? Don't we get paid for every day we work? If the barrels leak, our wages are not reduced."

The same is true of your sacred studies. You might forget them, but your reward is not reduced.

In the future God will make every one remember everything he ever learned, even if it was forgotten during his lifetime. In the future life, all souls will remember and understand everything they heard and studied in this world.

—*Rabbi Nachman*

Hasidic Tale

There was once a man who was very stupid. When he got up in the morning it was so hard for him to find his clothes that at night he almost hesitated to go to bed for thinking of the trouble he would have on waking. One evening he finally made a great effort, took paper and pencil and as he undressed noted down exactly where he put everything he had on. The next morning, very well pleased with himself, he took the slip of paper in hand and read: "cap"—there it was, he set it on his head; "pants"—there they lay, he got into them; and so it went until he was fully dressed. "That's all very well, but now where am I myself?" he asked in great consternation: "Where in the world am I?" He looked and looked, but it was a vain search; he could not find himself. And that is how it is with us.

The Maggid of Mezritch

Every lock has its key which is fitted to it and opens it. But there are strong thieves who know how to open without keys. They break the lock. So every mystery in the world can be unriddled by the particular kind of meditation fitted to it. But God loves the thief who breaks the lock open: I mean the man who breaks his heart for God.

—*Martin Buber,* Tales of the Hasidim
(New York: Schocken Books, 1947).

The Proof of Hard Questions

There has never been an easy answer, and it is known to be far more difficult in the doing than in the saying. Consider the story of Rabbi Meizlish of Cracow and Warsaw, who was a well-to-do merchant before he became a rabbi. Even then, when he was sending timber along the river to Germany to be sold there at a great profit, he was famous for his erudition, and he used to teach brilliant pupils at the yeshiva. Once the news came that the timber rafts were wrecked in a storm, and the whole of the rabbi's fortune was lost in one day. They did not know how to tell the rabbi and chose one of his favorite pupils to do so. The young man selected a passage in the Talmud and came to the rabbi with his question: "It says here that one has to thank God with blessings for the evil that befalls one as well as for the good. How can this be done?" The rabbi explained the matter in terms of its hidden meaning as well as in straightforward theology. To this the pupil replied, "I am not sure I understand. And if my rabbi were to learn that all his timber rafts were wrecked on the river, would he dance for joy?" The rabbi said, "Yes, of course." "Well then," said the pupil, "you can dance—all the rafts are lost!" Upon hearing this, the rabbi fainted. When he came to, he said, "Now I must confess I no longer understand this Talmud passage."[1]

—*Adin Steinsaltz*

Talmud

He who has been bitten by a snake is frightened by a rope.

Note:

1   From *The Long Shorter Way: Discourses on Chasidic Thought* by Adin Steinsaltz. Northvale, NJ: Jason Aronson, Inc., 1988.

Quoted in Rabbi Nathan of Nemirov's *Rabbi Nachman's Wisdom*, trans. and annotated by Rabbi Aryeh Kaplan (Brooklyn, NY: Breslov Research Institute, 1973).

Parabola
Volume: 12.4
Sense of Humor

Every Stick has Two Ends

Yiddishisms

With money in your pocket, you are wise and you are handsome and you sing well, too. —*Yiddish*

One chops the wood, the other does the grunting. —*Yiddish*

If the rich could hire others to die for them, the poor could make a nice living. —*Yiddish*

Sleep faster, we need the pillows. —*Yiddish*

If you can't get up, get down; if you can't get across, get across. —*Yiddish*

If you follow others' every stride, you are sure to sway from side to side. —*Yiddish*

Crabgrass grows overnight. —*Yiddish*

Many a man leaves heaven for hell just to be stubborn. —*Yiddish*

If it doesn't get better, depend on it, it will get worse. —*Yiddish*

If I try to be like him, who will be like me? —*Yiddish*

Parabola
Volume: 15.4
Hospitality

THE RICH MAN, THE BA'AL SHEM TOV AND KING DAVID

Pinhas Sadeh

In a town near Mezhivozh lived a very rich man who was also a scholar and an alms-giver. One day he decided to donate a Torah scroll to the synagogue—such a Torah scroll as, for sheer holiness, the likes of which had never been seen. So he bought some calves, kept them in a special pen, fattened them, slaughtered them, gave the meat free to the poor, and entrusted the hides to God-fearing tanners to be made into parchment. And when the parchment was ready, he brought an expert scribe, a God-fearing and scholarly man himself, provided him with room and board in his own home, in addition to the fee, and let him live there for days, months, and years until he finished the holy task. At last, when the scribe was done and the Torah scroll was perfection itself, the rich man gave a gala banquet in his house and celebrated the event as lavishly as he could.

All the Jews in town came to the rich man's house, among them a water drawer. Now this water drawer was an honest and simple soul who never shirked his work and was in the habit of always saying Psalms. After the host had honored the most prominent Jews by having them ink in the last letters of the Torah scroll, which had been left hollow for that purpose, and had given a speech in honor of the Torah and its scholars, rolls were passed out to all those present for the blessing over bread. The water drawer, who was seated at the far end of the last table, was given a roll too. And being ravenously hungry, because he had not eaten all day, he thought no one would mind if he washed his hands, said the blessing, and ate without waiting for the others. Yet in this he was mistaken, for just then his host passed by, saw him, lost his temper, and shouted in a very loud voice, "You numbskull! Who said you could go first? Do you think that saying Psalms all day makes you so important? Here you are among scholars and distinguished men, yet you push to the front of the line to wash your hands before them!"

When the poor man heard these words, which were spoken in great anger, he laid his roll on the table and walked out. Meanwhile, the other guests washed their hands and sat down to eat, none of them noticing the water drawer's embarrassment or absence. The host himself soon thought of other things and forgot him too. And so they sat there eating and enjoying themselves, and when the meal was over, each of the guests went home, leaving their host to study a page of the Talmud, as was his custom every evening. As he was sitting before the open book, he suddenly heard a voice calling him. He stepped outside and was seized by a gale wind, which carried him many a mile on its wings until it set him down in a wilderness.

When the man saw what a desolate place he was in, he was overcome with fear, and battered and sore from his earthward fall, he lay on the ground without moving. Once he had recovered and calmed down a bit, he glanced around and saw a light shining in the distance. Encouraged to stumble in its direction, he finally arrived at a great mansion in whose windows shone a bright light. He did not, however, knock on the door, but rather sat down outside, for he thought it must be the hideaway of thieves or else a haunted house. And as he was sitting there, he heard a voice call out within, "Make way for David, king of Israel!"

The rich man could not believe his ears and thought he must be imagining it, but almost at once he heard the voice call out again, "Welcome, David, king of Israel!" A few minutes later there was a great hubbub and the cry, "Make way for Rabbi Israel Ba'al Shem Tov!" The rich man strained to hear and heard someone say, "But why is that Jew there sitting outside by himself?" To which King David answered, "That man has been summoned by me to stand trial, and Rabbi Israel Ba'al Shem Tov will be his lawyer."

When the judges had taken their places, King David rose and said, "All my life I asked the Creator to consider my words as though they were His own until He promised me that whoever says even a few chapters of them every day will be in His eyes as one who has studied the entire Torah, Mishnah, and Talmud. And here, in a town in Poland, lives a simple, honest water drawer who recites Psalms all the time—yet in spite of that he has been humiliated in public! I wish to convict the man who did it in order to make sure it never happens again."

"The sentence for such a crime," observed the chief justice, "is death at the hands of Providence, but we had better hear what the counsel for the defense has to say."

The Ba'al Shem Tov declared, "Although the chief justice is right about the sentence, nothing stands to be gained from its being carried out, because the public will never know from that how mighty are the Psalmsayers and how heinous are those who mock them. I therefore move that the defendant be given a choice: either he can serve his full sentence by returning home and dying quietly in bed without anyone knowing the reason why, or he can have it commuted by inviting his fellow townsmen to a second banquet, at which he will beg the water drawer's pardon in public and tell everyone what happened to him here tonight, so that they themselves may know better than to mock such a one."

The chief justice ruled for the defense, and at once a messenger came to inform the rich man of his sentence and to inquire whether he wished to serve it in full. The man chose to have it commuted, but when, having said so, he wished to return home, he found he was unable to move. So the court sent a page to him with a pitcher of the water of Paradise, and after washing with it, he recovered. Then a pillar of cloud appeared and brought him home.

At the crack of dawn, the rich man assembled his household and told them to prepare another banquet for the whole town and to make sure to invite the water drawer. Halfway through the meal, the host rose in front of his guests, asked the water drawer to forgive him, and told everyone what had happened to him the night before. Hearing this, the guests were all stricken with the fear of God, and each said to his neighbor, "To think we didn't know how great is the merit of the sayers of the Psalms of David, king of Israel!"

The next day, the rich man traveled to the town where the Ba'al Shem Tov lived. As soon as he set foot in the Ba'al Shem's house and saw the great holy man himself, he fainted dead away. Upon reviving, he began to tell his story. "There's no need to go on!" said the Ba'al Shem. "I saw you sitting outside when I entered the courtroom last night."

This story was told by the *tsaddik* Rabbi Menachem Mendel of Kossov.

Excerpt from *Jewish Folktales* by Pinhas Sadeh, translation by Hillel Halkin, translation copyright 1989 by Doubleday, a division of Bantam Doubleday Dell Publishing Group, Inc. Used by permission of the publisher.

Parabola
Volume: 16.3
Craft

THE HOSE-MAKER

Martin Buber

Once, in the course of a journey, the Ba'al Shem stopped in a little town whose name has not come down to us. One morning, before prayer, he smoked his pipe as usual and looked out of the window. He saw a man go by. He carried his prayer shawl and phylacteries in his hand and set his feet as intently and solemnly as though he were going straight to the doors of Heaven. The B'aal Shem asked the disciple in whose house he was staying, who the man was. He was told that he was a hose-maker who went to the House of Prayer day after day, both summer and winter, and said his prayer even when the prescribed quorum of ten worshippers was not complete. The Ba'al Shem wanted to have the man brought to him, but his host said: "That fool would not stop on his way—not if the emperor called him in person."

After prayer, the Ba'al Shem sent someone to the man with the message that he should bring him four pairs of hose. Soon after, the man stood before him and displayed his wares. They were of good sheep's wool and well-made. "What do you want for a pair?" asked Rabbi Israel.

"One-and-a-half gulden."

"I suppose you will be satisfied with one gulden."

"Then I should have said one gulden," the man replied.

The Ba'al Shem instantly paid him what he had asked. Then he went on questioning him. "How do you spend your days?"

"I ply my trade," said the man.

"And how do you ply it?"

"I work until I have forty or fifty pairs of hose. Then I put them into a mold with hot water and press them until they are as they should be."

"And how do you sell them?"

"I don't leave my house. The merchants come to me to buy. They also bring me good wool they have bought for me, and I pay them for their pains. This time I left my house only to honor the rabbi."

"And when you get up in the morning, what do you do before you go to pray?"

"I make hose then, too."

"And what psalms do you recite?"

"I say those psalms which I know by heart, while I work," said the man.

When the hose-maker had gone home, the Ba'al Shem said to the disciples who stood around him: "Today you have seen the cornerstone which will uphold the Temple until the Messiah comes."

From Martin Buber, *Tales of the Hasidim, the Early Masters* © 1947, 1948 and renewed 1975 by Schocken Books, Inc. Published by Schocken Books, Inc. Reprinted by permission of Pantheon Books, Inc., a division of Random House, Inc.

Parabola
Volume: 22.4
Miracles

A SMALL MIRACLE

Retold by Diane Wolkstein

I heard this story from Rabbi Shlomo Carlebach during Rosh Hashanah. Before he told the story he said: "On the first day of Rosh Hashanah, we ask God for what is possible. On the second day, we are to ask for what is impossible. Rachel asked to marry Jacob, her sister's husband. Rabbi Nachman of Breslov asked to live each day as if he had gone to heaven and been granted one day of life to live on earth."

On a Thursday evening a week before the New Year, the holy Ba'al Shem Tov and his followers took off in a horse and carriage. They arrived at a small rundown hut in the woods. Before they got out of the carriage, the Ba'al Shem said to his followers, "You are to promise me that no matter what happens, you will not reveal who I am." The hasidim, who completely trusted their rabbi, agreed.

The Ba'al Shem knocked at the door. A simple man named Avi came to the door surrounded by his wife, Sarah, and their four daughters.

"We are hungry," the Ba'al Shem said.

"What an honor to serve you," the man said humbly. Avi knew they had no food so he whispered to Sarah to kill the cow.

"The cow's milk is all our children have to eat," she whispered back loudly.

"They are our guests," he hushed her. "It is an honor to have guests. Do not worry."

Sarah slaughtered and cooked the cow. The Ba'al Shem ate the cow. The others, knowing it was the man's only possession, could not eat it. The Ba'al Shem ate all night without thanking the man. In the morning the Ba'al Shem told Avi what he wanted to eat for the Sabbath: six loaves of challah, six kinds of vegetables, two kinds of fish, two kinds of meat, ten desserts, and three kinds of wine.

The followers of the Ba'al Shem were horrified. The Ba'al Shem, the master of the good name, was known for his teaching of loving-kindness. Again and again he told his followers that more than study or learning, what was most important was to treat every person with honor, respect, and kindness. The hasidim thought their rabbi had gone crazy. Every time they moved forward and were about to say something, the Ba'al Shem would raise his eyebrows in warning so that they would remember their promise.

If the Ba'al Shem's followers were horrified, what about Sarah? She had watched this rabbi eating all night and was filled with despair. Avi told his wife not to worry.

"Worry?" she said. "I am beyond worry. But what about our children? Who is thinking of them?"

There was no other solution. The man went into town and sold his house so he could have money to feed the rabbi and his guests. He only asked the banker to allow him to stay in the house until Monday.

Sarah prepared everything the rabbi had requested. The Ba'al Shem began to eat. He ate and ate. His disciples were so disgusted they could barely swallow. In the little hut everyone listened as the rabbi chewed each bite of his food. The three meals of the Sabbath passed excruciatingly slowly.

At last, the Sabbath was over. As he got into his carriage to leave, the Ba'al Shem called out to Avi, "I am the Ba'al Shem. I bless you to ask for all that you need."

The man was astounded. The Ba'al Shem, the holy Ba'al Shem, had been in his home. He had only dreamed of going to study with him, of being near him, and now to think that he, Avi, such an unimportant person, had been given the honor of serving the holy Ba'al Shem Tov. He glowed with joy and turned to his wife. For a moment a look of joy also crossed her face, but at once a cloud of worry replaced it. The family went to sleep without any food.

The next day Avi woke up before dawn and went into the woods. What could he do? He needed to provide for Sarah and the children. Who could help him? He went further into the woods. He knelt on the earth and he prayed, "Creator of the universe, I have never asked you for anything before, so please listen. My wife and children have no food. We have no house. I need money to feed them. I need money to buy back our house. And my wife would be so glad if there was money to send our daughters to school and for the weddings. Four weddings! And since I am asking, one more request. Creator of the universe, please make a small miracle and give me enough money so my house is large enough to provide for anyone else who might someday be in terrible need."

With this last request, he began to sob. As he was lying on the earth praying and crying, Ivan, the town drunkard, came by and said to him, "Whatever it is, don't worry. I can help you. You have always had a kind word for me. Everyone but you has treated me terribly. My children are the worst. I am not feeling well, and if I die, I want you to have my fortune. Come, I'll show you where I buried it." And he took Avi to a great stone nearby and showed him a box underneath it.

On Monday, the bank took Avi's home. The day after that, Ivan the drunkard died. When Avi went to open the box, he found it was filled with gold—enough gold to build a house even larger than the banker's.

But Avi did not forget his word. His house became a haven. Whenever anyone was in need, they went to see the simple Avi, for they knew they would be received with great honor and respect.

Then one day Sarah said, "Avi, it will soon be Rosh Hashanah. A year has gone by since the holy Ba'al Shem visited us. It was his blessing that brought our riches. We must go and thank him."

For a week she baked. Then they set out for Medzhibozh with loaves of bread and cake, as well as chickens and goats to give as presents to the Ba'al Shem. When their carriage pulled up before the home of the Ba'al Shem, some of his disciples, despite the couple's new clothes, recognized them.

"We have come to see the master," the man said simply. They brought Avi and his wife to the Ba'al Shem, and all the disciples came crowding around, eager to hear their story.

The Ba'al Shem recognized the man and his wife at once and invited them to sit down. "Tell us what happened since we last saw you," he asked.

Avi told him about meeting Ivan the drunkard and the box of treasure, and he and Sarah thanked the Ba'al Shem.

Then the Ba'al Shem said, "You see, this New Year it was decreed in heaven that you were to be a rich man, but since you were so humble and would never ask for anything, I had to eat you out of house and home so that you would ask for and receive the blessings that were waiting for you. Mazel Tov! The best of years!"

Parabola
Volume: 9.2
Theft

THE SEER OF LUBLIN'S SHIRT

Retold by Diane Wolkstein

One day, as the other members of his congregation were leaving the synagogue, the Seer of Lublin noticed Moshe. He was the last to leave. Tripping over his feet, bumping into chairs, he wore a shirt which had one green sleeve, one striped sleeve, and the rest of the shirt was patched together from the remnants of forty years of old pants, coats, shirts, and vests. He looked so bedraggled the Seer of Lublin could not bear it. He said, "Moshe, wait here for me." He went into his room and brought out a shirt. It was made of one piece of material and was blue, entirely blue. Moshe's eyes lit up. The Rabbi put the shirt into Moshe's hands. "For me, Rabbi?" Moshe crowed with happiness. "Yes, Moshe, for you. Wear it in good health and try to be a mensche."

Moshe put the shirt on and was filled with joy. He strutted down the road, happily stroking his shirt, the shirt of his holy Rabbi. Soon the town drunkard, Yoshele, joined him. He noticed Moshe's new shirt. How could he help noticing it? Moshe was stroking it as if it were a newborn chick. "Where did you get the new shirt?" Yoshele asked. "The Seer of Lublin," Moshe answered. "He gave me *his* shirt. Imagine! Me, Moshe, wearing the shirt of my precious Rabbi. And look, look at the shirt." "It's a beautiful shirt," Yoshele agreed. "A beautiful shirt." And he, too, began to stroke Moshe's shirt. After a while, he said, "Oh, if only I could have a shirt like that." Moshe, who loved to please others, said, "Do you want the shirt?" "Do I want the shirt! Oye, do I want the shirt!" "Then take it," Moshe said, "take it, it's yours."

Yoshele grabbed the shirt and ran. He ran into the town tavern and cried out: "What am I bid for the Seer of Lublin's shirt?" The bartender, who knew at once a good business deal, answered: "A year's supply of free drinks." "Sold!" said Yoshele.

The next day the bartender took the shirt to the market place and called out: "Whatever woman wears the Seer of Lublin's shirt will conceive twins! Whatever man wears the Seer of Lublin's shirt will double his fortune! What am I bid for the Seer of Lublin's shirt?"

Just at that moment the Seer of Lublin entered the market place. At the same moment Moshe also appeared in the market place. They were both drawn in the direction of the noisy crowd and watched in amazement as the Seer of Lublin's shirt passed from hand to hand and was sold for an amount as large as one week's salary! The Rabbi gave Moshe a thunderous look and hurried away. Moshe ran after him, trying to explain, but the Seer of Lublin shook his head saying, "No, Moshe, it's enough, not today."

Moshe was crushed. He had disappointed his holy Rabbi. He didn't know what to do with himself. His feet took him to the town cemetery. Moshe sat down on a grave and cried.

A stranger, passing by the cemetery, heard Moshe's sobs and went and sat down next to him. He waited a time, then he said, "Friend, tell me, what has happened? Was it someone close to you?" Moshe nodded. "Your mother?" Moshe shook his head. "Your father?" Moshe shook his head. "A child?" "It's me," Moshe said. "It's—whenever I try to help others—"And then Moshe told him the story. When he'd finished speaking, the stranger said, "But your story is not over. One can never tell what will come of helping others. Let me now tell you a story …

"Once there was a thief in our town. Not an ordinary thief but one with talent. Real talent. Just by looking at you he could tell what you had in your pockets. No one was exempt. He robbed from everyone in the town; yet no one could catch him. Soon he became rich. He married. He bought himself a fine house. He sent his children to school. He joined the synagogue. His life was wonderful, so he stopped being a thief. But then, with no money coming in, he became poor again. So he went to the people in the synagogue and asked for help. They laughed at him. They said, 'What? You steal from us, and now you want us to give you money. Give us back what you stole, and we will give it to charity.'

"Several weeks later, the richest man in the synagogue was passing the thief's house. He saw the thief sitting on the steps of his house, and he saw the thief was nearly dying of hunger. The rich man sent the thief some money to buy food for the Sabbath. The next week he did the same, and the next week and the next week; and every week after that he sent him enough money for food for the Sabbath.

"Many years later it happened that the rich man and the thief died at the same moment. Nearly everyone in the town attended the rich man's funeral. Maybe five people, if that, (probably his former students) went to the thief's funeral. The rich man went to heaven. His good and bad deeds were weighed, and he had so many sins the weight went entirely in one direction. The rich man realized he had no chance to enter paradise. Then, suddenly, there was a breeze, and he was pushed through. Once he was inside the gates of paradise, he asked, 'What happened, please, tell me, how did I get in?' He was told, 'Your friend, the thief, stole your sins.'"

Rabbi Shlomo Carlebach told this story on Yom Kippur, September, 1982 in synagogue. "Look to each other, bless each other," he urged his congregation.

Parabola
Volume: 3.1
Sacred Space

THE ALCHEMIST

Adapted from a Jewish folk tale

A certain alchemist, having come to a most puzzling passage in the weighty tomes he was consulting, took his problem before the rabbi.

"Rabbi," he said, "I have spent many years in studying alchemy, and have perfected my techniques beyond the capacities of any other man. Just now I am engaged in preparing the Elixir of Life, but I have come to a most puzzling and confusing passage and do not know how to proceed. Please, if you could, examine the passage in question and explicate it for me, and I will be sure that you are the first to taste of the Elixir when it is prepared."

The rabbi answered, "My son, there is no need to examine the passage, for the formula is well known."

"Take the roots of humility, together with the leaves of patience and hope. Add to them the twigs of the Torah and the roses of wisdom and crush them together in the mortar of penitence, using ample affection and love and also adding the waters of fear. This you must cook in the oven of thanksgiving, over the fire of suffering. When cooked, preserve the whole in the garment of understanding, pass it through the sieve of truth and faith, and drink it from the goblet of the will. This is the true formula for the Elixir of Life."

Parabola
Volume: 3.1
Sacred Space

The Physician

Adapted from a Jewish folk tale

It happened once that a group of physicians were in their cups and had fallen to quarreling about which part of the body was most important for life. As they could not agree among themselves, they decided to consult the rabbi.

"Of course it is the heart and blood vessels that are most important," said the first physician, "for on them the whole life of a man depends."

"Not at all," said the second physician. "It is the brain and nerves which are most vital, for without them, even the heart would not beat."

The third physician said, "You are both wrong. It is the stomach and the digestive passages which are important, for without the proper digestion of food, the body will die."

"The lungs are most important," declared the fourth, "for a man without air will surely die."

"You are all wrong," said the rabbi. "There are two vessels of the body only that are important, but you have no knowledge of them."

"What are they, then?" asked the physicians.

The rabbi replied, "The channel that runs from the ear to the soul, and the one that runs from the soul to the tongue."

Parabola
Volume: 29.3
Seeker

THE ANGEL OF LOSSES

Howard Schwartz

Late one evening, when Reb Nachman and his Hasidim were gathered together, a strong wind blew in the open window and extinguished all the candles. Some of the Hasidim rose to relight them, but Reb Nachman stopped them, telling them to remain in the dark. So they did. For a long time there was silence. Then one of the Hasidim said: "Tell me, rebbe, is the blowing out of the candles a good omen or bad?"

"Surely it is a sign that another presence is among us, an angel who watches over us even in the dark. This is Yodea, the Angel of Losses. Even now he is watching our lives unfold, recording every detail before it fades. This angel has servants, and his servants have servants. Some of these servants are angels, and some are not. Each of the angels carries a shovel, and they spend all their time digging, searching for losses. For a great deal is lost in our lives.

"So too is every *tzaddik* a servant of the Angel Yodea. That is because a tzaddik who searches after lost things is himself sometimes lost. And as you know, it is necessary to search in the dark, in the realm of the unknown. And with what do you search in the darkness? With the light of the soul. For the soul is a light planted in the tzaddik to seek after whatever has been lost.

"What kind of light is it? Not a torch, but a small candle. Yet even so, with it you can search inside deep wells, where darkness is unbroken, peering into every corner and crevice. So for once let us be guided by that light, small though it may be."

That is when the Hasidim all saw the flame that was burning before Reb Nachman's face. And even though they were in complete darkness, still they saw his face as if it were glowing in the dark. And indeed it was, for every one of them to see.

Parabola
Volume: 26.3
The Fool

THE WISE MEN OF CHELM

Retold by Josepha Sherman

It must first be understood that it's not that the people of Chelm are fools. It's merely that foolish things keep happening to them. And one day:

Oh, horror of horrors! Someone stole the *tzedokoh* box, the charity box, out of Chelm's one synagogue. Everyone in town went about red with shame. What could they do to see such a crime never happened again? The wise men of Chelm met with the rabbi to ponder the problem.

The rabbi of Chelm began, "We must make a new tzedokoh box."

"But, Rabbi," Aaron the baker protested, "How can we be sure that no one steals this one as well?"

The wise men sat in silence, thinking and thinking. Then Shlomo the butcher cried out, "I have the answer. We will hang the box from the ceiling of the synagogue entrance hall, so close to the ceiling that no thief will ever be able to reach it."

This was a good thing, a wise thing. Relieved, everyone began to disperse.

But then the rabbi called out, "Wait! I see a new problem. It is true that the new box will be safe. No thief will be able to reach it. But if the tzedokoh box is hung close to the ceiling, how will honest people ever reach it?"

This was truly a problem. The wise men of Chelm sat and thought, and thought, and thought. At last Simeon the carpenter cried, "I have the answer! I will build a ladder tall enough to reach the tzedokoh box. That way the charitable can get to it."

"But the ladder might slip!" everyone protested. "Some good and pious soul might fall and be hurt!"

"I have the answer," the rabbi said. "The tzedokoh box will be made. It will be hung close to the ceiling. A ladder will also be built, so that the charitable can reach it. And so that no one gets hurt—the ladder will be firmly fixed to both floor and ceiling!"

"How wise is our rabbi!" cried the men of Chelm. "How wise we all are!"

With that, they all dispersed, content.

There really is a Chelm, a perfectly normal town in Poland. Why it should have been chosen as the home of foolish people is one of the mysteries of folklore. But other towns have the same dubious distinction, among them Gotham in England and Lagos in Mexico.

CHAPTER NINE

•

REDEMPTION

The wolf also shall dwell with the lamb,
and the leopard shall lie down with the kid;
and the calf and the young lion and the fatling together;
and a little child shall lead them.[1]

—Isaiah 11:6

Parabola
Volume: 23.3
Fear

Fear No More

Viktor E. Frankl

But for every one of the liberated prisoners, the day comes when, looking back on his camp experiences, he can no longer understand how he endured it all. As the day of his liberation eventually came, when everything seemed to him like a beautiful dream, so also the day comes when all his camp experiences seem to him nothing but a nightmare.

The crowning experience of all, for the homecoming man, is the wonderful feeling that, after all he has suffered, there is nothing he need fear any more—except his God.

Parabola
Volume: 12.1
The Knight and
the Hermit

Jews, Myth, and Modern Life

Elie Wiesel

"And God himself buried Moses, and no one knows the place of his tomb." Why? All the commentaries are in agreement: it was to keep the prophet from becoming a myth and his tomb an idol.

One important aspect of Jewish tradition is the rejection of mythology: the greatness of Abraham consisted precisely in his ability boldly to demythify the divinities of his time. He carried on his search for truth within history, not apart from it. The Law, though God's work, is expressed in the language of human beings who have the right and authority to interpret it. Officially, there is no mythology in Judaism: our ancestors are human beings, as are our prophets. No one of them is perfect. They pass through crises, experience doubts and fears like everyone else, and like everyone else show themselves vulnerable, clumsy, often unlucky, not always attractive. Jacob's timidity is striking, as is the harshness of Moses, the fanaticism of Elijah, and the ambition of David; none of them is looked upon as beyond reproach. Scripture tells us that the just are not sinless; they are defined as human beings.

Therefore, Jews who assert their Jewishness find it difficult, or even impossible, to tackle the subject with which I am dealing here. Myth in modern life? The answer is simple: The Jew in me rejects it. But in rejecting it, do I not acknowledge its existence?

Myth accompanies the real and has a reality of its own as well as a duration of its own. Whether celebrated or suppressed, myth has its place
in the struggle of human beings to live out their destiny and gain the
upper hand over it. Wittingly or unwittingly, they vacillate between a
desire to discover a way of their own and a need to follow a way already
known. If they follow in the footsteps of their ancestors, they feel an
ambivalent sense of pride and humility. What shall they do to go beyond
their ancestors? Will they be satisfied simply to imitate them? Recourse
to myths makes each victory and defeat timeless if not eternal.

Just as human beings cannot live without dreams and legends, neither can they live without myths, which reflect both dreams and legends.
Through their relation to myth, men and women are linked not to other
lives they have experienced but to other lives not experienced. Is the link
satisfying or frustrating? Probably both, perhaps even both simultaneously.
As a result, they feel at once older and younger than they actually are; they
feel themselves to be both themselves and other than themselves.

In a sense, myth is the other within us. Being sufficiently distant and
yet surprisingly close to us, it is a guide that explains our impulsive acts
and our secret tremors. For some psychologists, complexes, manias, and
phobias find in myth an—often overfacile, simplistic—explanation and
point of reference. Myth presents the subject as if transformed into an
object, and thus helps us question ourselves about our actions and their
deeper motives, which lie buried in memories now concealed or forbidden. Flight from God, pursuit of illicit pleasures, dreams of domination
and power—all our problems were already known to the divinities and
demiurges of antiquity. We are sure of this, because we know what their
problems were. Does myth simply survive, or is it relevant as well? It
survives because it is relevant.

The life of myth varies, of course, according to period and context. It
reflects the mores of society more than it influences them.

Croesus and Oedipus, Venus and Diana, Orpheus and Hercules: to
what extent does our generation at century's end attempt to live out the
fantasies that connect it with other times and other heroes?

As of old, knowledge is linked to death and survival to remorse.
Hardly is a couple formed before it is threatened by the other: both
serpent and God drive it to actions that, sooner or later, will destroy its

unity. As of old, the happiness of the couple attracts the jealousy of the gods. As of old, the children will be the first victims.

The signs are not misleading: we live in an age that we cannot describe as Biblical. Events unfold with ever increasing rapidity and on an ever vaster scale. As in the past, history seems to speak directly to us, but, unlike our ancestors, we cannot decipher its message.

But is the message the same? Questions may travel the centuries unchanged, but the answers vary. In the memory that finds expression in the Bible, it is God who asks the first question when he says to Adam, "Where are you?" He asks each of us, no matter where, the same question. Is Adam a figure of myth? For me he is rather history's first refugee.

Refugees, the uprooted, victims of relentless persecution: the planet is full of these. Never since antiquity has society seen such a migration, voluntary or involuntary, across so many borders. Journey to paradise? Flight from hell? Some are drawn by an ideal of redemption; others have been expelled by evil forces. All go into exile with the feeling that they must begin all over again and rebuild everything. In other ages they were called nomads, wanderers. For them there is no return. Ulysses would have done better not to return home. There are only two possibilities: while he was away, everything has changed at home or nothing has changed. In either case, he will find himself a stranger. Was that what he was seeking on his journeys: to find himself a stranger?

The same demon resides in "modern" men and women. They are gnawed at from every side and want to be anywhere but where they are. All roads look good to them, provided they lead far away. In other times, people went to war if they wanted to travel; today they travel because they are no longer at war. The kings who of old went to Delphi to consult the oracle would go there today as tourists. Mobility, inspired by the attraction of picturesque distances or disgust with boredom at home, is a typical trait of our society, especially in the industrialized countries. Today it is not the gods but mortals who venture away from home in order to make themselves known.

What are the men and women of our day looking for? Success? Happiness? The young want noise, the elderly silence. All feel ill at ease with themselves. Adolescents try to appear older than they are; others try to appear younger. As a general rule, it is youth that seems essential to our generation, as advertising in all its forms makes clear. Actors and models are all vigorous and blooming, with their white teeth and fresh breath, their muscular bodies and smiling faces, their sensual lips open for love and their eyes reflecting ecstasy. They embody the ideal to be imitated and desired. Here the sun-god reigns, as he does in mythology, combining physical strength with beauty. If only we could find the secret of eternal youth! Some countries spend more on cosmetics than on education. New gods are also recruited, of course, from the scientific and financial worlds, but they are incomparably less numerous and less well known than the idols of screen or stage. Take any number of Nobel Prize winners in chemistry and medicine and together they will not enjoy the stardom of a twenty-year-old rock singer.

Wisdom on the one side, eroticism on the other. The former appeals to an elite; the latter excites the multitudes. To find a sensuous civilization comparable to our own, we must go back to the primitive tribes of Africa or the neighbors of Judea. Modesty has no place in our mores; there are no more taboos. The desire to bring everything out into the open smothers the imagination. No longer need one dream of naked women, because now we see them on television or in the flesh. Romanticism has departed from our relationships. There are no more preliminaries: boy meets girl and straightway asks her to spend the night with him; she for her part is hardly offended. A union that in the past took weeks and months—of play, meditation, preparation, hesitation, ardors, and despairs—to accomplish now requires only an hour. Long live simplicity! Taboos belong in the trash can. Let us, like the gods of nature, go straight to the point. Doubts are for old folks and old folks belong in a home. As with the Buddha, we try to hide them away.

For decades now, there has also been an effort to hide death from us. It has been cosmeticized, disguised, robbed of its element of sadness and truth. It has been made a subject for the theater, and for bad theater at that. The reaction to this is not surprising: today everything possible is being done to give death back its place in the social and psychological structures of society. Every university has its course in thanatology; death is openly discussed in hospitals. Human beings are seen as having a right to accept their death—I might almost say to *live* their death—which is thereby demythified.

Evident here is the chief preoccupation of moderns: to see through everything, understand everything, demystify everything. They seek to assume all phenomena under an immutable universal principle: the meaning of a dream derives not from the dreamer but from the dream itself. In other words: as in sickness, so here symptoms always have the same meaning. The classical cycles of love and hate, life and death, joy and despair, jealousy and nobility are detected at work in the actions of all human beings without distinction of race or culture. The psychoanalyst and the anthropologist work together to strip the mask from the rituals that underlie trivial actions.

Our preoccupation with dreams is another thing that links us with our ancestors. Like them, we give dreams a transcendent dimension. There is, of course, one difference between our ancestors and ourselves: they used to examine dreams in order to predict the future, while it is the past that intrigues us. Nonetheless time itself is the main issue for us: if we could look at it from the outside, we would see the invisible. Thus, what is hidden in human beings would help us glimpse what is hidden in the gods.

The gods descend from Olympus either to distract human beings or, on the contrary, to rouse them from their indifference. The names of the gods matter less than their unpredictable caprices. Men and women are always seeking to know what their role is in relation to the gods. In Greek mythology they are victims; in the Jewish tradition, partners in dialogue. In any case, they cannot do without the presence of the gods, even if the presence overwhelms them. Job protests against a heaven that is indifferent or distant; as soon as he hears the voice of God, he declares himself at peace. He prefers an unjust God to a God who remains apart from his creation. Was Job a mythical figure? Possibly; the Talmud does not simply reject the hypothesis. But there is this difference between Job and the figures of myth: the personages of myth are crushed by their encounter with the gods; Job is not. Instead, he arises and begins to journey again, to dream, to make plans and projects. This response captures the very meaning of the Jewish tradition: for human beings nothing is lost in advance; even when beaten down and chastised, they have the chance to repent. They can continue their ordeal, with the same fears and the same hope.

Of all the personages of the Bible, Job comes closest to the figures of myth. He is enveloped in mystery and belongs to more than one age and more than one country. Some Talmudic sages even doubt his existence: "He was only a parable," says one of them. Midrashic literature seems constantly concerned to separate fiction from reality. The imagination has its established place in Jewish thought, but it is traditionally important that it be seen as imagination. There is no prohibition against telling a mythical story, but its mythical character has to be emphasized. In this view, confusion brings danger.

Nonetheless, there is one case in which confusion seems to be sought or at least tolerated: the Messiah. What is he? A name? Perhaps a utopian dream? A prayer born of a people's melancholy waiting? Those who know do not say; those who say do not know. He is a mystical obsession and suggests the realm of what is forbidden and unapproachable. Living outside of time, he reminds human beings that time is not necessarily their enemy; the future is indeed permeated by anxiety, but anxiety is a vehicle for faith.

The Messiah: the ultimate permutation of words and actions, the result of suffering and consolation. The idea of the Messiah is as old as the Exile, for which it is the cure. The most poignant stories tell of his coming; the most heart-rending laments speak of his delaying. The Messiah is Israel's answer to tragedy and the Jewish gift to humanity.

The Messiah's "biography," however, is surprisingly lacking in detail. He is completely absent from the scriptures, barely mentioned by the prophets; he emerges only in the Talmud where poetry replaces fact when he is spoken of. He comes from the line of David, but his name, we are told, preceded the creation of the world; that name is not revealed to us.

In the school of Rabbi Shiloh the Messiah's name was said to be Shiloh. In the academy of Rabbi Yannai his name was said to be Yinnon (a derivative of Yannai). The disciples of Rabbi Hanina, for their part, swore that the Messiah's name could only be Hanina.

According to Maimonides, we will know nothing about the Messiah as long as he has not actually come among us. Legends about him abound, yet we cannot even imagine him. We can imagine his entourage, his heavenly palace ("the bird's nest"), his strolls from one shrine to another; but the person himself we can only conjecture. He is intensely present, but he eludes us. At once real and unreal, a creation of fantasy yet tangible, human yet transcendent, his person is easily confused with one that is condemned never to achieve existence. In other words: there seems to be an effort, conscious or unconscious, deliberate or indeliberate, to turn the human Messiah into a myth and the mythical Messiah into a human being.

On the other hand, we are given a mass of precise, descriptive details about his enemy. The cruel and bloodthirsty anti-Messiah is the son of Satan and a statue; his name is Armilus, and he is depicted as a monster: red hair, green face, eyes not matching (one very large, the other minuscule), six fingers on each hand, a stone for a heart. ...

The enemy is visible and makes us fearful; the Messiah is invisible but helps us overcome our fear. At the end of time, this fear will be vanquished for good, and humanity will enter the Messianic age when nothing will be as before. Time itself will have changed.

Time had a strange fascination for the ancient Jewish imagination. In fact, the Messianic age was more important to it than the person of the Messiah himself.

In the Messianic age, which will be preceded by a series of apocalyptic events, time will run backward: the Israelite people will regain their sovereignty, their temple will be rebuilt in all its splendor, God will be reunited with the *shekhinah*. Time will henceforth mean reconciliation and not separation. "Yom shekulo shabbat": it will be the day of the endless sabbath. It will bring the end of anxiety, the death of death, for all people, all nations, all the things that are.

But first, history will be shaken by terrifying tremors; these too are mythical. There will be the final convulsions of the beast, the final explosion of hatred, the final dance of the enraged demons.

Aharit Hayamim is the name given to that penultimate age: the end of the human journey through history. This final stage, the dividing line or boundary between exile and redemption, will plunge the world into the most murderous of all wars. There will be famine, plague, storms of fire and steel; wretchedness and shame will cover the planet. The Midrashic descriptions do not shun the fantastic: "In that age futility and arrogance will reign everywhere; the schools will harbor prostitutes and their clients; truth, humiliated, will be absent. Parents will be insulted by their children, and teachers by their pupils."

Baruch the Syrian says in the Apocrypha: "men and women will hate and kill one another. The condemned will rule over the mighty, the wicked over heroes, and imbeciles over the wise. ... And whoever is spared by war will perish in an earthquake; and whoever survives the earthquake will perish by fire; and whoever is spared by the fire will die of hunger."

And Ezra the Fourth: "The sun will shine at midnight. Blood will flow from wood, and stones will begin to speak. The peoples will be in confusion; the stars will fall from heaven. Lovers will fall upon one another like enemies."

Rabbi Israel of Ruzhin shares the anxiety of the ancients in the face of the end of time: "In that time human beings will stop hating others and will hate themselves. ... And the parable will have nothing to do with the meaning of the parable."

This confusion throughout creation will be succeeded by universal redemption. Time shattered will be followed by a different kind of time. Both times have a striking mythical resonance.

Meanwhile, the picture of the Savior, like the Savior himself, will be invisible but present. That is how it is, and we can do nothing about it. Perhaps it is as well that it should be so. For, knowing the Messiah to be unknown, it is incumbent upon us to look for him in every unknown.

It is difficult to await his coming while he is already present; yet without that presence the waiting would be absurd. And there is one point on which ancient mythology and Jewish tradition are in agreement: they deny the absurd. This, unfortunately, is not necessarily true of modern society.

Parabola
Volume: 23.1
Millenium

Before the Gates of Rome

Rabbi Joshua came upon the prophet Elijah as he was standing at the entrance of Rabbi Simeon ben Yohai's cave.

He asked him: "When is the Messiah coming?"

The other replied: "Go and ask him yourself."

"Where shall I find him?"

"Before the gates of Rome."

"By what sign shall I know him?"

"He is sitting among poor people covered with wounds. The others unbind all their wounds at once, and then bind them up again. But he unbinds one wound at a time, and binds it up again straightaway. He tells himself: 'Perhaps I shall be needed—and I must not take time and be late!'"

So he went and found him and said: "Peace be with you, my master and teacher!"

He answered him: "Peace be with you, son of Levi!"

Then he asked him: "When are you coming, master?"

He answered him: "Today!"

Thereupon he returned to Elijah and said to him: "He has deceived me, he has indeed deceived me! He told me, 'Today I am coming!' and he has not come."

But the other said to him: "This is what he told you: 'Today—if ye would but hearken to His voice.'"

From *A Jewish Reader: In Time and Eternity*, edited by Nahum N. Glatzer (New York: Schocken Books, 1961). Reprinted by permission.

Parabola
Volume: 10.2
Exhile

WE ARE ALL WITNESSES

Interview with Elie Wiesel

The long exile of the Jews, from the Babylonian Exile recorded in the Bible to the founding of the State of Israel in 1948, has been both a physical and a spiritual fact. From Biblical Prophets to medieval Kabbalists, eighteenth-century Hasidim, and twentieth-century Zionists, exile has never been forgotten. No longer a physical reality, it remains one of the deepest and most fruitful insights of Judaism, which still awaits the Gathering of the Sparks and redemption from the spiritual exile to which all human beings and the cosmos itself are subject.

"I am a stranger with thee, and a sojourner"—the ancient Hebrew poetry of exile is unforgettably powerful. But so too is the modern poetry. Parabola asked Elie Wiesel, internationally recognized as one of the great Jewish writers of our time, to share his understanding of exile with us.

Elie Wiesel was born in 1928 in Sighet, a small Transylvanian town with a richly traditional Jewish life. From his grandfather, he heard Hasidic tales retold as if the eighteenth and nineteenth century holy men and seekers in the tales were still alive, their lives still a dialogue between the above and Kabbalah and the Jewish mystical view.

In 1944, the Nazis occupied the region and deported the Jews of Sighet to their deaths in concentration camps. At Auschwitz and Buchenwald until the liberation in 1945, Wiesel lost his grandparents, his parents, and a sister, but survived, deathly ill and in despair, vowing not to speak of his experience in the camps until ten years had passed. He found his way to Paris, where he resumed his studies and in time became a journalist. In these years, he worked not only with teachers but with a Teacher, the inscrutable Rav Mordecai Shushani, whom he has memorialized in one of his most joyful stories, "The Wandering Jew."

In 1958, the prominent French author, François Mauriac, convinced him that the time had come to speak. The result was Night, *the brief and unforgettable account of his concentration camp experience which remains the most read and perhaps the most central work about The Holocaust. Thereafter, he continued to write—novels, stories, essays, plays, more than twenty books in all, ranging in theme from contemporary lives and issues to powerful recastings of Hasidic tales and the Hasidic world.*

Elie Wiesel is a witness and a survivor; this alone gives his work moral authority. But beyond that, he has incarnated the true vocation of the writer with a rare seriousness and power. When one meets him, any doubt we may have as to the essential dignity of man is erased.

—Roger Lipsey

Roger Lipsey: *Exile and the return from exile can be seen from many different levels. When the feeling appears of not quite belonging here, of being a stranger, that can be the beginning of a movement of return. What do you see as the real exile?*

Elie Wiesel: I cannot see any other exile but the real exile, and that exile is total. It envelops all endeavors, all explorations, all illusions, all hopes, all triumphs, and this means that whatever we do is never complete. Our life is not complete, and lo and behold, our death is not complete: one does not die when one should, or the way one should. As you know, in our tradition we speak of exile in absolute categories. Exile envelops God Himself; God Himself is in Exile. Language is in exile. The *Shekhinah*, of course, is supposed to be everywhere, and it is exile that carries it everywhere. So exile for us is something which is as absolute, as infinite, as life.

RL: *There is a feeling of being cut off, and yet there can be a thread, no more than a little thread to someone or something higher than oneself. When that is cut, that is the exile, don't you think?*

EW: Not necessarily. For example, exile has a link to solitude—why? Because we are away from home, we are away from our memories, we are away from security. But what is easier to bear—to be in exile alone, or with someone whom one loves? It may become worse to see the other person also suffering. So maybe the cutoff is a blessing and not a curse. One of the reasons why so many Hasidic rebbes sank into melancholy was precisely the *Galut ha-Shekhinah*, the Exile of the Shekhinah. They were ready to bear their own suffering, but not the suffering of God.

RL: *Is that your understanding today, or did they express that in their own way?*

EW: It's my understanding, which they didn't express. I discovered their melancholy, I was struck by it, and I couldn't understand why it was so. The greatest of the Hasidic masters, meaning the first generation, the companions and disciples of the Besht, all of them without any exception at one point in their lives had an encounter with melancholy, with deep depression. And I couldn't understand it, because all of them were speaking of joy and happiness and exhilaration. Why should they be in such danger of falling into depression? I studied it, I researched every case, always in their terms, with their books and stories. And the reason was a *transfer*, a transfer in the sense that they didn't encounter depression on their own account but because of the separation of the Shekhinah. And that's something, after all. If I suffer, maybe I've done something, but if God suffers, what right do I have to suffer for Him?

The real exile, the profound exile—where did it begin? It began with Adam, who fled God, and with Cain, who fled human beings. Or did it begin with Abraham, who fled his parents, or with Moses, who fled his enemies? There are categories in exile. God's exile also has many stages. In the Kabbalah, we read that God's exile—the Breaking of the Vessels—occurred very far back, at Creation. The Creation and exile were almost simultaneous. In the Midrash, we read that it happened during the destruction of the Temple, the first destruction.

RL: *God's exile from what?*

EW: We don't know about that, we only know that *we are* in exile; that, we know. And we ask ourselves, how did God our Father allow this to happen? There are many answers given. One answer was that God Himself is suffering.

RL: *Terrible trials and tests have been put in the way of the Jewish people, which are inseparably bound up with exile. After the concentration camps, someone said, "God saw that it was enough." After two thousand years, the Jews could return to their land. Does this mean the exile is over?*

EW: The entire period is a question. I envy those who think that God said it is enough. Maybe He said it's only a warning. I'm scared, I'm literally scared for the future of mankind. It seems to be the plan that whatever happens to the Jews later happens to the world. God gave the Law to all the peoples; we were the first to accept it, and then we shared it. Almost every phase in our civilization we later shared because we wanted to share; for after all, God said "I am your God," and we said, "Thank you, but don't be our God alone, be everyone's God." He gave the Torah, we are told in our tradition: He went from one people to another, from one nation to another, and nobody wanted it. And again, we accepted it—under duress, but we accepted. The moment we accepted, He said: everybody gets it!

There is a tendency in us: the more Jewish we want to be, the more universal we become. That is true in everything. There is a thesis to be elaborated about the connection, let's say, between the Inquisition in Spain and what happened to Spain, between the exodus of the Jews from Spain and the downfall of Spain. Somehow, when Jews left the country, it fell into bad shape. Very often, in Europe, they called them back.

RL: *What we've been talking about so far has more to do with all of us, with human beings in general. But when it comes to a man's own work on himself, then things have to be looked at in quite another way. A man learns enough about himself to see that something is lacking. He needs to live in the present, and not worry about past history or the future. Maybe the first thing he has to understand is that something in him is in exile from his true self.*

EW: Yes, but what you say about having no concern for past history or the future is impossible. How could human beings be human without the past?

RL: *Yes, but what about the present moment when I can be?*

EW: What is exile? What is *galut*? Whenever I have a problem, I go to the original Hebrew idioms. After all, the world was created in that language. Let's go back to the relations of that word: *gal*, move, *gil*, joy: it means *movement*, continuous movement. It means that everything is moving, except me; or the other way—I am moving and everything else stands still; or still a third way, we are not moving in the same direction. Then exile means to be displaced, I am here and I am not here. The content and form do not espouse one another. That means they are in exile. When a person is in exile, nothing fits.

RL: *Do you see a purpose in the exile?*

EW: We are told there is a purpose, the purpose is redemption. This is expressed in the Kabbalistic theory of the Gathering of the Sparks, after which the universe itself will be redeemed.

RL: *The Jewish people have had experiences which, had they stayed in one place, might never have occurred. And the rest of the world has had experiences because of the Jews which it might never have had. From the point of view of a return, could there have been something useful there?*

EW: Do you ask my opinion or the opinions of other people whom I could quote? In my personal opinion, I cannot bring myself to find a purpose to suffering, so much suffering. I am ready to accept my suffering, but not the suffering of others. Does it have a purpose, was it useful, two thousand years of suffering?

RL: *Yet there are individual stories of men growing as a result of their suffering. People suffer intentionally, perhaps, to reach another level, to come closer to God.*

EW: You find that phenomenon in every mystical movement; the self-inflicted wounds, suffering to reach a higher level, a higher sphere; then, variations occurred, you joined your suffering to the suffering of Christ, or you suffered for God, but it's still self-inflicted suffering. We never accepted it. You know in the Bible, when somebody renounces the usual, normal, everyday joys of life, he must make a sacrifice in atonement.

RL: *You said that the goal of exile is redemption. What does that mean?*

EW: I am told, I didn't invent it. My feeling is really that we did not choose exile, we never did. As long as we were in exile, we tried to rationalize it, and to see it in a larger context. We weren't satisfied to say that because Israel was in exile, the redemption would be only the redemption of Israel, a geographic redemption. We wanted to return to the Kingdom of David. In other words, we wanted the impossible. Only the impossible could explain or accept or justify so many sufferings. We speak of exile, and we speak of Messianic redemption, which is universal redemption—not only of the Jewish people but of Creation itself. And then all the imageries are possible: the wolf and the lamb at peace, there will be no slaves, justice will prevail.

RL: *Is there an exile within Judaism itself—not the exile of Jews in the diaspora versus Jews in Israel, but an exile within the religion? The religion of the successful American Jew often seems very dilute, and yet there is a longing to return to a more authentic Judaism. Have authentic Jews reached out to these economically successful and religiously failed Jews?*

EW: I don't know them! I know quite a few young people whom I teach (and I love them), who have a profound, authentic quest for something truthful. Not only in my classes at Boston University, but wherever I go, I meet people who want something. But there is no support anymore. The future is frightening, it is frightening.

I had to give a lecture two years ago in a seminar on the Year 2000. My topic was the future of language. So I worked on it, and never have I had to work so hard on a lecture, because I couldn't imagine the Year 2000. Yet it's only fifteen years away! Is this the feeling of the millennium? I'm not sure. It's the feeling that we are racing too fast; technologically, scientifically, we're going too fast, and in ethics and in philosophy we remain behind. Technology is never really pure, it's always at the expense of something. Maybe that is what the young people are afraid of: they see themselves running, thrusting into the future at a tremendous pace, and they look for support in the past, which is there, and the past after all is synonymous with survival: we survived the past. But can we survive the future?

RL: *Until modern times, traditions and customs made it possible for people to have more or less tolerable lives; they supported people, the possibility of living closer to one's center was there. Now, there is such a collapse of many traditions. You and a few other authors have restored the Hasidic tradition—*

EW: Well, I have not; I have tried to tell a few stories.

RL: *It seems as if, in the absence of traditions, the master is terribly important—the single individual who concentrates the knowledge and whose very presence in a room changes the way people think and feel.*

EW: Absolutely, absolutely, look at the Besht: when he came to a town, the simple fact that he was there influenced people. Moses—I would be afraid to meet Moses, but I would like to meet him. He was the one who was a watershed in everything, not only to his disciples but to all the people that he and his disciples had never met.

RL: *Is there a teacher to send people to now—a spiritual guide?*

EW: Ah, this is a disturbing question. I am looking for one. My own case is different, because I *had* teachers. The longing is not only for teachers but for what they represent, a whole world.

Hasidism is very beautiful, but to me it's amazing to see Hasidism in New York. It's so atypical here. Hasidism had to be in villages; it was born in villages, it was meant for villages. Hasidism is not only a structure of perceptions or of melodies or of stories, it is a geography. It had to be in the mountains of Carpathia, and in the villages there that were abandoned and forsaken. It was never a city movement, it was a village movement. You know, some streets in Brooklyn are structured like the villages in Eastern Europe. But the fact is that the Hasidic movement suffered most of the losses. I think three Masters survived among hundreds and hundreds.

RL: *There is a sense in which Hasidism was very healthy and alive even in 1930, but in your books you have also implied that there was a decline after the first three generations in the Hasidic movement.*

EW: I confess, I glorify them. I do it with love, because whenever I have to repeat something negative it hurts me so much. If I had written my books in the 1930s, like Martin Buber, I would have become an objective, neutral, critical historian of normative Hasidism; why not? But today this wouldn't do them justice. Of course, I know the truth—the first and second generations, and the third, were great. The fourth was less great.

RL: *The third generation was trained by the Great Maggid?*

EW: Yes, and then began the dynasties, families, and everywhere you found children becoming heads of schools. It was no longer in the tradition of the Besht. The Besht's successor was not his son, but a disciple. Moses left his succession not to his children but to his disciple Joshua.

That is the tradition: it goes from master to disciple, not from master to son. But in later Hasidism, it went from father to son.

RL: *So that people wouldn't fight and envy each other?*

EW: They fought! Why? Because really the generations became less worthy.

RL: *Isn't there always the "chain of tradition"? Doesn't someone always appear to maintain the life behind Judaism or behind any tradition—the* melamed vav *in Jewish tradition?*

EW: The melamed vav is by definition unknown. But that doesn't matter. There are always masters, but they change. That is of the very essence of Judaism. How was the tradition handed down? Moses gave it to the Elders, the Elders to the Judges, the Judges to the Prophets, then to the Teachers, then to other Teachers. Every generation has had its paradigmatic personage. Somehow, Jewish history has always managed to find those who kept it alive.

RL: *There has been something Biblical about recent Jewish history, hasn't there?*

EW: I think we live in Biblical times. This is the conclusion I have reached. We live in extraordinary times.

RL: *To see through the inner exile, to find oneself deeply happy to be here and to be what one is, accepting whatever burdens and suffering there may be—this requires a great deal of intensity. Where is the intensity in Judaism today? Where is the real quest?*

EW: Our times are Biblical, but also paradoxical. On one hand, you may say we have never been so poor because of what we have lost; on the other, when you see what is going on in Jewish life, it's amazing. Never has Talmud been taught in so many places as it is being taught now.

Never has there been such growth. Never has Hasidism been so popular. People want to study, they want to come along to communities.

In France, all those young people in '68 who belonged to the Maoists, the Trotskyites, etc.—what are they doing now? They are studying Talmud! Jean-Paul Sartre's adopted daughter just published a translation of *Eyn Ya'akov*, a huge Midrashic work. You can't imagine what's happening there.

RL: *Abraham Heschel once said that the "school" in the sense of "school of the prophets" is missing in Judaism.*

EW: It's difficult to evaluate, for geographic reasons again. In a small city with 15,000 Jews, sixty or seventy *shuls*, houses of prayer and study, it was easy—easier than it can be in New York or Chicago or Los Angeles. Here we need other methods. But the new methods must never be against the orthodox; a new method must be an outgrowth of orthodoxy but never *against it*. If the Talmud had been against the Prophets, there would be no Talmud; the Talmud came to complement. If the Midrash later came against the Talmud, it would never have grown; if Rashi had been *against*—but never *against*; it's always an adjustment, but not in opposition to. A new method is possible, it is necessary. We have to remember that we need also strong roots.

RL: *May I ask: you have been a witness, and—*

EW: We are all witnesses, I have no privilege.

RL: *But you have witnessed such things as most people don't see. As a witness, you help us all to remember: what is it we should remember?*

EW: Everything! We have to remember that we can't remember. My fear really is that memory is in exile. The only possible salvation of the Jewish people is to remember our whole experience. But this memory is so powerful, so exalted, that we can't remember fully: it is bigger than us, bigger than all of us, than all the people. So how do you transform it into memory? Memory must not stop. If I were to stop in, let's say, 1944, it would lead to madness. And then I realize that, after all, there was a

Jewish life before, and there I find my friends and my teachers, and I go back and find my grandparents, and go back and I find the Hasidim, and go back and find the Kabbalists, and I go back—memory must go back until it goes back to the source of memory. It is a creative channel.

RL: *Everything in Judaism says, "Remember."*

EW: Absolutely. We have lived through such events.

RL: *In a certain way, my life is not only the events of my life. Isn't this something that has to be faced?*

EW: Events are outside, reverberations inside. To be awake means to listen to these events. Each event is a code, history is telling us something, God is telling us something, and if we don't try to decode the message, then what will make us understand it?

Parabola
Volume: 20.4
Eros

THE LOVE OF GOD, THE LOVE OF MAN

Franz Rosenzweig

There is one commandment which gives meaning to and is the essence of all the other commandments that may issue forth from the mouth of God. Which is this commandment of all commandments?

The answer is well known. Millions of tongues declare it early in the morning and late at night: "Thou shalt love the Lord thy God with all thy heart, and with all thy soul, and with all thy might."(Deuteronomy 6:4) Thou shalt love. What a paradox! Can love be commanded? Is not love a matter of destiny, a state of becoming seized, a gift that comes in perfect freedom? And here you find it commanded? Yes, it is true; love cannot be commanded; no third person can command and force it. But He, the One, can. The commandment of love can only come from the mouth of the lover. Only the lover can, and indeed, does say: Love me! In his mouth love is not a commandment coming from without; it is the voice of love itself. The love of the lover has no other word in which to express itself but this commandment. Everything else is no longer an unmediated expression but rather an explanatory confession. There is something weak in a confession of love on the part of the lover; like any other declaration it lags behind the real issue, and, since love is utter presence, it actually comes too late. Had not the beloved her arms wide open to receive it, the declaration would fall flat altogether. But the imperative, the unmediated wish, born in this very moment and in this moment expressed, the "love me!" of the lover—this is an authentic expression, pure language of love. There is no provision here for a future. Nothing is in order but an immediate response. A contemplation of a future or of permanence would turn the (personal) commandment into a law. A law implies time, future, permanence. A commandment knows only this one present moment; it expects a response in the very moment of its utterance.

Any other commandment, viewed from the outside or, so to speak, after the event, could have originated as a law. The commandment of love can be a commandment, but never a law. The contents of all other commandments can be transformed or rephrased so as to be laws; this one would resist such transformation; its contents allows only this one form of unmediated presence, and of a unity of consciousness, expression, and expected response. Thus, as the only pure commandment it is the highest of all commandments. And, having its place at the head of the other commandments, the commandment of love has the power to turn into commandments everything that could be viewed (from without) as laws. Thus, God's first word to the human soul being "love me!" all other statutes which man may be given turn into words "which I command thee *this day*" (Deuteronomy 6:6), indicating the same immediate presence as in the commandment of love. All laws then become but explanations of the one and first commandment to love Him. The whole revelation on Sinai enters the realm of "this day," that great expression of presence. "This day" God issues the commandment, and it is up to "this day" to heed His voice.

From the mouth of the lover issues this imperative—and no other imperative can be imagined coming from Him. The "I" of this speaker, the initial word of the dialogue of Revelation ("I am the Lord thy God ...") is also the seal which concludes His words ("... I am the Lord"): it marks each single commandment as a commandment of love. The divine "I" runs through the whole realm of revelation; it resists being translated into a (far away, absent) He; it must remain an (everpresent) "I" which alone can say: "Love me!"

But the soul, ready, open, silently hearkening—what can it answer to the commandment of love?

The lover's demand is answered by the beloved's confession of her love. She, responding, can do what he, demanding, could not: she can confess. The soul, confirming her being in love, confirms also the being of her lover. All confession of faith has only this one content: He whom I, being loved, have recognized as the lover, He is (present, alive, existent). The God of my love is truly God. It is in the state of being loved that the soul becomes certain that God who loves her is truly God.

In the beloved's faith in her lover the soul becomes truly a human being. In the state of love the soul awakens and begins to speak; but only in the state of being loved does the soul win visible existence. God, too, free of His hiddenness, wins here, in the testimony of the faithful, His recognizable reality. "If you are my witnesses then I am God" (*Sifre* on Deuteronomy 33:5).

"Love thy neighbor." Jew and Christian alike affirm this to be the sum total of all commandments. With this bidding, the soul, pronounced of age, leaves the paternal home of divine love and goes on its journey in the world. It is a commandment of love like the one originally revealed ("Thou shalt love the Lord thy God ..."), and like the latter it vibrates in all the various statutes, turning them from rigid laws into living commandments. All commandments that stem from that original commandment flow into this, a commandment, too, of love (thy neighbor). ...

Love for our fellow-man is bidden by God. However, since love cannot be demanded but by the lover himself, therefore is the commandment to "love thy neighbor" immediately referred to the love of God. The love for God is to be expressed in our love for our neighbor. This love breaks forth again and again; it starts forever anew; disappointments will not deter it. Disappointments are even necessary so that this love will not petrify into a schematic, organized action but retain its freshness and its strength. ...

The one who is to be loved is called by Scripture "the neighbor." This word refers both in Hebrew and in Greek to the one who happens to be next to me at any given moment. It matters not what he was before and what he will be after this moment; now he is next to me, my neighbor. Thus he represents man at large. Since he happens to be near me I love him. Actually, my love comprises the sum total of all—humans and things—that can, at any given time, assume the place of the "neighbor." Ultimately, this love extends to everything, to the whole world. ...

The neighbor, the fellow man next to me, and only he, affects the relationship which spells redemption. ...

Thus love gives the world a soul. Whatever is touched by the breath of the love for fellow-man wins something that life itself cannot offer: eternity. Redemption originates in God; man knows only that he should love whoever is near him that moment; He endows it with eternity.

Reprinted from *Judaism*, Vol. 11. No. 2 (Spring 1962). Copyright 1962 American Jewish Congress.

Parabola
Volume: 8.1
Guilt

THE TWO MESSIAHS

Shlomo Carlebach

At the end of days, perhaps even tomorrow, two Messiahs will appear—one a son of Joseph, the other a son of David from the tribe of Yehuda. Both these Messiahs are needed to correct the world—Messiah ben Yosef for the *zaddik*'s holy *chuzpah* never to do wrong; Messiah ben David for the strength to do everything wrong and still find a way to return. The first teaches us not to destroy the holy ways we still have, the other not to give up even though we have destroyed so much already. The way of Joseph is to know, the way of the son of David, to do *tsuvah*, to repent.

Schlomo Carlebach, *Everybody Knows: A Collection of Chassidic Tales and Teachings* (unpublished).

•

CHAPTER TEN

DEATH AND RESURRECTION

Before his death, Rabbi Zusya said "In the coming world,
they will not ask me: 'Why were you not Moses?'
They will ask me: 'Why were you not Zusya?'"[1]

—Martin Buber

Parabola
Volume: 2.1
Death

The Death of Adam

Howard Schwartz

Adam lay in his tent, surrounded by his many sons and daughters. He had lived to be nine hundred and thirty when the sickness had seized him, and now even the days that had been numbered were drawing to an end. His first wife, Lilith, had left him long ago, and Eve, whom God had created for him from his own rib, had been dead for more than two centuries. In their last years Adam's memory of their life inside the Garden had become blurred, and when he had finally forgotten the lost splendor Eve had died of grief, and of the burden of bearing a memory that was too great for a single survivor. Now Adam alone was left. And strange to say, among the children of his children, there were those who had come to doubt the story of his origin, who could not bring themselves to believe that one father and mother had given birth to so many. But his sons and daughters had always shielded him from these sceptics, and among them the years he had toiled outside the gate that the angel still guarded were burned into their memory, as was the story of the death of Abel, his second son, and the punishment of Cain, his first. And now only Cain and Abel, among his many children, were missing. Instead it was Seth, himself an old man, who bent over his bed and spoke in his ear. But Adam had come to a place where he could not turn back. The words of his oldest living son were lost to him.

Neither did he notice the presence of the angel that had entered the room. His eyes had turned inward. At the last moment a luminous light passed through them and a bright glow surrounded his face. And at that very moment even those who had been uncertain that he was, in fact, the first father, felt the past become a blank wall behind them, and knew that the first era was finally past.

From *Midrashim: Collected Jewish Parables* (London: The Menard Press, 1976; distributed in the U.S. and Canada by Serendipity Books, 1790 Shattuck Avenue, Berkeley, California, 94709). © 1976 by Howard Schwartz and John Swanson. Reprinted by permission.

Parabola
Volume: 2.1
Death

Resurrection of the Dead

Ezekiel 37:1-14

The hand of the Lord was upon me, and carried me out in the spirit of the Lord, and set me down in the midst of the valley which was full of bones, and caused me to pass by them round about: and, behold, there were very many in the open valley and, lo, they were very dry.

And he said unto me, "Son of Man, can these bones live?"

And I answered, "O Lord God, thou knowest."

Again he said unto me, "Prophesy upon these bones, and say unto them, 'O ye dry bones, hear the word of the Lord. Thus saith the Lord God unto these bones: "Behold, I will cause breath to enter into you, and ye shall live: and I will lay sinews upon you, and will bring up flesh upon you, and cover you with skin, and put breath in you, and ye shall live; and ye shall know that I am the Lord."'"

So I prophesied as I was commanded: and as I prophesied there was a noise, and behold a shaking, and the bones came together, bone to his bone. And when I beheld, lo, the sinews and the flesh came up upon them, and the skin covered them above: but there was no breath in them.

Then said he unto me, "Prophesy unto the wind, prophesy, Son of Man, and say to the wind, 'Thus saith the Lord God: "Come from the four winds, O breath, and breathe upon these slain, that they may live."'"

So I prophesied as he commanded me, and the breath came into them, and they lived, and stood up upon their feet, an exceeding great army.

Then he said unto me, "Son of Man, these bones are the whole house of Israel: behold, they say, 'Our bones are dried, and our hope is lost: we are cut off for our parts.' Therefore prophesy and say unto them, 'Thus saith the Lord God: "Behold, O my people, I will open your graves, and cause you to come up out of your graves, and bring you into the land of Israel. And ye shall know that I am the Lord, when I have opened your graves, O my people, and brought you up out of your graves, and shall put my spirit in you, and ye shall live, and I shall place you in your own land: then shall ye know that I the Lord have spoken it, and performed it," saith the Lord.'"

Parabola
Volume: 2.1
Death

THE THREE ASPECTS OF THE SOUL

Zohar

The names and grades of the soul of man are three: *nefesh* (vital soul), *ruah* (spirit), *neshamah* (innermost soul, super-soul). The three are comprehended one within the other, but each has its separate abode.

While the body in the grave is decomposing and moldering to dust, nefesh tarries with it, and it hovers about in this world, going here and there among the living, wanting to know their sorrows, and interceding for them at their need.

Ruah betakes itself into the earthly Garden of Eden. There, this spirit, desiring to enjoy the pleasures of the magnificent Garden, vests itself in a garment, as it were, of a likeness, a semblance of the body in which it had its abode in this world. On Sabbaths, New Moons and festival days, it ascends up to the supernal sphere, regaling itself with the delights there, and then it goes back to the Garden. As it is written: "And the spirit [ruah] returneth unto God who gave it" (Eccles. 12:7), that is, at the special holidays and times we have mentioned.

But neshamah ascends forthwith to her place, in the domain from which she emanated, and it is on her account that the light is lit, to shine above. Never thereafter does she descend to the earth. In neshamah is realized the One who embraces all sides, the upper and the lower.

And until such time as neshamah has ascended to be joined with the Throne, ruah is unable to be crowned in the lower Garden, and nefesh cannot rest easy in its place; but these find rest when she ascends.

Now when the children of men, being troubled and sorrowful, betake themselves to the graves of those who are gone, then nefesh is wakened, and it goes out to bestir ruah, which then rouses the patriarchs, and after, neshamah. Whereupon the Holy One, be blessed, has pity on the world. ...

But if neshamah has for some reason been prevented from ascending to her proper place, then ruah, coming to the gate of the Garden of Eden, finds it closed against it, and, unable to enter, wanders about alone and dejected; while nefesh, too, flits from place to place in the world, and seeing the body in which it once was tenant eaten by worms and undergoing the judgment of the grave, it mourns for it, as the Scripture says: "But his flesh grieveth for him, and his soul mourneth over him" (Job 14:22).

So do they all undergo suffering, until the time when neshamah is enabled to reach to her proper place above. Then, however, each of the two others becomes attached to its rightful place; this is because all three are one, comprising a unity, embraced in a mystical bond.

Parabola
Volume: 13.2
Repetition and
Renewal

Sacred Echoes

Ecclesiastes 1:4-11

One generation passeth away, and another generation cometh: but the earth abideth forever.

The sun also ariseth, and the sun goeth down, and hasteth to his place where he arose.

The wind goeth toward the south, and turneth about unto the north; it whirleth about continually, and the wind returneth again according to his circuits.

All the rivers run into the sea; yet the sea is not full; unto the place from whence the rivers come, thither they return again.

All things are full of labour; man cannot utter it: the eye is not satisfied with seeing, nor the ear filled with hearing.

The thing that hath been, it is that which shall be; and that which is done is that which shall be done: and there is no new thing under the sun.

Is there anything whereof it may be said, See, this is new? It hath been already of old time, which was before us.

There is no remembrance of former things; neither shall there be any remembrance of things that are to come with those that shall come after.

CONTRIBUTOR PROFILES

S. Y. Agnon In 1966 he was the first Hebrew writer to be awarded
the Nobel Prize for Literature. A central figure in modern Hebrew
fiction, his works deal with the conflict between traditional Jewish
life and the modern world, and attempts to recapture the fading
traditions of the European *shtetl*, or township.

Mordechai Beck, Jerusalem-based artist and writer, immigrated to
Israel from England in 1973. His prose writing, poetry, essays and
journalism appear in newspapers and journals in Israel, the USA
and the UK. He is a founding member of the neo-Orthodox
community, Yedidyah.

Rabbi Philip Bentley is a writer and activist on Judaism and the
environment and involved with the Jewish Peace Fellowship. He
currently serves Agudas Israel Congregation in Hendersonville, NC.

Philip Birnbaum (also Paltiel Birnbaum) (1904-1988): author and
translator, best known for his translation and annotation of the
siddur (prayer book) which was first published in 1949. Birnbaum
was born in Poland and emigrated to the United States in 1923.
His works include translations (with annotation and introduction)
of the *Machzor,* the *Tanach*, the Torah and the *Haftarot* and the
Passover Haggadah.

Rick Blum, a licensed psychologist with an independent psychotherapy
practice, he is the author of *God for People with Brains: A Psychologist
Puts Judaism on the Couch.*

James L. Bull is a clinical psychologist with a background in sociology.
In addition to pursuing a private practice, he works at the Women's
Detention Facility in Las Colinas, California.

Martin Buber (1878-1965), Austrian philosopher and scholar whose
philosophy of dialogue has had a wide influence on thinkers of
many faiths. He resigned from the University of Frankfurt after

Hitler came to power in 1933 and immigrated to Palestine (now Israel) in 1938. There he was active in the Jewish and educational communities. His most widely known work, *I and Thou*, expresses his religious philosophy. Among his other books are *The Tales of Rabbi Nachman and The Legend of the Ba'al-Shem* (re-creations of Hasidic legends), *Good and Evil*, *The Origin and Meaning of Hasidism* and *The Knowledge of Man*.

Rabbi Shlomo Carlebach (1925-1994): Jewish religious singer, composer, and self-styled "rebbe" known as "the singing rabbi" in his lifetime. Although his roots lay in traditional Orthodoxy, he branched out to create his own movement, combining Hasidic-style warmth and personal interaction, public concerts and song-filled synagogue services.

Rabbi Geoffrey W. Dennis is rabbi of Congregation Kol Ami in Flower Mound, TX, and teaches Kabbalah at the University of North Texas. He received his M.HL and was ordained at Hebrew Union College-Jewish Institute of Religion. His first book, *The Encyclopedia of Jewish Myth, Magic, and Mysticism*, was released in 2007.

Lawrence Fine is chair of Religion and Director of Jewish Studies at Mount Holyoke College, scholar of medieval Judaism and Jewish mysticism. His most recent book is *Physician of the Soul, Healer of the Cosmos: Isaac Luria and His Kabbalistic Fellowship*.

Estelle Frankel is a psychotherapist and teacher of Jewish mysticism in Berkeley, California. She was ordained as a Rabbinic Pastor and spiritual guide by Rabbi Zalman Schachter-Shalomi and is the author of *Sacred Therapy*.

Viktor Emil Frankl (1905-1997): Austrian neurologist and psychiatrist as well as a Holocaust survivor. Frankl was the founder of logotherapy and Existential Analysis, the "Third Viennese School" of psychotherapy. His book, *Man's Search for Meaning*, chronicles his experiences as a concentration camp inmate and describes his method of finding meaning in all forms of existence, even the most terrible ones.

Irving Friedman is a scholar of the rabbinical tradition and translator of *The Book of Creation*.

Rabbi Abraham J. Heschel (1907-1972): Hasidic scholar and philosopher of religion. He was professor of ethics and mysticism at the Jewish Theological Seminary in New York. He is also the author of numerous articles and books, including *Man Is Not Alone*, *The Sabbath*, *God in Search of Man*.

Rabbi Abraham Isaac Kook (1865-1935) Born in Latvia, Rabbi Kook moved to what was to become the land of Israel in 1904 and later became the first chief rabbi of Israel. His works include *Of Societies Perfect and Imperfect* and *Orot*.

Rabbi Jonathan Omer-Man is president and founder of Metivta, an academy for adult religious education centered on the practice of meditation and the exploration of traditional Jewish spirituality. Omer-Man was involved in publishing in Jerusalem for many years. He now lives in the United States and lectures about Jewish mysticism and spirituality.

Isaac Loeb Peretz (1852–1915): Polish poet, novelist, playwright, and lawyer. He was a voice for *Haskalah*, or Jewish Enlightenment. In stories and pictures he wrote imaginative and sympathetic sketches of Jewish life.

Barbara Rohde (1925-2001): Writer, peace activist, community leader, mother of four and active Unitarian Universalist. She was raised in Nebraska and spent most of her adult life in Corvallis, Oregon. Her published work includes short stories, poetry, reviews, essays and a book of meditations titled *In the Simple Morning Light*.

Franz Rosenzweig (1886–1929) was a German theologian, author of *Der Stern der Erlosung* (*The Star of Redemption*) and, with Martin Buber, worked on a German translation of the Hebrew Bible.

Rabbi Zalman Schachter-Shalomi (commonly called Reb Zalman). Born in Poland in 1924 and raised in Vienna, he was interred in detention camps under the Vichy French and fled the Nazi advance by coming to the United States in 1941. He was ordained as a Lubavitch rabbi in 1947 but later left the Lubavitch community to pursue other ways of expressing the Jewish tradition. He initiated the Aleph Ordination Programs and the Aleph: Alliance for Jewish Renewal.

Howard Schwartz is a professor of English at the University of Missouri, St. Louis, and an author of fiction, poetry, essays, Jewish folklore and Jewish anthologies. Among his books are *The Four Who Entered Paradise, Reimagining the Bible: The Storytelling of the Rabbis, Sleepwalking Beneath the Stars* and *The Diamond Tree: Jewish Tales from Around the World.*

Rabbi Eliezer Shore is a storyteller, writer and teacher of Jewish mysticism and spirituality. He was born in New York but now lives in Jerusalem with his family where he teaches in a *yeshiva* (a school) for Talmudic studies. He publishes *Bas Ayin*, a journal of contemporary Hasidic thought.

Isaac Bashevis Singer (1904-1991). Storyteller and renowned writer of *shtetl* life, he began to write as a journalist in Poland between the world wars. His works include *The Magician of Lublin, Gimpel the Fool* and *A Crown of Feathers.* Singer received the Nobel Prize for Literature in 1978.

Rabbi Adin Steinsaltz is a scholar, philosopher, social critic, author and spiritual mentor of Russian Jewry. He is known for his interpretation, commentaries and translations of the Babylonian Talmud. Steinsaltz founded the Israel Institute for Talmudic Publications and was awarded the Israel Prize, Israel's highest honor, in 1988. Among his books are *The Thirteen Petalled Rose* and *The Essential Talmud.*

Jean Sulzberger is a Senior Editor of *Parabola*. She is the author of *Search: Journey on the Inner Path.*

Sir Elie Wiesel. Born in Sighet, Romania, he survived the concentration camps as a teenager and later became a citizen of the United States. He is the author of more than 30 books dealing with Judaism, the Holocaust, and the moral responsibility of all people to fight hatred, racism and genocide. His first book, *Night*, is one of the most powerful works in literature of the Holocaust. Wiesel was awarded the Nobel Peace Prize in 1986.

FOR FURTHER READING

Abrams, Judith Z. *The Talmud for Beginners.* 2nd ed. Lanham, MD: Jason Aronson Publishers, 1994.

Agnon, Shmuel Yosef, ed. *Days of Awe: A Treasury of Jewish Wisdom for Reflection, Repentance, and Renewal on the High Holy Days.* New York: Schocken Books, Inc., 1995.

Alter, Robert. *The Art of Biblical Narrative.* New York: Basic Books, 1983.

Appel, Gerso. *A Philosophy of Mitzvot.* New York: Ktav Publishing House, Inc., 1975.

Baeck, Leo. *The Essence of Judaism.* New York: Schocken Books, Inc., 1970.

_____. *God and Man in Judaism.* New York: UAHC Press, 1958.

_____. *Judaism and Christianity.* Philadelphia: The Jewish Publication Society, 1964.

_____. *The Pharisees and Other Essays.* New York: Schocken Books, Inc., 1947.

_____. *This People Israel: The Meaning of Jewish Existence.* New York: Holt, Rinehart and Winston, 1964.

Berkovits, Eliezer. *Not in Heaven: The Nature and Function of Halakha.* New York: Ktav Publishing House, Inc., 1983.

Bialik, Hayim Nahman and Yehoshua Hana Ravnitzky. *The Book Of Legends, Sefer Ha-Aggadah.* New York: Schocken Books, Inc., 1992.

Bickerman, Elias. *The Jews in the Greek Age.* Cambridge, MA: Harvard UP, 1998.

Blank, Sheldon H. *Jeremiah—Man and Prophet.* Cincinnati, OH: HUC-JIR Press, 1961.

Bokser, Ben Zion. *The Talmud: Selected Writings.* New York: Paulist Press, 1989.

Buber, Martin. *Good and Evil: Two Interpretations.* Farmington Hills, MI: Charles Scribner and Sons, 1953.

_____. *Hasidism and Modern Man.* Ed./trans. Maurice Friedman. New York: Harper and Row, 1966.

_____. *I and Thou.* New York: MacMillan, 1974.

_____. *Israel and the World: Essays in a Time of Crisis.* Syracuse, NY: Syracuse UP, 1997.

_____. *Kingship of God.* Atlantic Highlands, NJ & London: Humanities Press International, Inc., 1990.

_____. *Origin and Meaning of Hasidism.* New York: Horizon, 1960.

_____. *The Prophetic Faith.* New York: First Harper Torchbook Edition, 1960.

_____. *Two Types of Faith.* New York: Harper & Row, 1961.

_____. *Tales of the Hasidim Book One: The Early Masters and Book Two: The Later Masters/Two Books in One.* New York: Schocken Books, Inc., 1991.

_____. and Martin S. Jaffee. *Hasidism and Modern Man.* Atlantic Highlands, NJ & London: Humanities Press International, Inc., 1988.

Buttenwieser, Moses. *The Book of Job.* New York: The Macmillan Company, 1922.

_____. *The Prophets of Israel.* New York: The Macmillan Company, 1914.

Cassuto, Umberto. *Bible and Ancient Oriental Texts.* Jerusalem: Magnes Press—The Hebrew UP, 1975. Vol. 2 of Biblical and Oriental Studies.

_____. *A Commentary on Exodus*. Trans. Israel Abrahams. Jerusalem: Magnes Press—The Hebrew UP, 1967.

_____. *A Commentary on Genesis Part I: From Adam to Noah*. Trans. Israel Abrahams. Jerusalem: Magnes Press—The Hebrew UP, 1961.

_____. *A Commentary on Genesis Part II: From Noah to Abraham*. Trans. Israel Abrahams. Jerusalem: Magnes Press—The Hebrew UP, 1964.

Chafetz, Chaim. *Concise Book of Mitzvoth*. Trans. Charles Wengrov. New York: Philip Feldheim, 1990.

Cohen, A. *Everyman's Talmud*. New York: EP Dutton & Co, Inc., 1949.

Cohen, Arthur. *The Soncino Chumash*. Brooklyn, NY: Soncino Press, 1947.

Cohen, Norman J. *The Way into Torah*. Woodstock, VT: Jewish Lights Publishing, 2000.

Cohen, Hermann. *Ethics Of Maimonides*. Madison, WI: The U of Wisconsin P, 2004.

_____. *Reason and Hope*. New York: The Viking Press, 1971.

_____. *Religion of Reason: Out of the Sources of Judaism*. Oxford: Oxford UP on Demand, 1995.

Cohen, Shaye J. D. *From the Maccabees to the Mishnah*. Louisville, KY: Westminster John Knox Press, 1988.

Dan, Joseph, ed. *Jewish Intellectual History in the Middle Ages*. Westport, CT: Praeger Publishing, 1994.

Danby, Herbert. *The Mishnah: Translated from the Hebrew with Introduction and Brief Explanatory Notes*. Oxford: Oxford UP, 1933.

Dorff, Elliot. *To Do the Right and the Good: A Jewish Approach to Modern Social Ethics*. Philadelphia: Jewish Publication Society, 2002.

Efros, Israel I. *Ancient Jewish Philosophy: A Study in Metaphysics and Ethics*. Detroit, MI: Wayne State UP, 1964.

Epstein, Isadore. *Judaism*. New York: Penguin Books, 1966.

Finkel, Avraham Yaakov. *The Great Torah Commentators*. Lanham, MD: Jason Aronson Publishers, 1996.

Fox, Everett. *The Five Books of Moses*. New York: Schocken Books, Inc., 1995.

Fraade, Stephen. *From Tradition to Commentary: Torah and Its Interpretation in the Midrash Sifre to Deuteronomy*. Albany, NY: SUNY Press, 1991.

Gabirol, Solomon Ibn. *The Kingly Crown*. Trans. Bernard Lewis. Middlesex, Eng.: Vallentine Mitchell, 1961.

Ginzburg, Louis. *Legends of the Jews*. Baltimore, MD: Johns Hopkins UP, 1998.

_____. *On Jewish Law and Lore*. Philadelphia: Jewish Publication Society, 1955.

Goldberg, David J. and John D. Rayner. *The Jewish People and Their Religion*. New York: Penguin Books, 1989.

Halamish, Mosheh. *An Introduction to the Kabbalah*. Albany, NY: SUNY Press, 1998.

Halevi, Judah. *The Kuzari*. New York: Schocken Books, Inc., 1964.

HaLivni, David. *Midrash, Mishnah, Gemara*. Cambridge, MA: Harvard UP, 1986.

Hauptman, Judith. *Rereading the Rabbis: A Woman's Voice*. Jackson, TN: Westview Press, 1999.

Herberg, Will, ed. *The Writings of Martin Buber*. New York: Meridian Books, Inc., 1956.

Herford, Robert Travis. *Talmud and Apocrypha: A Comparative Study of the Jewish Ethical Teaching in the Rabbinical and Non-Rabbinical Sources in the Early Century*. New York: Ktav Publishing House, Inc., 1971.

Heschel, Abraham Joshua. *The Earth Is the Lord's: The Inner World of the Jew in Eastern Europe*. Woodstock, VT: Jewish Lights Publishing, 1995.

_____. *God in Search of Man: A Philosophy of Judaism*. New York: Noonday Press, 1997.

_____. *I Asked for Wonder: A Spiritual Anthology*. New York: Crossroad Publishing Co., 1983.

_____. *Man Is Not Alone: A Philosophy of Religion*. New York: Noonday Press, 1997.

_____. *The Sabbath: Its Meaning for Modern Man*. New York: Farrar, Straus, and Giroux, 1995.

_____. *Prophetic Inspiration after the Prophets Maimonides and Other Medieval Authorities*. Ed. Morris M. Faierstein. New York: Ktav Publishing House, Inc.,1996.

_____. *Who Is Man?* Palo Alto, CA: Stanford UP, 1965.

_____. and Samuel H. Dresner. *The Circle of the Ba'al Shem Tov: Studies in Hasidism*. Chicago: U of Chicago P, 1985.

Hirsch, Samson Raphael. *Horeb: A Philosophy of Jewish Laws & Observances*. Trans. I. Grunfeld. Brooklyn, NY: Soncino Press, 1997.

Horowitz, George. *The Spirit of Jewish Law*. New York: Bloch Publishing Co., 1994.

Ibn Pakuda, Bahya. *The Book of Directions to the Duties of the Heart*. Oxford: Oxford UP, 1988.

Kaplan, Aryeh. *Maimonides' Principles: The Fundamentals of Jewish Faith*. 2nd ed. New York: NCSY/OU, 1984.

Kaufmann, Yehezkel. *The Religion of Israel: From Its Beginnings to the Babylonian Exile*. Trans. and abr. Moshe Greenberg. Chicago: U of Chicago P, 1960.

Kehati, Pinhas. *The Kehati Mishnah*. New York: Phillip Feldheim, 2005.

Kehot Publication Society. *Likutei-Amarim-Tanya*. Bi-lingual ed. Brooklyn, NY: Soncino Press, 1973.

Klein, Isaac. *A Guide to Religious Jewish Practice (Moreshet)*. New York: Ktav Publishing House, Inc., 1979.

Kraemer, David. *Mind of the Talmud*. Oxford: Oxford UP, 1990.

Kushner, Lawrence. *Honey from the Rock: An Easy Introduction to Jewish Mysticism*. Woodstock, VT: Jewish Lights Publishing, 1991.

_____. *The River of Light: Spirituality, Judaism, and the Evolution of Consciousness*. Woodstock, VT: Jewish Lights Publishing, 1991.

Lachower, Yeruham Fishel and Isaiah Tishby. *The Wisdom of the Zohar*. Oxford: Oxford UP, 1989.

Lauterbach, Jacob Z. *Rabbinic Essays*. Cincinnati, OH: Hebrew Union College P, 1951.

Leibowitz, Yeshayahu. *The Faith of Maimonides*. Trans. John Glucker. Tel Aviv: Naidat Press, 1989.

Loewenthal, Naftali. *Communicating the Infinite: The Emergence of the Habad School*. Chicago: U of Chicago P, 1990.

Luzzatto, Moshe Chayim. *The Path of the Just*. Trans. Shraga Silverstein. 2nd edition, rev. New York: Philip Feldheim, Inc., 1969.

Maimonides, Moses. *The Guide for the Perplexed*. Trans. Shlomo Pines. Vol. 1. Chicago: U of Chicago P, 1974.

_____. *The Guide for the Perplexed*. *Trans*. Shlomo Pines. Vol. 2. Chicago: U of Chicago P, 1974.

_____. *Mishneh Torah*. Ed. Philip Birnbaum. New York: Hebrew Publishing House, 1967.

_____. *The Book of Knowledge*. Trans./ed. Moses Hyamson. Jerusalem: Boys Town Jerusalem Publishers, 1962.

_____. *The Book of Adoration*. Trans./ed. Moses Hyamson. Jerusalem: Boys Town Jerusalem Publishers, 1962.

Martin, Bernard. *Prayer in Judaism*. New York: Basic Books, 1968.

Matt, Daniel Chanan. *Zohar, The Book of Enlightenment*. New York: Paulist Press, 1988.

Mindel, Nissan. *As For Me — My Prayers*. 2 vols. Brooklyn, NY: Kehot Publication Society, 1984.

Mintz, Jerome R. and Dan ben Amos. *In Praise of the Ba'al Shem Tov Shivhei ha-Besht: The Earliest Collections of Legends about the Founder of Hasidism*. New York: Jason Aronson Publishers, 1994.

Montefiore, C. G. *A Rabbinic Anthology*. New York: Schocken Books, Inc., 1974.

Moore, George Foote. *Judaism in the First Centuries of the Christian Era*. 3 vols. Peabody, MA: Hendrickson Publishers, Inc. 1997.

Patai, Raphael. *The Jewish Mind*. Detroit, MI: Wayne State UP, 1996.

_____. *The Messiah Texts*. Detroit, MI: Wayne State UP, 1989.

Petuchowski, Jakob J. *Understanding Jewish Prayer*. New York: Ktav Publishing House, Inc., 1972.

Rivkin, Ellis. *What Crucified Jesus? Messianism, Pharisaism, and the Development of Christianity*. New York: URJ Press, 1997.

_____. *The Unity Principle: The Shaping of Jewish History*. Springfield, NJ: Behrman House Publishing, 2003.

_____. *Hidden Revolution: The Pharisee's Search for the Kingdom Within*. Nashville, TN: Abingdon Press, 1978.

Rubinstein, Jeffrey L. *Talmudic Stories: Narrative Art, Composition, and Culture*. Baltimore, MD: Johns Hopkins UP, 2003.

Rubinstein, Jeffrey L. *Rabbinic Stories*. New York: Paulist Press, 2002.

Sachar, Howard. *A History of the Jews in the Modern World*. New York: Alfred A. Knopf, 2005.

Safran, Alexandre. *Wisdom of the Kabbalah*. Trans. E. M. Sandle. New York: Philip Feldheim, 1991.

Samely, Alexander. *Rabbinic Interpretation of Scripture in the Mishnah*. Oxford: Oxford UP, 2002.

Schechter, Solomon. *Some Aspects of Rabbinic Theology: Major Concepts of the Talmud*. Peabody, MA: Hendrickson Publishers, Inc., 1998.

Schilpp, Paul Arthur and Martin Friedman, eds. *The Philosophy of Martin Buber*. Vol. XII. Chicago: Open Court Publishing Co., 1967.

Schneersohn, Joseph I. *Some Aspects of Chabad Chassidim*. New York: Machne Israel, 1961.

Scholem, Gershom. *Jewish Gnosticism, Merkvah Mysticism and Talmudic Tradition*. New York: Ktav Publishing House, Inc., 1960.

_____. *Kabbalah*. New York: New American Library, 1989.

_____. *Major Trends in Jewish Mysticism*. New York: Schocken Books, Inc., 1995.

_____. *The Messianic Idea in Judaism*. New York: Schocken Books, Inc., 1995.

_____. *On the Kabbalah and Its Symbolism*. New York: Schocken Books, Inc., 1996.

_____. *Sabbatai Sevi*. 2 vols. Princeton, NJ: Princeton UP, 1973.

_____. *Zohar: The Book of Splendor—Basic Readings from the Kabbalah*. New York: Schocken Books, Inc., 1995.

Seeskin, Kenneth. *Maimonides: A Guide for Today's Perplexed*. Springfield, NJ: Behrman House Publishing, 1991.

Seltzer, Robert. *Jewish People, Jewish Thought*. New York: Prentice Hall, 1982.

Shapira, Kalonymus K. *To Heal the Soul: The Spiritual Journal of a Chasidic Rebbe*. Trans. Yehoshua Starrett. Lanham, MD: Jason Aronson Publishers, 1995.

Shmueli, Efraim. *Seven Jewish Cultures*. Cambridge, MA: Cambridge UP, 1990.

Silver, Abba Hillel. *A History of Messianic Speculation in Israel*. Gloucester, MA: Peter Smith Publisher, Inc., 1970.

_____. *Where Judaism Differs: An Inquiry into the Distinctiveness of Judaism*. New York: Collier Books, 1989.

Silver, Maxwell. *The Ethics of Judaism from the Aspect of Duty*. New York: Bloch Publishing Company, 1938.

Singer, Solomon Alachua. *Medieval Jewish Mysticism—Book of the Pious*. Wheeling, IL: Whitehall Co. Publishers, 1971.

Slonimsky, Henry. *Essays*. Cincinnati, OH: Hebrew Union College P, 1967.

Soloveitchik, Joseph Dov. *Halakhic Man*. Lanham, MD: Jason Aronson Publishers, 1996.

_____. *The Lonely Man of Faith*. Philadelphia, PA: Jewish Publication Society, 1984.

Spector, Sheila A. *Jewish Mysticism: An Annotated Bibliography on the Kabbalah in English*. New York: Garland Publishing, 1984.

Sperling, Harry, and Maurice Simon, trans. *The Zohar*. 5 vols. London: Soncino Press, rpt. 1978.

Steinberg, Milton. *Basic Judaism*. San Diego, CA: Harcourt Brace Jovanovich, 1986.

Steinsaltz, Adin. *The Essential Talmud*. Lanham, MD: Jason Aronson Publishers, 1982.

_____. *A Guide to Jewish Prayer*. New York: Schocken Books, Inc., 2002.

_____. *The Talmud: The Steinsaltz Edition: A Reference Guide*. New York: Random House, 1996.

_____. *The Thirteen-Petaled Rose*. Lanham, MD: Jason Aronson Publishers, 1992.

Stern, David. *Midrash and Theory: Ancient Jewish Exegesis and Contemporary Literary Studies* (*Rethinking Theory*). Evanston, IL: Northwestern UP, 1998.

Tsevat, Matitiahu. *The Meaning of the Book of Job and Other Biblical Studies.* New York: Ktav Publishing House, Inc., 1980.

Twersky, Isadore, ed. *A Maimonides Reader.* Springfield, NJ: Behrman House Inc., 1972.

Unterman, Isaac. *The Talmud: An Analytical Guide to Its History and Teachings.* New York: Bloch Publishing Co., 1985.

Urbach, Ephraim E. *The Sages: Their Concepts and Beliefs.* Trans. Israel Abrahams. Jerusalem: Magnes Press—The Hebrew UP, 1975.

Weiner, Herbert. *9 1/2 Mystics, The Kabbala Today.* New York: Collier Books, 1997.

Weiss, Joseph. *Studies in Eastern European Jewish Mysticism.* Ed. David Goldstein. New York: Littman Library of Jewish Civilization, 1997.

Weiss, Raymond L. and Charles E. Butterworth. *Ethical Writings of Maimonides.* New York: New York UP, 1975.

Wirszubski, Chaim. *Pico della Mirandola's Encounter with Jewish Mysticism.* Cambridge, MA: Harvard UP, 1989.

Zalman, Shnuer. *Shulchan Aruch: Code of Jewish Law.* Vol. 1. Brooklyn, NY: Kehot Publication Society, 2002.

Chapter Citations

Call of the Tradition
1 Micah 6:6-9 Revised Standard Version (hereafter cited as RSV).
2 Jeremiah 9:23-24 RSV.
3 Isaiah 55:6-11 RSV.
4 Isaiah 58:6-9 RSV.
5 Bialik, Hayim Nahman and Yehoshua Hana Ravnitzky. *The Book Of Legends, Sefer Ha-Aggadah.* (New York: Schocken Books, Inc., 1992), p. 403:8.
6 *Ibid.*, p. 403:12.
7 *Ibid.*, p. 409:62.
8 *Ibid.*, p. 35:28.
9 *Ibid.*, p. 81:49.
10 *Ibid.*, p. 84:60.
11 *Ibid.*, p. 561:238.
12 *Ibid.*, p. 516:100.

Chapter 1
1 From *Your Word is Fire* (New York: Paulist Press, 1977). © 1977 by Arthur Green and Barry W. Holtz. Reprinted with permission of the publisher.

Chapter 2
1 From *Your Word is Fire* (New York: Paulist Press, 1977). © 1977 by Arthur Green and Barry W. Holtz. Reprinted with permission of the publisher.

Chapter 3
1 From *Philo: Philosophical Writings*, selections edited by Hans Lewy (Oxford: East and West Library, 1946), pp. 36-37.

Chapter 4
1 Proverbs 16:32 RSV.

Chapter 5
1 From *Your Word is Fire* (New York: Paulist Press, 1977). © 1977 by Arthur Green and Barry W. Holtz. Reprinted with permission of the publisher.

Chapter 6
1 From *Days of Awe* (New York: Schocken, 1948).

Chapter 7
1 Genesis 2:19-20 RSV.

Chapter 8
1 From *Hasidic Tales* by Elie Wiesel.

Chapter 9
1 Isaiah 11:6 RSV.

Chapter 10
1 From *Tales of the Hasidim: The Early Masters* by Martin Buber.. © 1947, renewed 1975 by Schocken Books, Inc. Reprinted by permission of Schocken Books, published by Pantheon Books, a division of Random House, Inc.

Photography Captions & Credits

Cover Photo
Menorah with 7 branches. Joseph Assarfati, Cervera Bible. 1299. Cervera, Spain.
Photo: Giraudon/Art Resource, NY.

Page xxxvii
Star of David on wall in Jewish district.
Photo: Juliet Coombe/Lonely Planet Images.

Page xxxix
Marc Chagall, *Moses Receives the Tablets of the Law*.
Photo: Réunion des Musées Nationaux/Art Resource, NY.
© 2007 Artists Rights Society (ARS), New York/ADAGP, Paris.

Page xli
The Great Synagogue in Budapest is the largest functioning synagogue in Europe.
Photo: ©Wolfgang Kaehler/Corbis.

Page xliii
Rembrandt Harmensz van Rijn, *Jeremiah Lamenting the Destruction of Jerusalem*. 1630.
Photo: Bildarchiv Preussischer Kulturbesitz/Art Resource, NY.

Page xlv
Print depicting Great Fish Vomiting Jonah onto Dry Land. 17th century CE.
Photo: © Historical Picture Archive/Corbis.

Page xlvii
Western Wall of the Temple in Jerusalem, built by King Herod the Great. 1st century CE.
Photo: Erich Lessing/Art Resource.

Page xlix
Synagogue in the Oranienburg Street in Berlin, Germany.
Photo:© Svenja-Foto/zefa/Corbis.

Page li
Trumpeter blowing the Shofar at the time of Rosh Hashanah and Yom Kippur, manuscript according to the German rite, 13th-14th century (vellum).
Photo: © Getty Images.

Page lii
Torah Case. Damascus, 1565/66. Copper: inlaid with silver.
Photo: The Jewish Museum/Art Resource, NY.